Not only is he a leading light on AI, but Donald Clark also practises what he preaches on real projects. This is a must-read on an issue all organizations have to wrestle with – productivity. We have gained from his expertise across many projects.
Alfred Remmits, CEO, Xprtise

Successfully adopting AI for productivity is uncharted territory, and it requires a wise, insightful guide. Few are better suited for this role than Donald Clark. Anyone looking to understand how AI can improve organizational efficiency should read this book.
Peter Shea, AI Integration Professional, Middlesex Community College of Massachusetts

Donald Clark has been ahead of the curve on AI for years, not just predicting the revolution but helping organizations worldwide put it to work. He has supported countless practitioners and leaders in making AI practical, effective and transformative. His willingness to share knowledge and his hands-on approach make him a rare and invaluable guide.
Rebecca Stromeyer, CEO, ICWE

I've worked with Donald Clark on productivity and seen firsthand how sharp his insights are. He has always had a rare ability to cut through the noise. Knowing him, it's no surprise this book does the same. It's clear, comprehensive and genuinely useful for anyone wanting to understand AI and productivity.
Dave Tucker-Diaz, CEO and Founder, Genio.co

Donald Clark makes an impressive, well-researched case for AI to improve human productivity in many areas. Along the way he thoughtfully tackles all of the leading issues around the technology, from politics and ethics to economics and culture.
Bryan Alexander, Senior Scholar, Georgetown University

AI and Productivity

Using artificial intelligence to improve processes and unlock potential

Donald Clark

KoganPage

First published in Great Britain and the United States in 2026 by Kogan Page Limited

Kogan Page

Kogan Page Ltd, 2nd Floor, 45 Gee Street, London EC1V 3RS, United Kingdom
Kogan Page Inc, 8 W 38th Street, Suite 902, New York, NY 10018, USA
www.koganpage.com

EU Representative (GPSR)

Authorised Rep Compliance Ltd, Ground Floor, 71 Baggot Street Lower, Dublin D02 P593, Ireland
www.arccompliance.com

Kogan Page books are printed on paper from sustainable forests.

ISBNs

Hardback	978 1 3986 2333 0
Paperback	978 1 3986 2331 6
Ebook	978 1 3986 2332 3

British Library Cataloguing-in-Publication Data
A CIP record for this book is available from the British Library.

Library of Congress Control Number
2025034253

Typeset by Integra Software Services, Pondicherry
Printed and bound by CPI Group (UK) Ltd, Croydon CR0 4YY

CONTENTS

PART TWO

Jagged frontier

PREFACE

AI has surprised everyone, as the script has flipped.

Technological escapism has flipped over into productivity. Two decades of selling us ads, fractious social media, games, gambling, filters on photos, hailing Ubers, ordering fast food and porn and pandering to the attention economy have been flipped into finding things out, researching and getting things done – a productivity tool in the real economy.

Traditionally technology was top-down. This has been flipped into being bottom-up. Top-down technology was printing, steam, electricity, TV, radio and the internet. Yet AI adoption has been bottom-up, by enthusiastic individuals in their hundreds of millions with over a billion monthly uses, on the back of its obvious utility. It has been a sleeper revolution.

Another flip is in having moved from the fields to factories, then factories to offices, it is not blue-collar, but white-collar work that is under threat. AI is a cognitive, not physical, technology. Yet there may be another flip in the script, as its cognitive capabilities, embodied into robots, steel-collar workers and vehicles, also puts blue-collar jobs at risk.

Productivity comes from never-ending small flips, as we don't go back to written ledgers, typing pools, VHS tapes and cheques.

We have intelligence on tap. You can talk to it, get it to do things for you, even create. It is there 24/7, can communicate in almost any language, written and spoken. Yet I still come across people who see it as a fad, of no relevance in the real world of work. To be frank, anyone who thinks that AI will have little or no impact on productivity is delusional.

It took billions of years for *Homo sapiens* to evolve, yet AI in just a few years has challenged, even surpassed us, on many psychological and physical tasks. The last 200 years have been the most productive in the history of our species. The next 20 may outpace what we did in those 200, as AI becomes the most important catalyst and accelerator of productivity in history. It has been a quiet engine of transformation, outpacing expectations. Underestimated at every turn, it has advanced further than we dared imagine. Some deliberately and persistently downplayed what it could do; the brick wall, plateauing, stochastic parrot narrative. Many are still stuck in this Pythonesque parrot narrative, so refuse to accept arguments for increased productivity.

My starting point is the simple reality that productivity gains have been evidenced for some time. This book will take you to places where productivity is more than just a hypothetical promise, with real research, academic papers, analysis, market reports, implementations, projects and projections.

Productivity may seem a soulless, mechanical word, but it has the advantage of making AI practical and useful. It is an interesting word, because it can be used in a number of different contexts. One can apply it at the level of the individual, tasks and processes, organizations and nations, even see it in terms of loftier goals such as global sustainability. AI has become a central focus for world leaders, organizational leaders and nearly everyone else. There has never been a moment in human history quite like this.

As the raw power of practical functionality pushes us towards more concrete, analytical and consequential thinking on AI, this focus on productivity will, I hope, allow us to see AI through a more practical lens and help us apply it within our own lives and organizations.

This is not an academic tract, but rather a capture of a fast-moving topic. It is not what we think that matters, but what we do. Strategic decision making very often settles on concrete acts, decisions and solutions to improve process, innovate, pivot and automate.

We must move to a more nuanced account of these practical networks of causality and consequences in productivity. Our human relationship with created intelligence will be complex and will vary, from continuous agency to accepting complete automation, but there is a whole constellation of complex relationships in-between. My thesis is that productivity will accelerate as AI becomes more potent, and floods into more and more areas of human endeavour.

This is my fifth book on technology and after two editions of *AI for Learning* published also in South Korea and China, I wanted to do something eminently practical, hence my focus on the great issue of the day – productivity.

Productivity is the new focus, as we have moved from early adoption and wonder to real use in real organizations to get things done, quickly, cheaply and better. There was a switch in 2025 from angst to utility, from personal use to organizational attention and strategy. The technology confounded its critics by getting better at a blistering pace. It did not slow down, hit a brick wall or plateau. In fact, it was difficult to keep up, as it added memory, reasoning, research, speech, image creation, agents and then full-blown lip-synched video.

Part 1 gives a wide definition of *productivity*, with evidence that the age of AI is a radical shift away from the age of technological escapism. AI is a bottom-up technology that flips everything, and will practically and radically change all of our lives.

While there was much published on utopian or dystopian views of the technology, there was little focus on the middle ground, and its actual use to increase productivity is now its primary driver. There was no long, hard, cold look at the research and nature of its actual use in the real world. Big words like critical thinking, creativity and collaboration were bandied about, but it was unclear how they actually related to AI, which itself had critical, creative and collaborative capabilities. The human-in-the-loop trope appeared everywhere but few seemed to analyse what that actually meant. It turns out to be surprisingly complex, with humans, more usefully experts, in various relationships with AI, not merely 'in' the loop.

Part 2 deals with the *jagged frontier* and a focus on productivity to bring us back to earth into the behaviour of real people in real organizations in the real world. A journey along the jagged frontier shows sectors that were resistant, some static, others spiky, moving forward on a broad front or seeing breakouts. A deeper examination exposes many paradoxes of productivity. Why has it not ripped through all sectors and economies? Well, we humans are messy, we procrastinate, we bring all sorts of biases to the table and put up a stout resistance whenever radical technologies appear. Organizations are systemically structured to defend their bureaucracy and embedded practices. At the economic level, these paradoxes are well known. Progress will be in fits and starts across the jagged frontier but a general technology eventually triumphs and we will enter a new era of economic progress.

Part 3 is all about *action*: prompting, experts-in-the-loop, deployment and metrics. Real methods on strategic, tactical and practical ways to get productivity gains from AI.

Part 4 is about *ethics*, not as negative moralizing but split into weak issues which have relatively small impacts on productivity, such as plagiarism, prejudice, persuasion, privacy and passivity, and are solvable. Then it examines strong ethical issues, where the spotlight is now on several ethical issues around the consequences of this gear change in productivity. Privileged access and control may result in immiseration and poverty; there is danger to the planet through energy demand, paramilitary drone wars, even the risk of perishing as a species.

Based on the research, productivity in its widest sense is used to bring a practical perspective to AI. It will change the world but not as many suggest, by simply swapping out people for software and tasks for automation. It will be complex as individuals, organizations, teams, sectors and whole nations adjust unevenly to the change. But adjust they will, as this is a global, general technology and Artificial 'General' Technology moves us into uncharted territory. Use this book as a guide, and we may just get there... unscathed.

ACKNOWLEDGEMENTS

My thanks go to the many people whose AI projects we have worked on over the last decade, along with my son Carl, the CEO of Digital Khaos, who uses AI constantly in his business, and Callum, my other son, who has built all of our AI technology. Callum was awarded a 30-under-30 award in Berlin and remains my primary source for AI expertise. I would also like to thank and acknowledge AI, which, for this book, has been used to search, expand on, critique, find references, citations and proofread. This is the new normal in writing, using AI as a productivity tool, not to do the writing but to leave me the time and freedom to write. Lastly, a nod to Doug, my dog, who often nestled up to me while I was alone typing, and to my wife who gave me the time and space to write another book.

PART ONE

Productivity

01

What is productivity?

For the first two decades of the 21st century, technology drifted into escapism, creating a surplus of ever more exotic distractions. Smartphones, social media, entertainment and endless apps fed a culture of distraction, not productivity. Silicon Valley catered more to hedonism than solving hard problems. Online technology fed a sedentary consumer culture that, far from delivering sharp productivity gains, was content to satisfy the soft underbelly of consumer capitalism: ad revenue through search, fractious social media, hailing cabs, fast-food delivery, sharing and filtering photos, games, entertainment, gambling, porn and a zillion apps. Devices, especially those designed to entertain, such as tablets and smartphones, delivered the product. The iPhone was worshipped as the peak of technical achievement.

If anything, this technology was largely satisfying an attention and addiction economy, not productively solving problems in the real economy. Often counter-productive, it tended to distract us from productivity in life, education and the workplace.

Doing good in the world was replaced by base, self-gratifying and monetary goals. As a consequence, the talent from our universities marched lockstep into speculative finance, consulting and startups that shovelled out apps. One sign of the decadence was the get-rich-quick cryptocurrency speculation, laden with fraud, money laundering and criminal activity, using emission-heavy energy to mine coins.

Even work and office tools seemed stuck in word processing, presentation software and spreadsheets. Word does not make one a novelist, PowerPoint a presenter nor Excel a financial wizard. There was no higher purpose, little interest in the tough problems of productivity in healthcare, education, criminal justice, construction, clean energy, transport, manufacturing, research and problem solving – just more apps that gathered your data to sell you more stuff.

Did Silicon Valley serve us well with over two decades of selling ads, memes and social media? Was any progress made in productivity or did it distract and undermine productive work and loftier goals? We seemed to languish in a world of low productivity but high entertainment, where we talked endlessly about box-sets and not human achievements.

Curated commons

Still, amid the distractions, free digital services quietly reshaped productivity. Tools like Google Search, Gmail, Wikipedia and Duolingo created a new 'curated commons', a mix of public and private platforms offering a useful consumer surplus. Globally, the savings in time and cost run into hundreds of billions.

Some were privately built and managed, what Hoffman and Beato (2025) call the 'private commons', services such as Google Search, Gmail, Docs, Sheets, Slides, Maps, Earth and the Android operating system. Microsoft developed or acquired Outlook, Teams, GitHub and OneDrive. Even Amazon offered Alexa, free ebooks, Twitch and Open datasets on AWS. Meta had Facebook, Instagram, WhatsApp and Messenger. Beyond this, the free use of Zoom rocketed during the pandemic. Below the popular tech, lay Slack, Discord, Signal, Telegram and lots of free and useful downloadable apps.

Others were philanthropic. Knowledge and learning benefited from the not-for-profits Wikipedia and Khan Academy. Wikipedia replaced large sets of very expensive encyclopaedias, almost overnight, and continues to grow in breadth and depth, providing value and productivity gains for its global audience. Wikipedia remains one of the most extensive and multilingual knowledge resources on the internet, with millions of articles in hundreds of active languages, all maintained by a global community of volunteers. Duolingo emerged to provide language learning on a global scale.

All of these function as 'commons', in being free to use. They blurred the boundary between private and public. Some were completely free, others under a freemium model, with costs for premium services. Many private platforms delivered over a public network. The reciprocal exchange between capitalism and consumers had become something different from traditional economic exchange.

In economics, all of this can be translated into what is called 'consumer surplus'. This measures the benefit a consumer gets from buying a good or service for less than the maximum amount they were willing to pay. In the case of these free services, it is all surplus, as they pay nothing.

Can we meaningfully calculate the productivity value of this 'curated commons' in terms of the consumer surplus it generates? One can certainly calculate the time saved. Even early estimates (Varian, 2011) put this between $65 billion and $150 billion on Google Search alone. In the UK, Public First (2018) estimated at least £37 billion of consumer surplus from free Google services to the UK each year. In productivity terms, we can calculate time saved as additional work or leisure hours and multiply by the average wage or value of leisure. Globally, this undoubtedly yields a consumer surplus in the hundreds of billions of dollars a year.

AI explosion

Then... out of the blue, came a technology that seemed to soar above whimsical ad revenue and social media, something compelling, wondrous and terrifying – generative AI.

This new species of 'curated commons' acted as a springboard for trained models, using huge corpuses of text, to provide generative AI. Google's Colossal Clean Crawled Corpus swept up Wikipedia, scribd.com and PLOS papers. Commoncrawl, a not-for-profit dataset, had over 2.7 billion web pages, along with Pile, with Books3, GitHub and scientific papers from PubMed Central, arXiv, legal documents and much more. This was used by OpenAI and others to train their models. A lot of other sources were used, such as OpenWebText2's Reddit-linked web content and DM Mathematics for symbolic reasoning. The cultural knowledge of our entire past was used to provide tools that were about to shape the future.

We made the sudden leap from stupid to smart tech, from technological escapism to technological pragmatism. Generative AI marked a shift from merely entertaining or distracting ourselves with technology to deploying it as a tool for real-world productivity. Within days people were using it to do in minutes what used to take hours. Where previous tech often diverted attention from systemic challenges, generative AI endowed individuals and organizations with the tools to tackle them head-on. This technology suddenly supported a pragmatic mindset. It moved us toward a future where technology is not just a novelty, but a partner in meaningful output and change. Within days, users in their millions, in months, hundreds of millions, immediately used the technology, not on idle, social chat, but to get things done.

A backlash came, but exponential progress silenced the sceptics. AI was ridiculed as basic, a mere stochastic parrot about to hit a brick wall or plateau at any minute. There was even an attempt to kill it or at least delay it for half a year. Then came an obsession with guard railing and policing its language, as if those were imminent threats to civilization. But the mood shifted, and the sceptics retreated in the face of astonishing exponential progress. Software had at last found a purpose, through AI, as a generator of productivity.

As its capabilities rocketed and costs plummeted, it was obvious that it had much deeper roots in human purpose, with the possibility of solving hard problems in productivity in almost every sector. Governments recognized this by encouraging its use. The goal of Artificial General Intelligence (AGI) suddenly became very real as the Turing test was smashed into irrelevance. The word 'General' really mattered, as it could be applied to almost anything. Every sector could be reimagined, even politics and economics.

It held an interesting promise, to free us from the tyrannies of 9-to-5 work, low-satisfaction jobs, unaffordable healthcare, expensive education, repetitive bureaucracy and economic stagnation. Increased productivity started to come into focus as a useful, not utopian, goal. As of early 2024, around 67 per cent of the global population (5.35 billion people) have access to the internet via a device such as a smartphone, tablet, laptop or desktop computer. For those aged 15 to 24 it is 75 per cent. Although it is unevenly distributed, with some regions having a penetration near 100 per cent while others, like East Africa, are at 26 per cent, the number with access has surged in recent years. It grows every year, especially through mobile devices, with estimates suggesting a rise to 7.9 billion users by 2029 (DataReportal, 2025). This growing audience now has access to free AI services.

Then came another surprise: embodied AI, through the rise of the robots. Suddenly there was the ambition to solve problems of productivity in both the cognitive and physical domains. Having freed ourselves from the tyranny of technological escapism, we could look forward to smart software, doing smart things, making us all more productive in many senses of that word, in both the cognitive world and physical world.

AI has opened up a new form of 'commons', with free intelligence on tap, within a freemium model. The physical commons – land – was finite, but the digital commons is infinite, so potentially endlessly productive. Add to this that AI also gets faster, better, with lower costs, and we have the prize of productivity.

This focus on 'productivity' anchors and grounds AI in the real world, moving us from escapism to efficiency. It stops us from drifting too far into abstruse, utopian and dystopian fantasies. We are no longer narcissistically staring into the mirror; we have walked through a door into alternative ways to work, to reinvent ourselves, our organizations and the world we live in.

What is productivity?

As Krugman put it in 1994, productivity is not everything, but over time, it is almost everything. Economic prosperity hinges on turning resources into value efficiently. While policy tools like taxes or tariffs come and go, lasting gains come from improved output per worker, and AI may be the biggest leap yet.

Krugman states a solid truth about what drives prosperity. Economies rise or fall, not because of short-term political decisions or sudden market trends, but because of one fundamental force: how efficiently people, organizations and businesses can turn resources into value.

Countries have tried all sorts of ways to get their economies moving: cutting taxes, raising taxes, imposing tariffs, reducing tariffs, increasing public spending, reducing public spending, tightening or loosening regulations. Krugman argues that none of it matters in the long run unless it translates into higher productivity. Without actual gains in efficiency and output, wages stagnate, businesses struggle to compete and economic growth slows and stagnates.

AI represents the next great leap in productivity, with mind-boggling and enhancing tools that promise to augment, and to some degree automate, all sectors, some faster than others, but eventually almost everything – exactly the kind of productivity growth Krugman described as essential for long-term economic success.

Krugman had one other thing to say about growth: that the key is continuous reinvention. Countries and companies that embrace AI and train workers for the new era will see sustained growth. Those that resist AI technological change and cling to traditional methods will fall behind.

History of productivity?

As Daniel Susskind (2024) noted, the last 200 years saw explosive growth thanks to steam, electricity and computing. AI now joins this list but doesn't just augment human labour; it can replicate and even replace it. This raises new questions. What happens when we outgrow field, factories and offices?

AI, like these past paradigm shifting technologies, is also a 'general' technology but with a difference. It does not just make us more productive, it has the potential to replace much of what we see as uniquely human forms of production. Commoditized intelligence does more than just augment what we do; it can replace much of what we do.

Long periods of rising productivity have characterized the last few centuries. As productivity improved in agriculture, technology freed us from the fields and we moved to factories, then as the knowledge economy flourished on the back of computer technology, from the factories to offices. Now we face a future with AI, where we may free ourselves from white-collar work but seem to have no place to go. White collar, not blue collar, or perhaps both, are under threat.

Advances in large-language models (LLMs) are poised to flip the economic, even reorder the political map, because they will reorder where, and for whom, productivity grows.

The most exposed jobs to generative AI tools are the white-collar roles that power the service economy: management consultants, accountants, analysts and recent graduates who once counted on a safe salary premium. When those occupations can be augmented, automated or replaced by software, their productivity is likely to rocket for a small group of first-mover professionals but then stagnate, or collapse, as the technology becomes commoditized and headcount is cut. Graduate wages have already been flattening; student loan burdens and housing costs leave these workers little margin if salaries stop rising. In short, the promise of stable, high-productivity office work is dying.

The flip side is that jobs with the lowest automation risk, and the clearest long-run productivity path for humans, are physical, manual and local: roofers, plasterers, plumbers, sports professionals, servers in restaurants, physiotherapists. AI cannot easily replicate dexterity, on-site problem-solving or hands-on service, so these roles will keep their scarcity value. They will enjoy the job security and bargaining power once associated with graduates.

We may see an economic 'collar flip', where blue collar becomes the reliable engine of real output while white collar enters a period of uncertainty. With people and capital dispersing outward, we could see downward pressure on current high property prices and rises in other regions.

In a landscape where productivity gains arrive unevenly and unpredictably, the winners will be those who can translate AI-driven productivity into secure, dignified livelihoods, and the losers those who see their traditional advantages evaporate.

Oddly, the concept of economic growth, as a focal point in economics and policymaking, is a relatively recent development, with growth and gross domestic product (GDP) becoming obsessions in the modern age. Surprisingly, before the 1950s, discussions about pursuing economic growth were virtually non-existent.

Economists John Maynard Keynes and Simon Kuznets developed the concept of GDP during the Second World War, which later became the key metric for economic growth during the Cold War, in many respects an economic war, one which the more productive West won.

At its core, productivity measures how efficient goods and services are produced – essentially, the output generated per unit of input, such as labour, resources or capital. When productivity rises, using less labour, resources or capital, we get an increase in overall economic output. Heightened productivity acts as a catalyst for economic growth and societies achieve higher standards of living and greater prosperity. While the emphasis on economic growth is a relatively recent phenomenon, the interplay between productivity and growth has become a central theme in how we think about how economies develop and thrive.

As Figure 1.1 shows, it is no accident that this growth followed the European Enlightenment. That cultural transition towards reason, empirical inquiry and the systematic pursuit of useful knowledge was a necessary condition for productivity, innovation and sustained growth. The last two hundred years of economic growth have been propelled by the discovery of better ways to use finite resources, on the back of relentless innovation. This resulted from the endless intellectual ferment around progressive science and economics.

FIGURE 1.1 Global GDP per capita, 1–2008 CE

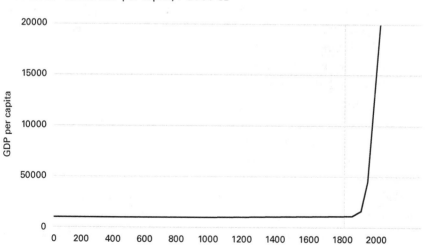

AI is the latest product of Enlightenment ideas, the growth of science and mathematics, coupled with a belief in progress through innovation and economic development, not as a physical invention, like the steam engine or electricity, but a psychological extension, the replication and improvement of our cognitive capabilities. These capabilities can also be embodied, placed inside physical robots that mimic and exceed our physical capabilities.

Growth and productivity

Growth has become the aim of all economies, yet it is hard to see how economies can square the circle of growth with the switch to clean energy, rising inequalities, pricey education, expensive healthcare and supporting a huge welfare state and ageing populations. AI could offer a way out of these conflicting forces and dilemmas, with a focus on using created intelligence to solve problems, optimize and innovate at breakneck speed.

This book is about this growth sweet spot, the idea that AI can bring improvements to individuals, teams, organizations, sectors and nations, using AI to increase productivity with a humane approach to growth. As soon as you personally use this technology, you become more productive. This can be realized at scale in organizations and nations.

Of course, more GDP does not always mean people are actually better off, as growth can be reckless and cruel. A country can grow its economy by adding more people, pumping out more fossil fuels or stacking up debt. That does not mean life is improving. Productivity, on the other hand, is about getting more value from growth. Productivity can also mean higher wages, lower costs and stronger businesses, not just thoughtless expansion. You do not have to cut down more forests or push people to work longer hours to succeed. You can innovate, automate and train workers better to get more out of what is already there. Productivity increases can lead to people working fewer hours, with less stress and more time for life.

If we extend the idea of productivity into the production of ideas, research, innovation and entrepreneurial activity, productivity can mean progressing beyond poorly optimized process, procedures and production. It fuels even more startling growth. More than just optimizing processes and doing the same thing more productively, productivity then becomes an agent for advancement and societal progress.

Without productivity, growth is also fragile. It is not just about getting bigger – it is about getting bigger but also better. Organizations can find that the pursuit of growth means rising costs and commitments that can harm you when the market turns or circumstances change. We saw this with the financial system in 2008, where companies were seen as being too big to fail, but fail they did. Also in higher education, where forecasts on student numbers, home and abroad, suddenly failed to materialize. Growth in itself can get bloated and turn chaotic, whereas sustainable productivity brings control and makes organizations and economies more resilient.

Seeing growth in terms of wider definitions of productivity also redefines it as sociologically and ecologically sustainable, reducing waste and strengthening economies without environmental harm. While growth as a goal in itself can be destructive, using up scarce resources, producing waste, billowing out pollution and destroying the planet, carefully calibrated growth, sensitive to solving these problems, is positive progress.

Growth is too often focused on reaching numbers, whereas productivity focuses on better outcomes. This is the difference between chasing bigger numbers and building a future where people benefit from those numbers, a future that creates a cycle where industries get stronger, wages rise and economies become more competitive, without needing to rely on cheap labour or endless population growth. Meaningful growth comes from a world that does not see growth as an end in itself but rather as enhancing efficiency and a better work–life balance. It drives innovation, makes businesses competitive, reduces reliance on resource exploitation and gives long-term economic stability.

Productivity meanings

Despite the focus on GDP, the word 'productivity' has come to have a number of meanings. It does not have one fixed definition but stretches across a family of related uses, bound not by a single rule but by a web of contexts, practices and purposes. To pin it down would be to miss its flexible nature. We must focus on 'productivity' not just in its narrow, economic and mathematical form but on both its quantitative and qualitative forms.

That said, there is often a similar lack of appreciation around the meaning and complexities of AI. There is a distinction to be made between generative AI and its predecessors. Such is the pace of its explosive evolution, it is difficult to keep up with developments, from improved quality of output, memory, increases in context windows, reasoning, deep research and agentic AI. Then there is multimodality, producing astonishing images, audio, avatars and video from text.

There is wild speculation about where AI is going, from the extremes of transhumanism, where some welcome our becoming slaves to this new evolved form of intelligence, to the doomsters who want it crushed – now! The truth, of course, lies somewhere in-between and does not lie on some simple, linear spectrum of use but within a complex range of uses. Rather than a single, tunnel vision on the nature of AI, we need to see it as a *constellation* of personal, organizational, state and global ideas around 'productivity'. Each have their own complex, multifaceted forms; the personal often translates into the team, organizational, sectoral, then national to international dimensions.

If we take the constellation analogy further, AI is the new sun at the centre of the productivity solar system, first energizing those planets nearest to this sun: places of broad breakthrough and surges of sector and domain-specific productivity. For others, more distant, it will take time. In this constellation, some productivity gains from AI may be huge spikes, like AlphaFold, that save unimaginable amounts of research time. Others may be sector-specific gains based on specific sets of domain data, and others will be a general rising tide in organizations and personal tools, useful to anyone and everyone. Progress will be somewhat fragmented and ragged. And this is also uncharted territory, outside of our known world, into the unknown.

Think of words related to the word 'productive': industrious, prolific, dynamic, fruitful, creative, constructive, bountiful. Then we see relatable forms of productivity, something we can feel as beneficial. Productivity is not a single essence, but a shared sense of productive progress. We need not be loyal to precise economic and mathematical definitions – better to see it as a general, multifarious sense of productive development.

Taxonomy of productivity

Productivity is about getting things done, but it takes on countless forms and manifests across a wide array of activities. It is not just about work in the traditional sense; productivity spans personal development, organizational growth, teamwork, societal and cultural progress, even the natural world. To truly appreciate its diversity, let's explore the different species or categories of productivity and how they interact with our lives.

Economic productivity

- National productivity
- Sectoral productivity
- Organizational productivity

- Team productivity
- Personal productivity
- Task productivity

National productivity

When an expert chastised an audience in Newcastle over them voting for Brexit, on the basis of a potential loss in GDP, a woman shouted back, 'That's your bloody GDP, not ours.' She had a point. This macro metric can mean little at the level of a sector or organization, as it is too high-level. At the individual level it can be almost meaningless.

Measuring productivity and GDP is a relatively modern idea, born out of our growing need to quantify economic performance and progress. It has its roots in the Industrial Revolution, when mechanization and factory systems dramatically reshaped economies. For the first time, societies needed tools to assess the output of these new industrial processes and their impact on national wealth.

Yet, the story of GDP and productivity measurement is not without criticism. Over time, many have pointed out their limitations. GDP does not capture inequality, environmental damage or the value of unpaid labour and more intangible services. Productivity metrics often ignore the human, cultural and social dimensions of work. Despite these criticisms, these measures remain central to our understanding of economic performance.

GDP gives you the big-picture view. It measures the total monetary value of all goods and services produced in a country over a specific period. This includes consumer purchases, business investments, government spending and exports. GDP is therefore a snapshot of a nation's overall economic health, giving a broad idea of how the economy is performing.

Beyond GDP, productivity measurement through AI becomes more detailed at lower economic levels. Exploring productivity down to individual businesses, even workers, helps to identify exactly where and how value is created most efficiently, enabling more targeted improvements and better economic outcomes. As this book is primarily about AI and productivity, we will focus on the mid-level and micro-levels, down through sectors, organizations, teams and personal productivity.

Sectoral productivity

The next step down is productivity in specific sectors of the economy, such as healthcare, manufacturing or technology. Here we can measure how efficiently each sector transforms inputs such as labour, capital and raw materials, into outputs. For example, in the automotive industry, where steel, assembly-line machinery and labour are the main inputs, are manufacturers now turning out more cars per worker or per machine?

Sector analysis is useful for policymaking, in deciding which sectors to support in your industrial and economic strategy. Most governments in developed economies have stated openly that they see AI playing a major role in increasing growth. The UK's AI Opportunities Action Plan, with 50 concrete recommendations on using AI to accelerate growth, and concrete financial and other levers to encourage sectoral growth, is typical (Department for Science, Innovation and Technology, 2025). Trade associations and conferences have also issued reports, showcased sector-specific exemplars and stimulated debate and action.

These policy shifts tend to focus on applying AI to increase productivity in both the public and private sector, with most focused on economic development, but also on education, health, innovation, data, robotics, ethical concerns and regulations. They play to the strengths of a nation's strongest sectors, those with the most potential for growth.

Organizational productivity

Drilling down further, we can look at productivity at the business, organizational and institutional levels. This is often explicit in reported accounts where the health and growth of an organization is laid out and audited. Additional metrics, such as margins and repeat business, are also useful. An organization's annual report is a good starting point for identifying areas and metrics where productivity improvements through AI can be targeted.

Inside an organization, productivity is, of course, spread across many functions. Departments may be responsible for productivity within their fields, while HR and Learning and Development are more focused on general people development but rarely have a direct focus on productivity metrics. Responsibility for productivity tends, therefore, to be spread thinly across the organization. Pushing for increases in productivity also tend to be reactive, addressing the issue only when there is a perceived problem.

At its heart, basic economic productivity is about getting the most bang for your buck. You start with your inputs, such as time, money or effort, then see how well you turn that into something useful. But this can be broken down into several types of economic productivity.

Let's start with *labour productivity*, which is all about how much work a person can get done in a given amount of time. Many spend hours on repetitive, low-value tasks, such as entering data, sorting emails, filing reports, arranging meetings and doing compliance. But with AI, these same tasks can be completed in a fraction of the time.

Capital productivity, on the other hand, is about how effectively we use investments in physical and digital assets like computers, software and office equipment. AI assists with this by getting more out of the same tools. The same software and hardware can produce more output by making it faster and smarter.

But perhaps the greatest gains come in *total factor productivity*. This is the holy grail of productivity, reflecting not just labour or capital productivity alone, but the overall efficiency when we combine them. When AI is integrated into workflows, it is not just the employees who are working smarter and getting a lot more out of the software and hardware; it is the system as a whole that becomes more streamlined and effective. It is the integration of several productivity factors that lift total factor productivity.

Of course, it is pointless optimizing something that does not need optimizing, so the first step in increasing productivity in organizations is often to eliminate what is unnecessary. A general principle that can be applied is Occam's Razor, minimizing the number of entities to reach your goal. Many organizations have superfluous steps, rules or bureaucracies. One can use AI to identify and eliminate such processes, paperwork, even roles. A good start is to separate critical from non-critical entities. There is slack in most systems, so one can use AI to identify tasks that are essential and critical; the rest can be available as resources to be accessed by people or software. It may not be automation that is needed but elimination.

There are also often layers of institutional inertia, reflected in outdated processes, bureaucracy, even fears and backlashes from leaders and those worried about losing their jobs. Yet some leaders have recognized the need for a radical shift into being an AI-first company, with AI as the primary strategic concern. This is obviously true in major global technology companies but also many in health, finance and retail organizations. This was explicit in emails and memos from CEOs in Fiverr and Shopify (more of them later) (Clark, 2025a, 2025b).

We may eventually see total organizational productivity when AI-run companies become common. Here individuals or small groups use AI to ideate, create, build, code, market, do the accounts, report and adapt in a market.

Team productivity

Organizations are social entities and social behaviour within organizations is most often executed in teams. It is teams that execute projects and teams that are managed; their optimal structure, in terms of types and competences, is often the key to productivity. Organizations that want to fully unlock AI's productivity potential must move beyond seeing AI as merely a personal efficiency tool and treat it as a collaborative partner that actively amplifies knowledge, output and value across teams.

An IT team, for example, can deliberately identify coding tools that clearly improve productivity. It is often a matter of targeting specific teams or departments that are ploughing the same furrow, stuck in old practices and tools.

No matter whether a team is fixed, temporary, in the same place or virtual, teamwork and collaboration are on the rise. Unfortunately, much teamwork is sub-optimal in productivity, as teamwork is not easy and does not always come naturally to people. Peruvian Eduardo Salas is fascinated by 'teamwork', as he thinks teams really matter in most organizations, especially in the military, aviation and healthcare, where they can be critical (Salas et al, 2008). What makes a good team? How do you develop teams and train for teamwork? Better team processes and training increases performance, saves money and saves lives.

Clear roles and responsibilities, driven by compelling purpose with a vision, goals and objectives, matter (Belbin, 2012). AI can be used to create and track this, in a culture of psychological safety, where people can be open and admit their mistakes. This also means there must be permission, mutual trust and complete openness on the use of AI.

AI can be used to develop team norms and performance conditions that are clear, known and appropriate, including the use of AI. Salas is a fan of huddles and debriefs, as they are error-correction methods, and AI can be used to summarize and set expectations that are clear and understood; it can also be used to share any unique information and methods, including efficient AI prompts and tools, and give access to relevant documents, information, policies and procedures interrogatable by AI.

Given the ubiquity of online collaborative tools, like Microsoft Teams and Slack, Salas reminds us that what is also needed is a clear view of what teams are and how they should be supported and trained. This includes knowing how they utilize and work with AI.

We are entering an age when AI is becoming an invaluable member of teams, not just a tool or resource used by teams. One study on 'The

Cybernetic Teammate: A Field Experiment on Generative AI Reshaping Teamwork and Expertise' by Dell'Acqua et al (2025) showed that teams using AI produced the best outputs, particularly top-quality outputs, and benefited from improved morale.

Personal productivity

In one of the most successful time management books of all time, Dave Allen (2002) gave us his 'two-minute rule'. If something can be done in two minutes, do it, rather than adding it to endless lists that get longer as deadlines pass. Allen's whole approach was to get rid of the psychological weight that procrastination brings. With AI, many more things can be done within that two-minute envelope: emails, memos, quick reports, summaries, translations and so on.

In fact, you have been using AI for that two-minute rule for decades to increase personal productivity, as whenever you write, use autocorrect, search Google and see predictive text, use Google Scholar, Google Maps, translation, online shopping and pricing, call an Uber, engage with social media, streaming choices, home voice assistants, pass through a passport gate or take a photograph on your smartphone, you have benefited from quick productivity gains through AI.

You constantly benefit from AI productivity without knowing it. Like water, intelligence is creeping in at the personal level to get things done. With some of these services, you are still in the loop; with others, you can choose to be or not to be in the loop. Increasingly, however, the mundane aspects of everyday life and work are being intelligently augmented and automated.

Procrastination is one of the most pervasive obstacles to personal productivity. It sneaks into our lives at every level, personal and organizational, delaying progress, and often leaving us uneasy. It is easy to dismiss it as laziness but procrastination is often rooted in fear, poor practice or a feeling of being overwhelmed. It is a daily battle for many. Whether you put off studying for an exam, delaying physical exercise, doing a tax return or avoiding that difficult conversation, procrastination creates a cycle of guilt and stress that saps your energy and motivation. The tasks pile up, the deadlines loom larger, and the mental toll grows heavier, making it harder to even begin. AI is being used across the board by individuals to solve the problem of procrastination by getting done in minutes those things that used to take hours.

AI also brought opportunities for individuals to inject doses of productivity directly into their workflow. Whether it was researching a topic, getting a quick answer, summarizing, creating concise communications or writing reports, we discovered that, just as the calculator produces numbers as solutions, so generative-AI produces words, and now images and video, as solutions.

AI enters at this deeply personal level, making tasks quicker and easier. The billions of uses of AI started with personal productivity and remain its base power. Many have been using AI on the sly, as their organizations and institutions make it uncomfortable for them when using it, limit it or ban its use. This is a rearguard action, as rising personal use shows that AI is proving its worth, primarily as a productivity tool.

We would do well to teach employees how to fish in this increasingly deep and wide lake of concrete productivity tools, related to what they actually do in work, rather than abstract, over-long courses which are de-anchored from their personal reality. Allowing them to exercise agency aligns learning with their tasks and their work.

We see rapid improvements in its quality, memory, reasoning, agentic abilities, accuracy, being up to date and accessibility. It is also multilingual and multimodal. We all felt that sense of personal agency through prompting. This shifts significantly when AI memory kicks in, as that increases context, relevance and intention. The location of agency shifts again when agentic AI executes a series of tasks and actions, with varying degrees of human oversight, from continuous, through occasional to rarely and almost never. AGI will be an even greater step.

Task productivity

AI tools boost productivity by optimizing the task(s) between your intention and the output. For draft emails, reports or marketing copy, you can instantly rephrase, shorten, translate or expand it, in seconds. In coding, autocomplete systems generate whole functions, tests and bug fixes, letting engineers spend more time on design. Real-time assistants in call centres surface answers and suggested phrasing mid-conversation, raising the number of cases resolved per hour.

Because AI can turn free text into slide decks or spreadsheet formulas, they act as your automatic interface to strip out many micro-tasks of data handling and formatting. Similarly, designers and marketers can use image, text and video generators to create dozens of visual concepts, ad variants or alternatives for testing.

Productivity gains are already being seen in many common and mundane tasks, but more sophisticated gains are being seen in research and high-level tasks in sectors such as healthcare and the law. Agents can pursue these higher-level goals further, largely on their own, planning, deciding and acting with only light human interventions. These increase productivity further.

Each level of productivity measurement feeds into the next. Improved task-level productivity increases personal productivity, which enhances team performance, leading to better organizational outcomes and stronger sectoral performance. All of this ultimately rolls towards higher GDP. But one common denominator across all levels of using AI to increase productivity is asking a basic question. To what problem is AI a solution? Productivity increases emerge when problems are solved. Seeing AI as solutions to problems is how nations, sectors, organizations, teams and individuals achieve the best results. It is the problems that come first.

Productivity plus

My TED talk in 2012 (Clark, 2012) claimed that 'we had more pedagogic change in 10 years than the last 1,000 years', stating that the internet had changed how we access, use and learn knowledge, reshaping our lives and future. My stronger claim now is that we will see an even more significant technological shift in the next 10 years than the last 1,000 years, through AI. This is by far the most important century in the history of our species, as AI is likely to be a general, global, civilization-shaping force affecting what technology does in our lives in general, fuelling many types of innovative change – physical, cultural, even ecological.

There is more to productivity than work and workflows. Technology, as we have seen since the start of this century, has drifted somewhat aimlessly into escapism, entertainment and diversion. That is not bad in itself but we now have a chance to use technology as a force for good, with innovations that are much bigger than mere increases in output.

Productivity plus

- Innovative productivity
- Physical productivity
- Cultural productivity
- Ecological productivity

Innovative productivity

Beyond simple organizational productivity are dimensions of productivity that have attracted a lot of academic attention, namely the productivity of innovation, which looks at how entrepreneurship and innovation can be made more successful to fuel future productivity.

A hidden force behind technological and economic progress, across these last 200 years, was innovative and practical productivity, not a wholly top-down process but rather an organic, trial-and-error phenomenon driven by human creativity and sometimes government support, research and market incentives. At its core, innovation is often about increasing productivity, finding smarter, faster and more efficient ways to solve problems, reduce costs and improve lives.

This is not just the story of lone geniuses or government mandates. Incremental improvements, often made by many contributors over time, are often the true drivers of progress. Steam engines, electricity and digital technology all show how each new wave of innovation helps productivity by allowing people to do more with less: less labour, less energy and fewer resources, and it was the practical implementation of these general technologies that gave us the productivity gains.

The best ideas often emerged from competition, experimentation and collaboration. Markets provided constant feedback, rewarding ideas that worked and discarding those that did not. This trial-and-error approach ensured that the most productive solutions rose to the top. History shows that societies that embrace innovation and productivity thrive, while those that try to control or restrict it fall behind.

Productive innovation is therefore a massive driver of human prosperity. It has given us better healthcare, cheaper energy, faster communication and more efficient production methods, all of which have freed up time, expanded economies and amplified productivity across industries.

Predictive productivity is an offshoot from innovative productivity, but could be one of the most potent and potentially disruptive forms of productivity. An AI forecasting tool can be trained on past data, measured against already proven historical outcomes. This intense training could produce powerful forecasters. It is already forecasting in the financial markets, where it could, with agentic AI, outperform humans. In health, predictive medicine may become the norm. Almost all organizations could do with better forecasting, on everything from demand for products to societal trends. Predictive productivity takes productivity into the future, based on past data; it may also prove potent in predicting climate change and other currently intractable problems.

Physical productivity

When thinking about AI and productivity there is a tendency to imagine that everyone works with text in an office, so all jobs are augmented or eliminated by digital output. This is a conceit, as many do not work in offices but have jobs doing physical things in the physical world. We get so enamoured with thinking about AI as software that we ignore the potentially much greater growth in embodied AI. In the physical world this could have dramatic effects, such as automated vehicles, robotaxis, drones, domestic robots, social care robots and dark factory manufacturing.

We will have robots that are relatable to humans, as that is their functional design, but most will be purely functional with no need for relatability to humans beyond ease of use. Robots can also create other robots; therefore, anything robots can produce, from cardboard boxes to computer chips, can be subjected to significant increases in productivity using these low-cost 24/7 workers.

Physical productivity brings ethical issues in its wake. Dark factories can be directed towards dark ends. The risk from the production of drones is already being realized in war. Biological weapons and a massive escalation in nuclear weapons are also frightening possibilities. Cybersecurity risks also multiply. We could see the exploitation of the high seas, with vast solar farms and data centres, where fusion and other energy capture methods may allow even more AI dominance. Space becomes important, in terms of power and resources and, as humans find space difficult and robots do not, it is ripe for progress and dominance through embodied AI. The earth may even end up being dominated from above by a space-dominant nation.

An intriguing question is what it will mean to share our world with a huge number of AGIs. Their replicability and scale have very few limits, making that future look very different from our current world.

Cultural productivity

Cultural productivity is a category often overlooked in traditional definitions but no less vital. This is the productivity of artists, writers and creative inventors who transform ideas into tangible forms. Much harder to quantify, driven by inspiration rather than efficiency, its impact is profound. We should not overlook the recognized role of cultural and creative productivity in shaping our cultures, sparking innovation and providing the emotional resonance that makes productive progress meaningful.

An enormous pool of data stretching back in history, the cultural output from our species has been used to train huge multimodal models that we can commune with to create a new future. With new forms of AI, we are borrowing from the past to create the new. It is a new beginning, a fresh start using technology we have never seen before in the history of our species, a powerful, bottom-up technology that has given us fresh agency.

AI, along with us, does not simply copy, sample or parrot things from the past: together we create new outputs. Neither does it remix, reassemble or reappropriate the past: together we create the future. This moves us into genuinely new forms of production and expression. We should avoid seeing it as reproduction, reinterpretations or simple syntheses; rather, it is the ground for genuinely new work. It should not be too readily reduced to one word, but rather should be pre-fixed with 're-': to re-imagine, re-envision, re-conceptualize, re-contextualize, re-vise, re-work, re-vamp, re-interpret, re-model, re-define and re-invent new cultural capital.

Creation as a uniquely human endeavour has all along been a drawing upon the past, deeply rooted in what the brain has experienced and takes from memory whenever you think, speak or write anything new. We are now, together, taking things from the entire memory of our cultural past in new acts of cultural creation.

This new world or new dawn is more communal, drawing from the well of a vast shared, public collective. We can have a common purpose of mutual effort that leads to a more co-operative, collaborative and unified effort. There were some historical dawns that hinted at this future – the Library at Alexandria, open to all, containing the known world's knowledge; Wikipedia, a huge, free communal knowledge base – but this is something much more profoundly powerful, productive and communal.

The many peoples, cultures and languages of the world can be in this communal effort, not to fix some utopian idea of a common set of values or cultural output, but to create beyond what just one group sees as good and evil. This could be a more innovative and transformative era, a future of openness, a genuine recognition that the future is created by all of us, not determined wholly by the past, but from an amalgam of cultures. AI is not a machine; it now 'us' speaking to 'ourselves', in fruitful dialogue.

How do we find meaning in a world where AI can do everything better than we do? One could argue for automating people out of the economy, but that is an arid goal. Using AI to do communally interesting things, such as the advance of beneficial education, healthcare, science and technology, along with the blossoming of the arts and culture, for the benefit of all, may be more important goals. This is still a consequence of increasing productivity, but it redefines what productivity means.

Ecological productivity

Ecological productivity, which should not go unnoticed, is the deep well of productivity from which we, as humans, evolved. In nature's fight against entropy, we are the most fascinating product of its bountiful productivity. Its primary productivity, the creation of energy at the base of the food chain, fuels a secondary productivity, where consumers of that energy take energy and transform it, grow, move around and reproduce. Ecological productivity is clearly sustainable, unless we make it unsustainable, as nature has its own recycling system with decomposers that turn organic material back into soil.

It has been steadily productive for billions of years, eventually producing us humans, the only thing we know in the universe that uses ideas, language and intelligence to increase our own productivity. Superbly successful, adaptive and resilient, we are part of this vast intertwined ecosystem. So, wherever these thoughts take us on productivity, we must not destroy the productivity of nature itself, which has nothing to do with profit margins or increasing value but is the foundation upon which all human productivity rests.

Wake up!

Let me try to bring the complexity of productivity to life, covering many different dimensions of productivity we have mentioned, to show that too tight and linear a treatment can be limiting.

A shepherd once discovered a plant that made his goats quite lively and used that plant to stay awake himself. That plant was coffee. This everyday substance owes its spread and popularity entirely to its productive effects on the mind. A fascinating drink, with a long history, that has dramatic cognitive effects and has more recently spread around the planet through a coffee-shop culture, it is the most widely consumed psychoactive drug in the world. But what is its role in work and productivity?

Since that Yemeni goatherder observed his goats frolicking around after eating coffee beans, coffee grew in popularity in the Middle East. It allowed Islamic Sufis to get through long nights of prayer and Islamic students found they could keep awake to recite and learn the Koran. The port of Mocha eventually opened up the trade in coffee in the 16th century, to Constantinople and on into Europe. As a marker of hospitality, it encouraged social activity and conversation, especially in an Ottoman Empire where alcohol was prohibited.

Trade across the British Empire led to the first London coffee house in 1652 (*innovative* productivity), right by the Royal Exchange, which was an immediate success, and within 10 years there were dozens of coffee houses in London, fuelled by Puritan attitudes, when alcohol was frowned upon. By the late 17th century coffee houses charged a penny a cup and were called 'penny universities', places of cross-disciplinary debate. Drinkers sat at a long table, next to and opposite people, to encourage conversation. Pamphlets and newspapers were available, all adding to *societal* productivity. Indeed, they became such hothouses of political debate, Charles II wanted them shut down, to repress political dissent.

Edward Lloyd's coffee house became Lloyds of London. Jonathon's Coffee House in 1698 listed stock prices, which eventually became the London Stock Exchange. Similarly in New York, a coffee house became the New York Stock Exchange, all of which aided *organizational* productivity. Coffee houses were also seen as sharpening the wit. The *Tatler* (1709) and *Spectator* (1711) drew content from that source, as coffee stimulated thought and cultural output, so contributing to *cultural* productivity. Pepys went to a coffee house three or four times a day and Voltaire drank 40 cups a day!

To drink a coffee in the morning to become alert, and then after meals to combat post-prandial lethargy, is an established social ritual. Espressos, an Italian habit, came with the technological invention of compressing water through coffee, an example of *technological* productivity, making it quick to produce.

Quick and easy to make, with psychoactive qualities, coffee was also incorporated into the workplace, as a regular break from work but also as a method of staying productive and getting through the working day, a form of *organizational* productivity.

Urban, corporate coffee chains, and now more artisanal small coffee shops, have seen a global revival, picking up on the digital revolution, popular with mobile laptop workers and students, offering free Wi-Fi. Many have people deep in thought, writing, coding, emailing and doing their jobs, stimulated by coffee and the general social environment of a warm and inviting place, giving *societal* productivity.

There is now evidence that coffee improves short-term memory and reaction times, improving personal productivity. Koppelstaetter et al (2008) looked at a group of 15 volunteers who were given 100 mg of coffee. Testing and scanning showed improvements in memory in the caffeine-fuelled group.

Coffee also reveals *ecological* productivity. Caffeine is an evolutionary adaption that benefits the plant, a natural fungicide that stops it being eaten by insects. When the plant leaves fall and decompose, they release caffeine into the soil, inhibiting the growth of nearby plants. Its stimulant effect also attracts pollinating bees. This is a beautiful example of evolved, *ecological* productivity.

Conclusion

Productivity is not just economic output – it is solving problems efficiently. AI helps us do this at scale. Rather than fear change, we should channel it. Like steam or electricity, AI offers an era-defining opportunity but only if we use it to unlock real-world value. Productivity is no longer a numbers game; it is about doing more with less, and doing it meaningfully.

The coffee story shows how complex the productivity nexus can be. Productivity issues often have a long history, with cognitive aspects, human behavioural features, societal impact, political consequences, even biological and ecological dimensions.

Abstract words, like 'productivity', tend to suffer from a definition problem. We would do well to not see it in terms of some pure essence, a thing in itself, but rather a constellation of concerns, issues and problems. Rather than talking about productivity as one purely abstract economic term, we can reframe productivity as the art of solving problems through efficiency, a shift in mindset that changes everything.

It is never as simple as one assumes. Our deep dive into AI and productivity in this book takes a wide-angle lens to the problems, in exposing the paradoxes, problems and solutions of productivity. By understanding these wider issues, we see productivity not as a single concept but as a multilayered phenomenon that touches every corner of life. Rather than seeing it as a dry economic calculus, we should see AI as being productive in many dimensions, allowing us to flourish in our world.

We will now explore the many paradoxes we face when AI hits not the brick walls of technical, data or energy constraints, or even regulations, but the morass of confusion and paradoxes that arise whenever great change sweeps though the world of work.

References

Allen, D (2002) *Getting Things Done*, Piatkus Books

Belbin, R M (2012) *Team Roles at Work*, Routledge

Clark, D (2012) More pedagogic change in 10 years than last 1000 years, YouTube, https://www.youtube.com/watch?v=dEJ_ATgrnnY&t=10s (archived at https://perma.cc/9W95-78VY)

Clark, D (2025a) Fiverr CEO's stunning letter to all, April, https://donaldclarkplanb.blogspot.com/2025/04/fiverr-ceos-stunning-letter-to-all.html (archived at https://perma.cc/98JH-9FW2)

Clark, D (2025b) Memo from CEO of Shopify: Reflexive AI, April, https://donaldclarkplanb.blogspot.com/2025/04/memo-from-ceo-of-shopify-reflexive-ai.html (archived at https://perma.cc/5523-83TP)

DataReportal (2025) Digital around the World, DataReportal, https://datareportal.com/global-digital-overview (archived at https://perma.cc/5Z7U-QQUR)

Dell'Acqua et al (2025) The cybernetic teammate: A field experiment on generative AI reshaping teamwork and expertise, Harvard Business School Working Paper No 25-043, March

Department for Science, Innovation and Technology (2025) AI opportunities action plan (UK), https://www.gov.uk/government/publications/ai-opportunities-action-plan/ai-opportunities-action-plan (archived at https://perma.cc/SX54-ZYED)

Hoffman, R and Beato, G (2025) *Superagency: What Could Possibly Go Right With Our AI Future*, Authors Equity

Koppelstaetter, F et al (2008) Does caffeine modulate verbal working memory processes? An fMRI study, *NeuroImage*, 39 (1), 492–99

Krugman, P (1994) *The Age of Diminished Expectations: US Economic Policy in the 1990s*, MIT Press

Public First (2018) Google's impact in the UK: At home, at school, at work, https://www.publicfirst.co.uk/wp-content/uploads/2018/10/GoogleImpact2018.pdf (archived at https://perma.cc/25LJ-DNA7)

Salas, E, Goodwin, G F and Burke, C S (2008) *Team Effectiveness in Complex Organizations: Cross-Disciplinary Perspectives and Approaches*, Routledge

Susskind, D (2024) *Growth: A History and a Reckoning*, Harvard University Press

Varian, H R (2011) The economic value of Google [Presentation], San Francisco, 29 March

Further reading

Elliott, L (2017) The blunt heckler who tells economists they are failing us, *The Guardian*, 10 January, https://www.theguardian.com/commentisfree/2017/jan/10/blunt-heckler-economists-failing-us-booming-britain-gdp-london (archived at https://perma.cc/AM4A-MY3U)

Maddison Project Database (2020) Angus Maddison economic growth data, University of Groningen, https://www.rug.nl/ggdc/historicaldevelopment/maddison/releases/maddison-project-database-2020 (archived at https://perma.cc/HMR9-QLJL)

02

Productivity paradoxes

Many expect AI to deliver instant productivity miracles or dismiss it as useless. There is a paradox! But real progress is uneven, what is called the 'jagged frontier'. AI excels in some tasks, struggles in others. Understanding this non-linear progress means understanding and confronting the paradoxes that arise in practice: technological, organizational and human.

Productivity paradox

Since 2008, productivity has remained stubbornly flat despite waves of technological innovation. Covid-19 briefly promised a digital acceleration, but the long-standing paradox remains. Technology progresses, yet productivity gains lag. AI throws this into sharper relief. Why is it not having a uniform impact? The puzzle remains because its adoption is filtered through a web of behavioural, institutional and economic contradictions.

A paradox is a statement or situation where something seems to contradict itself. Paradoxes are useful in exploring the limitations of an approach in productivity, even opening up our minds to new possibilities. The whole field of productivity is full of surprising paradoxes: behavioural paradoxes at the personal level, adoption paradoxes at the level of technological implementation, organizational paradoxes, as well as economic paradoxes at the societal level.

Investigating these productivity paradoxes is useful because paradoxes reveal deeper complexity and causes. You have to question your assumptions about how easy it is to apply AI to productivity problems. It may seem superficially obvious that people, organizations and nations will behave rationally and work towards increasing productivity but psychological and organizational bottlenecks intervene. You cannot take anything for granted, as the world is not a purely rational place. It opens your mind up to complexity, to explain why things do not happen in a predictable fashion. Above all, paradoxes provoke curiosity about a subject and force us to think beyond obvious conclusions.

Behavioural paradoxes

Despite its appeal, productivity often meets resistance. People procrastinate, rationalize inefficiency and even moralize against automation. Bureaucracies multiply tasks instead of eliminating them. We cling to rituals, meetings, paperwork, procedures, not because they are useful but because they are familiar. We humans wrongly assume that we always play the starring role. Our sense of human exceptionalism makes us anthropomorphize or behave in ways that are counter to actual productive value. Humans are experts at finding ways not to be productive.

One paradox of productivity is that despite it being obviously desirable, it is paradoxically difficult. You have to have respect for the problem, look at the apparent paradoxes, try to understand and unravel them, then accept there are trade-offs.

At times we seem to enjoy not being productive, getting satisfaction from the mundane repetition of work. We also find all sorts of excuses, some simple, some elaborate, to avoid even thinking about becoming more productive. At the simplest level we have instincts that manifest themselves as biases towards avoiding productivity, especially through technology. Procrastination is commonplace because we fall into habits of unthinking behaviour.

At a more rational level, we find ways to defend the indefensible, as 'just the ways things are done', or justify inefficient behaviour with ad hoc excuses. We even imagine that AI is somehow being underhand or cheating and we come up with full rationales, ways of convincing ourselves, that productivity is somehow ethically wrong, so we put up stout resistance to change.

We even invent all sorts of processes, procedures and practices to waste time, through documentation, forms, sign-offs, meetings, policies, regulations, the famous red tape. The term 'red tape' has a long history, reaching back to the 16th century, when documents were tied up with red ribbons. 'Red tape' no longer refers to ribbons but to bureaucracy, especially excessive government documentation and procedures, but also more generally for unnecessary obstacles to getting things done.

Paradoxically, the solution to the paradox of production is often to automate it out of existence. If we can minimize the need for humans-in-the-loop, even automate the process completely, the paradox no longer exists! Things get done with little or no effort. If only it were that simple.

Bias paradox

AI triggers deep-seated cognitive biases. Intrinsic human traits, such as inherent biases and sticking to fixed narratives on the back of those biases, shape our decisions and perceptions. This interplay between the human need for stability and technological change helps us understand technological progress.

Most AI in the world remains invisible, working its magic behind the scenes, in autocorrect, correcting images, searching, reading your passport, number plate reading, securing access to your online bank account or phone. AI often succeeds when it is no longer seen as AI. You don't have to find AI, as it will have found you.

Yet when visible, AI is a technology that sparks equal measures of fascination and dread. On one hand, it is a marvel of human ingenuity, promising solutions to problems we once deemed unsolvable. On the other, it is the bogeyman, conjuring fears of runaway robots, mass unemployment and a world where humans become obsolete. But why do we feel this way? Why do AI and its advances so often trigger our nervousness, suspicion, even outright hostility? The answer lies in a battery of cognitive biases that shape our perception and reactions.

It is always easier to see biases in others than admit to our own and even easier to attribute biases to AI, if we see it as a new, strange and threatening technology, especially a technology that seems closer to us than anything we have ever seen before, something that even challenges us as a species.

The most common bias is *confirmation* bias, our habit of seeking evidence that supports what we already believe. Many see AI as strange, unfamiliar and not fitting into our confirmed world. Linked to this is *status quo* bias. We have an unconscious preference for things to stay the way they are. As creatures of habit, we like predictability and control, and AI threatens both. When a machine starts behaving like us, answering questions, writing, speaking, even driving, it unsettles that expectation.

We are evolved creatures, so also have a strong *anthropocentric* bias, a belief that we humans sit at the top of the pyramid, exceptional creatures with by far the highest intelligence and creativity. Suddenly AI challenges this belief by doing things we thought only we could do. When it started to write stories and poems, create images, even video, we got very defensive. A similar but more considered reaction is *loss aversion* bias, which gives us anxiety when we think about or encounter AI. This is more reasoned, as we fear losing what we have, our jobs, our privacy and our sense of human exceptionalism. As we see it do things faster, even better, we fear the consequences and want to avoid losing what we hold dear.

Then we have a tendency to dream up worst-case scenarios, as we have *negativity* bias, seeing threats more readily than opportunities. Suddenly, AI is an existential threat; runaway AI takes control and extinction looms, wiping out humanity. The benefits in education, science and healthcare are pushed to the side. One accident and self-driving cars are all over the news, whereas the real numbers of people who die on the roads are rarely mentioned.

It is not that these feelings and biases come up one by one. It is a swirl of confusion and mixed emotions, but the overall effect is one of resistance to change. Overall, one's reaction is full of contradictions, a mixed sense of wonder and fear, seeing AI as both exciting and terrifying. It is also difficult to grasp, as the technology is opaque and immediately challenging, as something different from anything we have experienced in the past. AI is therefore uniquely challenging in the history of technology as it seems so human.

We should not assume, therefore, that the benefits of productivity should be obvious, even when we show studies and evidence that significant gains can be realized. Changing minds and behaviour is a matter of both heart and head, emotion and reason. This gives rise to lots of paradoxes in productivity.

Procrastination paradox

Productivity is fundamentally personal. We all know from personal experience that productivity is a real thing and can be improved. Psychologically, we've all had those pangs of guilt about not getting things done: filling in your taxes, switching that savings account. We are natural-born procrastinators. We go make that cup of coffee, check our social media, do anything but get on with stuff.

This paradox of procrastination is puzzling as it seems to act against our best judgement and interests. It seems almost irrational, certainly counterproductive. Many organizations are similarly plagued by long meetings, perhaps the most common procrastination technique.

Procrastination is widespread, affecting around 20 per cent of adults and 50 per cent of students (Steel, 2007). Wang et al (2023) suggest 30–65 per cent of workers spend time web browsing or doing things unrelated to work, even when faced with urgent work. Employers clearly expect some non-productive time, but poor productivity can be costly.

The irony is that the psychological weight of avoidance often exceeds the burden of the task itself. Paradoxically, the longer you resist, the more unbearable the burden becomes. Of course, the actual task is rarely as difficult as you imagine and it would seem that fear of failure, along with worry about not meeting high standards, or others' expectations, cause procrastination. Beyond its impact on productivity, it is also linked to higher stress, anxiety and guilt. Chronic procrastination is even linked to prolonged distress.

Perfection paradox

As Shakespeare said in King Lear, 'Striving to better, oft we mar what's well'. Striving for perfection can kill productivity. Spending hours tweaking an email, document or report that is already good enough wastes time and energy. Perfection becomes the enemy of the good. *Do not procrastinate by waiting until the next version of an AI tool is launched, as there will always be a next version.*

Perfectionism, often seen as a sign of high standards and excellence, can backfire, reducing efficiency, delaying decisions and harming your wellbeing. Perfectionists can show high levels of indecisiveness and that leads to procrastination and missed opportunities. These are direct hits to productivity. They suffer paralysis through analysis, constantly refining, resulting in delays that kill productivity. Perfectionism also takes a toll on mental health, resulting in stress, anxiety, even depression, all of which further impair productivity.

According to Hewitt and Flett (1991) there seem to be three interrelated components in perfectionism: self-oriented, other-oriented and socially prescribed. Self-oriented perfectionism is when individuals set and become driven by self-imposed high standards. Other-oriented perfectionism holds others to unrealistic expectations. Socially prescribed perfectionism is the belief that others hold you to standards that you cannot reasonably meet.

Patterson et al (2021) found that between 1989 and 2016, perfectionism increased by 32 per cent among students in the US, Canada and UK, damaging results on productive output.

In organizations, Swider et al (2018) found that perfectionist employees spend far too much time getting stuck in endless revisions, refining work beyond what is necessary, leading to delays, missed deadlines and lost opportunities.

AI can produce high-quality work in record time. It does not have an intrinsic psychological problem with perfectionism, and it doesn't care about others or social pressure. And it can be calibrated to produce output at whatever level is required. It therefore eliminates the paradox of procrastination and perfection.

Organizational paradoxes

Busyness paradox

Being busy is not the same as being productive. Parkinson's Law reminds us that work expands to fill time. Without prioritization, we fall into the trap of chasing low-value tasks. AI excels here, not by working harder, but by eliminating redundant effort, structuring focus and compressing time.

When it comes to productivity, there are some common mistakes people make that cloud their perceptions of what productivity means. Just because you are writing documents or attending endless meetings does not mean you are pushing out the productivity boat. Productivity is about results, not how much you do along the way.

Not all tasks are equal in terms of productivity, but many people treat their to-do list like a shopping list, giving everything equal weight. Without prioritization, you spend all your energy on trivial tasks while the big, meaningful ones remain unfinished. The Pareto Principle, also known as the 80/20 rule, reminds us that 80 per cent of results often come from 20 per cent of effort.

Being practical, are you a slave to notifications? In this age of smartphones and endless pings and red notifications, many let their time be dictated by whatever pops up on their screen. These constant interruptions sabotage productivity. It is often better to turn off the alerts and take control of your attention. Many never stop to evaluate what is working and what is not. Without reflection, you are doomed to repeat the same mistakes over and over. True productivity is about working smarter, not harder, aligning your time and energy with your goals, learning to prioritize. When you avoid these common distractions, you will get more done.

The main productivity hack is not to see productivity as just about effort but to think about amplifying productivity through AI, systems, technology aids or automation. Efficiency comes from a well-oiled process, not brute force.

Parkinson's paradox

Parkinson's Law, more correctly a paradox, was first defined by British naval historian Cyril Northcote Parkinson (1955) in *The Economist*. It states that 'work expands to fill the time available for its completion'. This highlights a critical paradox in productivity: that the more time or resources allocated to a task, the more that task will inflate in complexity, often reducing overall efficiency.

He developed his theory on observations of inefficiency in the British Civil Service, seeing that bureaucracies tend to grow, irrespective of actual workload, which undermines productivity. In the British Colonial Office, for example, staff numbers increased even as the British Empire shrank. Parkinson argued that this was due not to more work but to administrators creating work for each other, a cycle of inefficiency where productivity is sacrificed in favour of process. This is sometimes called bureaucratic bloat.

Many are familiar with the meeting paradox, where the more meetings an organization holds, the worse progress and productivity becomes, as real work gets displaced by performance. Collecting more data and reports is meant to improve oversight, but it ultimately blinds decision-makers with information overload, preventing decisive action. Expanding an organization is meant to improve productivity, yet it can introduce layers of complexity that make actual decision making slower. The more an organization creates rules and oversight mechanisms to ensure accountability, the harder it becomes to actually hold anyone accountable, as responsibility is diffused across committees.

In his later work, *Parkinson's Law: The Pursuit of Progress* (1959), he introduced another brilliant observation with his Law of Triviality, which explains how teams and organizations often spend more time on small, relatively unimportant decisions while neglecting major strategic priorities.

Boiled frog paradox

The paradoxes of productivity show that, often, people can't see, do and often don't want to increase productivity. The boiled frog paradox describes a frog placed in gradually heated water, not noticing the slow rise in temperature until it is too late to escape. In other words, gradual negative changes often go unnoticed until it is too late.

Applied to human and organizational resistance to productivity improvements, the paradox says that people often fail to notice slowly worsening inefficiencies and outdated processes, bureaucracy and practices.

Employees and leaders resist productivity improvements simply because they have grown accustomed to existing systems, no matter how problematic. Like the frog in slowly boiling water, they fail to recognize the gradual decline in productivity, comforted by familiarity, until eventually, significant competitive disadvantages become undeniable, even fatal.

Organizations often avoid making necessary changes to improve productivity, such as adopting AI, because employees perceive these changes as disruptive or threatening. The subtle accumulation of wasted time, bureaucratic bloat and operational rigidity feels tolerable because it happens gradually, leading to complacency and resistance to new solutions. The boiled frog paradox illustrates how incremental acceptance of poor productivity can blind individuals and businesses to the urgent need for change, ultimately hindering adaptation and growth.

Clark Paradox

AI aids individual productivity, yet institutions often suppress its use. This 'Clark Paradox' reveals a deep contradiction: tools that empower workers are treated as threats by legacy structures. On the border between personal and organizational productivity, this fascinating and unique paradox often goes unnoticed. So unnoticed, I have claimed it for myself. AI empowers individuals to perform at higher levels, yet that empowerment is, paradoxically, treated as a threat by institutions designed to promote hierarchical, top-down control.

Despite the remarkable productivity gains that AI offers, there has been a growing undercurrent of unsanctioned AI use in the workplace. In one study, by SHRM (2024), which surveyed 31,000 employees, a surprising 78 per cent admitted to using AI tools not provided by their organizations. This shadow adoption is not driven by rebellion but by necessity, with employees turning to external AI tools to meet work demands and save time where their company tools fall short. A significant 29 per cent of respondents were classified as AI power users, engaging with these tools several times a week and achieving significant productivity gains, with over 30 minutes saved daily.

These power users found creative ways to integrate AI into their workflows, optimizing task completion and improving efficiency.

This highlights a gulf between corporate policies and employee needs. Workforces are independently seeking out tools to fill the void created by their organization's inaction. To avoid the censorious comments and censorship, people in all areas of human endeavour use it while not telling anyone, without the knowledge of their teacher, lecturer, recruiter or employer.

Utility drives use. By providing employees with sanctioned, high-quality AI solutions, companies can gain from productivity gains while also maintaining security and consistency.

Technology paradoxes

We tend to assume that obviously productive technology, which saves time, money and resources, will sweep through organizations with ease, relieving us from the pressures of work. Paradoxically, history tells us that the various technological revolutions in the past took longer than many imagine; even general technologies that have widespread applications take longer than expected to result in actual rises in productivity.

Often it is just capability overhang, the concept of a technology that has not yet realized its productivity potential due to the lag of adoption. AI is evolving faster than even its creators imagined, with rapid increases in the breadth and depth of functionality, along with massive falls in costs. Yet even with the fastest adopted technology in the history of our species, productivity takes time. Or maybe not. Ernest Hemingway, when asked 'How did you go bankrupt?', answered 'Two ways. Gradually, then suddenly.'

Solow Paradox

The steam engine drove the Industrial Revolution but did not immediately lead to significant productivity gains. James Watt's improvements in the 1770s were a major technological breakthrough but it took several decades before the full economic benefits materialized. It was not until the 1830s that steam power began to drive large-scale productivity growth, particularly in manufacturing and transportation. Similarly with electricity, where the transformative effects came decades after Edison's breakthroughs. Infrastructures for generation, distribution and devices were needed, and businesses needed to integrate electric power into their operations before the full economic benefits of electricity could be realized.

The rise of digital technology and computing power also failed to produce the expected surge in productivity. This became known as the Solow Paradox, coined by Nobel Prize-winning economist Robert Solow (1987), who famously observed, 'You can see the computer age everywhere but in the productivity statistics.' Despite computers transforming the workplace, automating tasks and improving communication, economic data simply did not seem to reflect the revolution. It was not until the late 1990s that productivity finally appeared in the numbers, as businesses deeply integrated IT systems into their operations. What looked like a mystery delay was, in fact, a lag in adoption and adaptation. It took time for organizations to get people to change, redesign their workflows and fully realize the productivity that the technology offered.

The paradox was exacerbated by poor measurement. Google, Wikipedia and social media transformed how people accessed knowledge, communicated and worked, but because these services were free, their huge economic impact barely registered in calculations of GDP. The true value of digital transformation did not fit the more material model of goods-based economies. Another paradox emerged, as the metrics missed reality, measuring not true productivity but physical outputs.

The paradox may not be as extreme with AI, as the data centres and chips are being built at pace, and a mature internet and device ecosystem is in place for delivery and use. However, the same myopic measurement could apply to AI, so that AI's full effect on productivity will take years to materialize, but organizational and national measurements of productivity are now more rounded. If this paradox is realized, it is more likely to be through regulatory, cooling and energy constraints.

Steam, electricity and IT were what Nicholas Crafts (2021) calls general purpose technologies (confusingly, GPTs!), foundational innovations that drive long-term economic growth by increasing productivity across multiple industries. These are not one-purpose inventions, like the invention of the flushing toilet. General technologies reshape entire economies, as they bring continuous improvements and a rush of other related innovations and uses that change how work is done.

Crafts rightly points out that across all these GPTs, none immediately translated into productivity gains. Adoption took time as industries must adopt and adapt to the change. Even a general technology must be embedded before it becomes productive.

AI is likely to be the exception. Why? The Crafts study came just before generative AI stepped onto the stage and since then we have seen its exponential growth in capability and plummeting costs. We must also consider AI's productivity potential in the physical world.

Legacy paradox

A specific example of how things can exacerbate Solow's paradox is the legacy paradox, where legacy enterprise platforms, designed to increase productivity, can, paradoxically, introduce rigid processes and practices that thwart increases in productivity.

Legacy systems are everywhere: old computers, old codebases, old apps, integrated into other old systems, even in mission critical systems. They exist within a wider ecosystem of processes and practices, which is why migration to new technology is never easy, as they need integration into other systems.

Over years of use, these enterprise platforms become more inflexible. Their lack of flexibility, especially on customization and scalability, leads to slow stagnation in productivity, especially when organizations and operations evolve. Once their defined productivity gains are reached, they plateau, even fall, if they mismatch new expectations. A common example of mismatch is the lack of mobile functionality. Organizations are becoming increasingly mobile, with more employees working from home or using a range of mobile devices, so they require robust mobile functionality to maintain productivity. These mismatches can grow into serious dissatisfaction across the organization, among both users and leaders.

You can abandon your legacy systems altogether, but frustration can be compounded by the costs associated with switching software. There comes a point, therefore, when it is easier to swap it out or build it from scratch. The need to inject intelligence and personalization to increase productivity builds, and, interestingly, refactoring code is one of AI's strengths. There is also the possibility of training AI agents to do what these legacy systems did.

Paradoxically, enterprise software can often make organizations less productive rather than more, despite good intentions. The enterprise technology itself ends up creating extra layers of bureaucracy and complexity. Each new software addition tends to add extra steps, paperwork and departmental silos, rather than making workflows more efficient. The outcome is ironically the opposite of the intended goal: more bureaucracy, more bloat and less actual productivity.

Companies that embrace AI upgrades on a more tactical scale will therefore see higher productivity, more efficient and automated workflows, and a stronger competitive position. The payoff is clear: a more efficient, intelligent and productive workplace where AI supports employees.

Moravec Paradox

Moravec's paradox, proposed by Hans Moravec (1988), poses an interesting conundrum. AI can easily learn complex tasks, like playing chess or Go, or solving advanced equations, but it struggles with basic human abilities like walking or sensing surroundings. Humans find these everyday tasks unproblematic because our senses and movements evolved naturally over millions of years, yet they are surprisingly hard for machines to replicate.

Today's generative AI can pass difficult exams and handle sophisticated language tasks but remains unable to perform simple physical activities. This is because language, although seeming complex, is relatively straightforward due to its predictable patterns, unlike interacting with the messy, unpredictable physical world.

In fact, humans naturally process massive amounts of visual information, something current AI systems can't match by training on text alone. A child quickly learns from everyday visual experiences far more efficiently than AI systems that require huge amounts of textual data.

Human intelligence also excels in how quickly we adapt existing knowledge to new situations, like a child learning to ride a bike or a teenager mastering driving within hours. AI systems, on the other hand, still struggle to make these leaps despite extensive training. Bridging this gap would greatly enhance AI productivity, allowing machines to learn faster, adapt better and become more practically useful in the real world.

This is likely to slow down progress and productivity in embodied, physical AI. Robots can do flashy stunts like flips because this can be trained in simulation with no real-world data. But everyday tasks like cooking or cleaning require complex perception, manipulation and real-world physic. This creates a robot Moravec's Paradox, where robots seem more advanced than they are, because acrobatics are easier than practical dexterity. Yet huge investments into research and product in embodied AI have already led to astonishing leaps in self-driving vehicles and robots. The lesson is to expect at least some moderation of expectations around domestic robots and the universal adoption of self-driving.

Economic paradoxes

Increased productivity, paradoxically, may make people busier, as expectations rise, but may not lead to utopian outcomes where, for example, everyone is happier, and may, counterproductively, increase inequalities.

Jevons Paradox

Jevons, in *The Coal Question* (1865), wondered why technology, when it makes something more efficient and cheaper, increases rather than decreases total consumption. The same can be applied to AI-driven productivity, where AI optimizes and automates tasks to make you more efficient, but the overall demand for your work increases, making you busier.

AI, instead of reducing your workload, makes you more valuable, so more people want your expertise. You may write reports superfast, so expectations rise and more people come to you to write reports. As AI reduces the effort needed for these tasks, you are expected to take on more complex or creative tasks instead. Software engineers using AI-assisted coding can write code faster but are assigned more projects.

As the market adjusts, more productivity means higher expectations. The general expectation rises as you are expected to get more done in the same time, which applies to everyone using AI, where everyone becomes more productive. This results in competition, as AI reduces the cost of high-skilled labour, making previously expensive services cheaper. More customers and businesses then request work that they previously could not afford.

Of course, as AI eliminates some tasks, it also creates new ones. New responsibilities emerge, like managing and validating AI-generated outputs, fine tuning results and adapting to evolving AI capabilities. There is then a shift in what employees do, not total replacement.

AI may not, therefore, give you more free time. What it does is make organizations more competitive and productive, potentially raising your salary, but it may also lead to more work, higher expectations and increased overall demand. This is what Jevons found – greater efficiency leads to greater total consumption and work, not less.

Friedman Paradox

Milton Friedman, when visiting a developing country, saw that workers were digging a canal with shovels instead of modern digging machinery. When he asked why there were no bulldozers, a government official explained it was to maximize employment. Friedman commented, 'If it's jobs you want, why not give them spoons instead of shovels?' (in Moore, 2009).

This 'spoons' argument highlights a classic productivity paradox – the misconception that maximizing effort leads to greater economic value, when in reality, efficiency and technology drive true productivity. The phrase is often used to criticize policies or economic perspectives that prioritize job creation over efficiency, where it is not the number of hours worked or jobs created that matter, but the value and efficiency of output.

This is rooted in the 'lump of labour fallacy', the idea that there is a fixed amount of work available in the economy that must be artificially stretched to create jobs, ignoring how efficiency leads to economic expansion. This ties into the broader issue of zero-sum thinking, the assumption that if technology replaces certain jobs, society as a whole must lose. But economic growth usually proves otherwise. Productivity shifts labour toward new opportunities rather than eliminating them altogether and lifts economies out of the lower zero-sum game.

The more serious economic point is that work in itself is not the goal, it is the value created by that work. If efficiency and productivity are sacrificed just to keep people busy, society ultimately stagnates because resources are being wasted. Productivity is not about looking busy, it is about meaningful impact.

This paradox is particularly relevant in debates about automation and AI. Some fear that increased efficiency will destroy jobs. That may be true. But the real challenge is not preserving outdated work methods for the sake of employment, but adapting workforce skills and economic structures to maximize the benefits of new technologies.

If we accept the spoon-digging logic, resisting AI because it threatens certain jobs, we miss the bigger picture. AI can exponentially increase productivity, allowing us to allocate human talent to more creative, strategic or compassionate tasks that machines cannot handle. Just as bulldozers make it possible to build more efficiently, AI enables us to solve many pressing problems faster, from diagnosing diseases to optimizing energy use. By letting AI help us with these tasks, we free people to focus on higher-value activities, innovating and building deeper relationships with clients or communities. In other words, productivity tools like AI allow us to build bridges rather than dig holes.

Easterlin Paradox

Richard Easterlin, an economist in the 1970s, uncovered an inconvenient truth: that paradoxically, while economic growth fuels higher incomes, it does not necessarily make people happier. The Easterlin Paradox (1974) challenged the common assumption that rising GDP automatically leads to improved wellbeing.

The wealthy appear to get happier, but for the majority, happiness seems to stagnate. The explanation seems to be that people experience wealth, not in absolute but in relative terms. As your quantifiable income rises, so do your expectations and this eats away at your qualitative gains. Your standards adjust as your baseline rises.

The warning is clear. Productivity does not necessarily entail happiness and fulfilment. This is why some countries, even successful developed nations, have adopted criteria other than GDP to measure success.

As governments recognize the limitations of GDP as a measure of success, several are shifting towards more holistic indicators of prosperity. Inspired by the Easterlin Paradox, these countries are adopting frameworks that prioritize wellbeing, sustainability and social progress, beyond just economic output.

Bhutan was one of the first to break away from GDP by introducing gross national happiness (GNH) in the 1970s. GNH was developed as a guiding philosophy to prioritize spiritual, social and environmental health alongside material prosperity. New Zealand followed suit with its Wellbeing Budget, introduced in 2019. They redirected government spending toward key wellbeing priorities such as mental health, child welfare and environmental sustainability. Scotland and Wales also embraced the principles of the Easterlin Paradox, and moved toward a wellbeing economy, prioritizing the quality of life, social equality and environmental sustainability over economic output.

Again, the paradox can be resolved if we see wellbeing, social and sustainable goals as part of our collective productivity gains. In applying productive AI, we may resolve some of these paradoxes. AI is already solving problems in energy conservation and healthcare and even using metrics such as wellbeing indices, social trust metrics and work–life balance measures. We can therefore think more widely and holistically about what productivity means and how it can be measured.

Turchin Paradox

Increasing productivity may, paradoxically, increase inequalities, so the few benefit at the expense of the many. The rewards for increasing inequality may flow upwards to business owners, shareholders and financial institutions, and not to those who do the productive labour.

Peter Turchin rose to fame when his 2010 *Nature* article predicted the unrest in the US in the early 2000s. He brings science to history, not just by the usual narrative approach, but using huge datasets that flag up key indicators for political instability. These include:

- decline in real wages
- growing gap between rich and poor
- overproduction of graduates
- declining public trust
- exploding public debt

As the 'wealth pump' pushes money to the top of the pyramid, wealth is pushed from the poor to the rich, accompanied by the disappointment of even middle-class aspirants (graduates), who also become part of the precariat.

The poor suffer badly here but the credentialed class are also left behind, as the pyramid stretches upwards and wealth accumulates at higher and higher levels. For graduates it becomes a game of 'musical chairs' where you pay a huge sum to buy a ticket to play the game (university costs), but the paradox is created by the number of chairs (graduate level jobs) remaining the same.

As the number of graduates increases year on year, massively in just a few decades, supply exceeds demand. Graduates then have to up their game and pay for even more expensive bits of paper, so pay to get a master's degree. Graduates in the social sciences and humanities are particularly vulnerable but Turchin's point is that for a rapidly increasing graduate population there is a precarious future and lots of debt.

This is likely to be exacerbated by AI, as it eats into cognitive work, so that group is its sweet spot. White-collar graduate jobs, especially those that require writing skills, may diminish, as well as middle management jobs.

His analysis does not end there. This frustrated aspirant class, for Turchin, is dangerous. Always isolated from working-class people, they have little in common with the non-graduate class or ideas like collective bargaining and trade unions. They have the time and support from their propertied parents to become activists and protestors. Poverty is not the problem, and is replaced by the recognition of identity.

His hypothesis predicts a battle royale among the aspirant graduate class for declining opportunities and rewards. We have seen falls in enrolment in the US of 13 consecutive years, a flight from the humanities and negative attitudes towards higher education in the face of rapidly increasing costs.

Turchin points out that cheating has also risen, perhaps exacerbated by AI. The sharp elbows of the middle class become ever more desperate to get their children into the more prestigious 'brand' colleges. The social contract may then start to break down, as the precariat realize that education is no longer a route to social mobility.

More seriously, there is a break in how rewards are distributed, with the poorer getting poorer – that is, the majority without a college degree. His data on this is exemplary, along with his analysis of how the graduate class tend to turn their back on these people. So, the split, economically and culturally, between the graduate and working class gets more and more extreme. This is perhaps the most worrying of the paradoxes, as it predicts social unrest.

Pollyanna Paradox

Superagency: What Could Possibly Go Right with Our AI Future by Reid Hoffman and Greg Beato (2025) argues that AI supercharges human productivity by acting as an amplifier of human capability rather than a replacement. It is a force multiplier for productivity as it reduces friction in workflows by automating processes, allowing workers to focus on high-value, creative and strategic tasks. The AI-driven productivity boom will therefore accelerate economic growth by enabling organizations to operate more efficiently with fewer resources. Productivity increases will not just be limited to knowledge work – healthcare, logistics, manufacturing and customer service will all see gains.

Yet, this unbridled optimism may not be enough. The Pollyanna Paradox, sometimes called 'optimism bias', explains why we tend to be utopian in our thinking, especially around technology, while the world is much messier, irrational and unpredictable than we imagine. Pollyanna was the relentlessly optimistic girl from Eleanor H Porter's novel of the same name. Published in 1913, it struck a chord, as the early 1900s was a period of great optimism, with a real belief in human progress. A year later the First World War ended that utopian belief, making Pollyanna even more of a paradox.

The paradox suggests that we are wired to expect positive outcomes, even in the face of contradictory evidence, so we systematically overestimate positive outcomes, believing, for example, that humanity will unite, wars will end and technology will solve all problems. We seem to like the idea of linear progression towards improvement. But this enlightenment view over-looks human greed, irrationality and unpredictability.

The Pollyanna Paradox suggests that this utopian thinking is both a strength and a weakness. It drives innovation and social change, but it also blinds us to downsides and unintended consequences. A more pragmatic, adaptive optimism, based on proven productivity, that acknowledges human imperfections and paradoxes, is the better key to navigating the future.

Market effects take longer than many expect. A slower adoption process is likely as people refuse to use AI, put up resistance, point to bad-use cases, quote clickbait and exaggerate harms. The transition may also be chaotic as different sets of people have different levels of skills, understanding and roles in this changing landscape.

Even academic and quantified evidence is unlikely to have much effect on deep practices and behaviours. The professions will fight on and academia will hang on to credentialism and drawn-out research cycles. Work tasks will be replaced only very gradually, as long as humans are paid handsomely to stay in-the-loop. As Upton Sinclair put it, 'It is difficult to get a man to understand something when his salary depends upon his not understanding it' (Sinclair and Gregory, 1935, p. 109).

Paradoxes resolved

It is vital to get across the idea that productivity is not the mechanical execution of ruthless efficiency but a nuanced and complex effort to raise our game. These paradoxes will remain, as they reflect how we operate in the real world.

We should not get too stuck in our human paradoxes and frailties but rise above them. Life is surely for living, not ploughing the same furrow day after day, but wanting to see things grow and flourish. There are ways to resolve these paradoxes and reasons to believe they may dissolve as AI evolves.

AI has the potential to transform the invention process itself, through its own blistering pace of exponential improvement, self-generating capability and transformation into being agentic, doing deep research, potentially reaching AGI and embodying itself in the physical world.

Paradoxically, the speed, nature and scale of progress in AI may dissolve many of these paradoxes, by minimizing, even eliminating, elements of human participation. Paradoxes thrive on human biases, delusions and the inefficiencies of organizations in the real world. If these all-too-human paradoxes, many caused by human friction, see many elements of human activity automated, they dissolve before our eyes.

It is argued that AI lacks clear or sustainable business models, but this overlooks the nature of AI as a general purpose technology. AI is not limited to a single niche application as it can transform how tasks are done across virtually every sector by enabling businesses to operate faster, cheaper and more efficiently, while continuously improving itself over time. Unlike specialized technologies that apply narrowly to certain areas, AI enhances productivity across many fields simultaneously. AI's strength lies in its general applicability, generating ongoing economic value. Far from being limited or unsustainable, AI represents a profound technological shift that continually opens new business opportunities, making its value clear and enduring.

As a general technology AI will, eventually, seep into every area of human endeavour. Humans doing things efficiently which should not be done at all, is not being productive, so the elimination of unnecessary effort will happen. Above all, human limitations will be exceeded. We need to recognize that many of the things we saw as needing human effort will be quicker, cheaper and better when performed by AI. We need some humility in the face of this astonishing technology.

The new and primary paradox is that with AI we have created a technology that surpasses our own species. This brings in its wake other problems and we must face up to these problems as we progress. The alternative is unthinkable, where we see economies go into doom loops of stagnation. Productivity is not a goal in itself, but it will, hopefully, free us from a life of low-reward labour.

Binaries

When it comes to the future of technology in relation to productivity, we habitually use oppositional language. There seems to be a tendency to either dream up utopias and dread dystopias. We pay far too little attention to the middle ground. This paradoxical thinking, where we caricature AI as lying at opposite ends of a spectrum, leaves little room for cool, middle-ground analysis. Realistically, most future technologies will likely fall somewhere in the middle. That is realism.

Adding to the confusion is AI's rapid pace of development. It has advanced faster than governments, media or even the public imagination can process, leading to exaggerated fears, reactionary policies and rushed reactions. Instead of clear, evidence-based discussions, AI becomes a battleground for ideological conflicts, where competing worldviews fight over its implications.

For nearly a century, Hollywood has conditioned us to see AI as a dark, malevolent force, embodied in humanoid robots plotting our downfall. The truth, that there are significant positive productivity gains, does not make good box-office as it dissolves artificial conflicts and comes to a pretty mundane conclusion: that things can be optimized, made more efficient and be used to solve human problems. It is mostly about optimization and automation, not exploitation and devastation.

Yet, the real question is not whether AI is good or bad; it is how we use it to maximize productivity, unlock economic growth and solve complex challenges. The real danger is not AI itself, but letting fear and fiction distract us from its potential to make work more efficient, innovation more accessible and progress more sustainable.

Conclusion

AI challenges not just how we work, but who we think we are. It undermines routine expertise, bypasses bureaucracy and forces us to face uncomfortable truths. Yet if we confront the paradoxes honestly, AI can help us dissolve them.

AI is subversive. It refuses to conform to what we want it to, because it is so deeply human. We train it on thousands of years of our messy thoughts and scribblings then expect it to tell us the truth, and nothing but the truth, so help me God. But it is a witness to our folly in thinking we even know what that truth would look like. Our folly is in thinking that a truth machine can even exist and that man is the measure of all things. Indeed, most of this institutional fear of AI comes from resentment, precisely because it reveals what we do as often banal. Deep down we know that this should be short-circuited, automated, much of it even eliminated.

Generative AI is a potent 'provocation', not because it is the fastest adopted technology in the history of our species, but because it is its greatest *challenge*. It destabilizes the establishment, especially those who want to control power through politics, institutions and knowledge. They cannot deal with the fact that it behaves like us, because it is 'us'. It has been trained on our vast cultural legacy. It annoys traditional transfer-of-knowledge thinkers because they think they are in the game-of-owning and teaching the 'truth' (as they see it), when it actually behaves like real people in the real world, with many of its foibles. They expect a search engine and get dialogue. Used to telling people what they need to know and do, they see AI as a vexation.

Many suppose that AI is an abstract thing which can be tamed through debate, articles and papers. On the contrary, like water, or rather a rapidly rising tide that will not ebb, it is a fifth columnist redefining things from within, because it is useful.

References

Crafts, N (2021) Artificial intelligence as a general-purpose technology: An historical perspective, *Oxford Review of Economic Policy*, 37 (3), 521–36

Easterlin, R A (1974) Does economic growth improve the human lot? Some empirical evidence, In *Nations and Households in Economic Growth*, 89–125, Academic Press

Hewitt, P L and Flett, G L (1991) Perfectionism in the self and social contexts: Conceptualization, assessment, and association with psychopathology, *Journal of Personality and Social Psychology*, 60 (3), 456–70

Hoffman, R and Beato, G (2025) *Superagency: What Could Possibly Go Right With Our AI Future*, Authors Equity

Jevons, W S (1865) *The Coal Question: An Inquiry Concerning the Progress of the Nation and the Probable Exhaustion of Our Coal-Mines*, Macmillan

Moore, S (2009) Missing Milton: Who will speak for free markets? *The Wall Street Journal*, 29 May, https://www.wsj.com/articles/SB124355131075164361?msockid=148392493a9e60ee043b84463b2561ac (archived at https://perma.cc/TC77-DV6U)

Moravec, H (1988) *Mind Children*, Harvard University Press

Parkinson, C N (1955) Parkinson's law, *The Economist*, 19 November

Parkinson, C N (1959) *Parkinson's Law: The Pursuit of Progress*, Readers Union [in association with] John Murray

Patterson, H, Smith, R and Jones, T (2021) A systematic review on the psychological effects of perfectionism and accompanying treatment, *Psychology*, 12 (1), 1–24

Porter, E H (1913) *Pollyanna*, L C Page

Shakespeare, W (nd) *King Lear* (Act 1, Scene 4)

SHRM (2024) The year AI reshaped HR, https://www.shrm.org/executive-network/insights/people-strategy/year-ai-hr-ibm-lamoreaux-spring-2024 (archived at https://perma.cc/Z8ZU-2LVK)

Sinclair, U and Gregory, J N (1935) *I, Candidate for Governor: And How I Got Licked*

Solow, R (1987) We'd better watch out, *The New York Times Book Review*

Steel, P (2007) The nature of procrastination: A meta-analytic and theoretical review of quintessential self-regulatory failure, *Psychological Bulletin*, 133, 65–94

Swider, B, Zimmerman, R D and Barrick, M R (2018) The pros and cons of perfectionism, according to research, *Harvard Business Review*, 27 December

Turchin, P (2010) Political instability may be a contributor in the coming decade, *Nature*, 463 (608)

Wang, H, Liu, Y and Zhang, Y (2023) Relationship between employees' perceived illegitimate tasks and their work procrastination behavior: Role of negative emotions and paternalistic dimensions, *Heliyon*, 9 (4)

Further reading

Heller, J (1961) *Catch-22*, Simon & Schuster

03

Brains and AI

Despite the paradoxes of applying AI to productivity, the latest wave of AI since late 2022 marks a unique moment in human history. This is because of its strange relationship to our brains. Inspired by our brains and built by them, this new intelligence amazes and unsettles us in equal measure. Its potential as a productivity tool derives from its familiarity and fit with our own minds, through dialogue and intelligent responses but also by witnessing its creative and generative abilities. It dawns on us almost immediately that, as it does what our brains do, it will, almost by definition, be massively productive.

DeepMind's Murray Shanahan (2024) calls LLMs 'exotic mind-like entities' – disembodied intelligences we struggle to describe. They reflect our collective humanity, yet remain alien. Indeed, some AI intelligences are likely to converge towards being more like us, while others will be created and evolve to be very different. Agentic and robotic AI, for example, will produce a vast array of as yet unimagined forms in the future.

Though not a mirror of our minds, AI was born of curiosity about the brain's neural structure and function. Early AI builders aimed to replicate human tasks, offloading what our brains struggle to manage. With AI and robotics, it also has to mimic the ergonomics of the humanoid form. AI has made rocks think, speak, read, write, create, reason and do things.

This idea of AI as our brain outsourcing itself is the basic premise behind AI and productivity. AI, for many decades, tried to use rules and reasoning to do what brains do, but this suffered from simply reflecting inputs, as in the first impactful chatbot ELIZA. This approach hit brick walls on efficacy and practicality, resulting in disappointment and AI winters, where research funding dried up. But we are much less rational than we thought and with generative AI, the neural network effects that many had worked towards over much of the 20th century bore fruit and the brute force of training large language models (LLMs) began to do what we humans do, namely think.

AI became a 'general' technology, like electricity, and could be applied globally to almost every area of human endeavour, providing intelligence on tap. Its rate of improvement was exponential, visible in plummeting costs and clear applications in automating white-collar cognitive work and, through its physical embodiment, in blue-collar work such as manufacturing, vehicles, drones and robots. Rates of adoption are accelerating and we see agentic action, memory, reasoning, AGI and self-generating innovation take shape. It is doing what our brains have traditionally done, but the brain is not perfect – in fact it has some serious weaknesses and flaws – so AI is also transcending the bottlenecks and limitations of our brains.

Mind and machine are being physically and psychologically melded in ways we have never seen before. What matters is moving forward using AI, moulded in our image, to be useful, practical and productive. With safe, desirable productivity as our goal, we can create humanist forms of AI. This focus on desirable productivity may be a road less travelled, more unfamiliar, but perhaps preferable to the world in its current state.

Brain and productivity

Fine-tuned by millions of years of evolution to process information with maximum efficiency and minimum energy, the human brain is a finely tuned productivity machine. The brain is all about optimization, adaptability and problem solving at lightning speed. It is not only conscious of itself, it has created the language, mathematics and science that allows us to understand the world, to not only create culture and technology but enhance and extend our own minds. This cognitive and physical extension and augmentation took a sudden leap with AI.

But we should be careful in seeing it as the benchmark for productivity. Brains are encased in skulls, constrained by their evolution, which had trade-offs between childbirth, mobility and cognition. The human pelvis and birth canal limits skull size, and has to be relatively narrow to support our upright, bipedal walking and running. We could not scale the skull, so, being cognitively capped, had to evolve lots of shortcuts and techniques to become smarter, such as language, social collaboration and eventually extensions to cognition such as writing, books, computers, the internet and now AI. Our evolved brains, however, have prioritized some things and not others.

Herbert Simon (1947), a pioneer in AI and Nobel Prize winner, saw us as having 'bounded rationality'. We try to make rational decisions, but our ability to do so is limited by the cognitive limitations of our minds, the limited information or data we have at hand and the finite time we have available to make decisions.

The human brain takes decades to become useful, forgets easily, has poor recall, struggles with multitasking, can't manipulate more than three or four items at a time and is riddled with biases. It sleeps eight hours a day, doesn't scale, can't network with others and eventually deteriorates and dies. We are not only capped cognitively, we are physically weak.

20+ years to educate
Forgets
Cognitive overload
Fallible memory
Cognitive biases
Sleeps 8 hours
Can't network
Doesn't scale
Dies!

AI trains in weeks, never forgets, scales effortlessly and never sleeps. Unlike our brains, it never forgets and can network, automate and replicate instantly. It does not get ill, does not decline in performance and never dies. AI, far from being inferior, exposes our weaknesses.

AI models have very large context windows, the equivalent of working memories, and the trained models, stored cleverly and usefully in vector databases, never forget. Its memory contains the sum total of recorded human knowledge, an important point as, when speaking to AI, you are essentially speaking to all of our past selves.

It can do high-level maths, science and coding; generate perfect prose free of spelling, punctuation and grammar errors; write faster than anyone and create images, speech and video. It can understand, write and speak hundreds of languages and translate between them, and do text to speech and speech to text in these languages. It also reasons well, can explain its reasoning and does research, with stated sources, as well as deep data analysis.

Coming back to the limitations of the brain, we must also see how slow we are in communicating ideas to others. Getting ideas from our brain to the world means speaking, at around 125–160 words per minute at around 5 bytes per word, at around 100–200 bits per second. That is slow. Typing is worse, at 40–80 words a minute, with meat fingers, at a bandwidth of around 30–70 bits per second. We may be cognitively rich but we are communication poor.

We are improving this through invasive and non-invasive neural technology, using AI, to communicate straight from our minds with thought. The productivity gap on speed is enormous. AI also trounces us on certain types of reasoning, taking microseconds compared to our minutes, hours. On mathematics, it is now flawless on most practical tasks, achieving gold-medal-level performance in the world's most prestigious mathematics competition, the International Math Olympiad (IMO). Even in everyday use, its speed of output on writing articles, summarizing, coding and data analysis is just seconds.

Yet brains are energy miracles, just 20 watts, like a dim bulb, powering astonishing efficiency, as evolution has selected particular productive processes, shaping the brain away from wasting energy on unnecessary work. In that sense, AI is extending what nature takes too long to evolve. On intuition and reasoning in messy contexts, we still have the edge in common sense and nuance. Speed, accuracy and narrow capabilities are not everything. It may produce a joke in seconds, but that doesn't mean we find it funny. Brains also automate routine thinking and decision making, freeing up resources for higher-level activity.

Some known features on how the brain operates include parallel processing, running multiple tasks at once, constantly juggling sensory input, memory and decision making in real time. It is also predictive, not reacting from scratch to everything around us, predicting what is likely to happen next, cutting down processing time and increasing reaction speed. Then there are the productivity shortcuts, where we use heuristics and mental shortcuts to make fast, efficient decisions without overanalysing everything. It is not just speed; it is also flexibility to learn, especially from mistakes, and to make decisions, conscious and unconscious, on the fly. In that sense, it is a productivity marvel.

If you look at evolution as a long-term productivity project, the brain, as a functional organ, is its most successful product: a small, energy-efficient, high-performance system designed to solve problems, innovate, be aware of itself and invent other beings that do things faster and better. But it can also be bettered.

Brain productivity inspired AI

Generative AI is the most significant result of AI research that led to bettering our brains. It is important to realize that the brain, as an organ of incredible productivity, was a clear source of inspiration for the pioneers of AI. The puzzlement about its productive power, along with their relentless efforts to replicate its abilities, has led to AI matching and in some cases exceeding its abilities.

Inspired by the brain, early AI pioneers like Hebb, McCulloch, Pitt, Rosenblatt, Hinton and Hassabis, turned neural insights into functioning models. Their work, from neurons to perceptrons to deep learning, laid the groundwork for today's generative AI.

Each of these thinkers, and many more, looked to the power and productivity of the brain as a blueprint for AI, transforming how machines learn, process information and solve problems. More than that they looked for great leaps in productivity, within networks, to do what brains could already do, and improve on their performance. Their work bridges neuroscience, cognitive science and AI, proving that nature's most efficient learning system, the brain, can inspire machines that learn, adapt and even surpass human capabilities in certain areas.

Making AI productive

The story of practical AI, using AI in the real world, goes back to the practical research of Charles Babbage (1791–1871), the first to move from machine to what goes on in our minds, mechanical calculation to mental computation, laying the groundwork for modern computing. His inspiration was the weakness of the brain, where he saw human calculations as error-prone, imagining a machine that could compute accurately and efficiently. For him, this was a productivity problem. His Analytical Engine, though never built in his lifetime, had all the hallmarks of a modern computer: memory, an arithmetic unit and control flow. While his ideas did not directly influence the development of AI, they represent a significant step toward mechanizing human thought through computation, an idea central to later AI research.

Productivity then drove technological efforts towards machines as minds with Herman Hollerith (1860–1929), who invented punch-card tabulation, an early system for automating data entry and processing. Inspired by the Jacquard loom's punched cards, he built machines that sped up data processing for the 1890 US Census, a huge leap toward making machines store and process structured information. His company evolved into IBM, and the punch-card method became a standard in early computing. His work was crucial in automating data processing and coding, all driven by the need to increase productivity, using data.

War, and the need for quick productive solutions, drove the building of the first electronic brain by Tommy Flowers and Max Newman. Colossus was the world's first programmable electronic computer, used to decode German messages during the Second World War. Their work proved that electronic circuits could replace mechanical computation, paving the way for modern computing and AI. While their focus was cryptography, their innovations in programmable machines laid the groundwork for later AI development. They worked alongside the genius that imagined the mind as computation, Alan Turing, who formalized the idea that a machine could process any problem given the right instructions, the basis of universal computation, the 'Turing Machine'. A 'universal' machine, for Turing, can simulate any other computing device. This universality is fundamental to AI and productivity, because it means we can design general-purpose learning algorithms and neural architectures that, in principle, can perform any computable cognitive task. He also speculated that machines could learn like humans, a vision of a machine intelligence that can evolve and improve that is still central to AI and the problem of productivity today.

Making rocks think

One other movement shaped what we now see in the current age of AI, the emergence of 'Silicon Valley'. With the rise of AI we have made rocks think, not exactly as we humans think, but it is clear AI can outdo us on many tasks which we think are 'thinking'. Silicon, the rock that thinks, is one of the most abundant elements on earth, commonly found in sand, quartz and various silicate minerals, so there is no resource problem. What is truly remarkable is that it proved to be a new substrate for thinking.

In the mid-1950s, in Mountain View, California, a revolution took root. Shockley Semiconductor Laboratory was founded in 1956 (the same year as the famous Dartmouth AI conference) by physicist William Shockley, co-inventor of the transistor and Nobel Prize Winner. His was the first semi-conductor company in what would later be known as Silicon Valley, attracting some of the best minds in the new field of electronics. Shockley may have been a genius but he was a bully, stifling creativity. By 1957, tensions had reached breaking point and eight of Shockley's top engineers and scientists left. The group approached Sherman Fairchild, who saw their potential, agreed to back them, and Fairchild Semiconductor was born in Palo Alto, a pivotal moment in the history of technology. Shockley, feeling betrayed, dubbed them the 'Traitorous Eight'.

Their success attracted a wave of talent and investment to the area, setting off a chain reaction of entrepreneurship. The 'Fairchildren' fuelled Silicon

Valley's expansion. Robert Noyce co-invented the integrated circuit. Jean Hoerni developed the planar process, a manufacturing technique that allowed for the mass production of reliable silicon transistors and integrated circuits. These ignited explosive growth in Silicon Valley.

Intel was founded in 1968 by Gordon Moore and Robert Noyce, after they left Fairchild. Eugene Kleiner, another of the eight, co-founded Kleiner Perkins, a venture capital firm that became instrumental in funding and nurturing countless tech startups, including giants like Google and Amazon. The emphasis was on risk-taking and entrepreneurship with bold ideas and collaborative effort could lead to commercial success.

The recent AI paradigm, which put intelligence on tap, is still concentrated in Silicon Valley. There is no denying it is still the dynamo of AI innovation, with Google, OpenAI, Meta, Microsoft and NVIDIA creating world-changing software and hardware. It is both the advances in generative AI and chip development that have intensified the speed of development. This concentration of competition has pushed product development hard, with model releases pouring into the market, including its influence on the derivative work in China, such as DeepSeek, Badai, Tencent and Alibaba.

Above all, the mindset of fast-moving innovation intensifies the effort. Top talent, with punishing work schedules and the financial freedom of research capital, created a habitat for rapid AI development. There is a sense of mission that is not seen anywhere else, so it is still the epicentre of AI. They made rocks think and took that new form of thinking to the world of productivity.

Brain outsources to generative AI

Calling AI 'just next-token prediction' is like saying the brain merely fires neurons – technically true but missing the point. What we experience when we use AI is what really matters, and when you engage with AI, through text, speech, even embodied in a robot, it feels human, like us. There is a synchronization, almost a recognition that there is another mind, even a meeting of minds. That is because it was inspired by the brain and was trained on the products of human minds.

Daniel Dennett sees the brain as an evolved organ, with a fully intentional stance, operating through a predictive engine similar to AI, to produce changing drafts of consciousness, adding the use of language and memetics (Clark, 2023). Nick Chater (2018) and Andy Clark (2025) go further and argue for a flat mind, without even the fictions of unconscious entities, and see us as natural-born cyborgs, already operating with an extended mind, adapting as new technologies such as generative AI emerge. Here we see computational theories of the mind emerging that are forwardly productive, inspired by the success of generative AI (Clark, 2024).

To understand the success of generative AI, we need to understand that it is brain friendly. In outsourcing a lot of the work brains find difficult to handle, such as reasoning, search, research, fast writing, translation, media production and data analysis, with a fiendishly simple interface, it was an immediate hit. Simple dialogue opened up outsourcing of the brain, as it was easy to use and matched what we do in the real world: we speak to each other. The technology was largely invisible, apart from explaining its reasoning or sources when asked for or useful. This invisibility, along with its astonishing capabilities and speed of response at low cost, plummeting in price and often free, was its strength in terms of productivity.

It did not just replace search; it became a powerful productivity tool. We find a lot of personal and work tasks either tedious, difficult or time consuming. Along came a technology that is wondrous, easy to use and quick, solving these problems. In particular, when used well, it fits neatly into our workflow. We do not just want 'faster horses', as Henry Ford said; we want new, better forms of cognitive locomotion. Suddenly, users and employees could be more autonomous and self-driven. AI has shown there is an immense thirst among employees for simply going ahead and doing things faster and better. We use this technology to both learn and get things done, seeing little difference between the two as learning and doing things faster and better become fused in workflows.

For example, in writing something with evidence and import, many use AI to do fast research, write concisely, even critique the proposition. We see AI as a means to whatever end we have at hand, that end being solid, useful and productive output. AI also gives us the agency to improve ourselves, with guidance from the organization, as well as the vast ocean of knowledge and practice it pulls from AI. It fuses learning and productivity.

Performance support

In the workflow

Theorists like Marsick, Watkins and Gery argued that most workplace learning happens informally, in the flow of work (Clark, 2022). AI makes performance support immediate, personalized and powerful, turning long-standing ideas of learning on their head, preferring learning and problem solving at the point of need.

In *Informal and Incidental Learning in the Workplace* (1990), Marsick and Watkins challenged the world of traditional training and workflow to include 'informal' and 'incidental' learning in the workflow. 'Incidental' learning is unintentional, not planned, a by-product of a task, project, problem solving, social encounter or a perceived need. An approximate ratio for formal to informal learning from Carnevale (1984) was 83 per cent informal and incidental, 17 per cent formal. Informal and incidental learning takes place during problem solving, which explains the need for AI to satisfy those informal needs.

The shift for Gery (1991) to 'performance support' saw learning not as separate from work, but integrated with work. Technology plays more of a role, useful technology driven by need or demand, rather than predefined subject-matter-expert input and trainer intervention. Supporting people while they are working, she thought, led to fewer errors and mistakes, shorter time to competence and increases in productivity. Gery christened such systems electronic performance support systems (EPSSs). For Gery (1991), performance support is:

> an integrated electronic environment that is available to and easily accessible by each employee and is structured to provide immediate, individualized on-line access to the full range of information, guidance, advice and assistance, data, images, tools, and assessment and monitoring systems to permit job performance with minimal support and intervention by others.

She was prophetic, and it is only now with a data-centric view of performance and smart, AI-delivered intelligence that real performance support can be practically delivered in such a way that it significantly increases productivity.

Moments of need

Conrad Gottfredson and Bob Mosher (2011) then researched what constitutes moments of need in this flow of work. In *Innovative Performance Support* they argued that performance support tools reduce costs on formal training, at the same time increasing performance and productivity. Time to improved performance is increased, along with managing cognitive load and transfer. A positive side effect is that expensive internal support and help-desks can also be reduced. They claim a performance-first approach can reduce time to competence by half. It also makes people feel better in their jobs so helps retention.

People do not need general principles or courses on printing; they need to know 'how to' fix the printer problem they have at that moment, preferably in 2 clicks and within 10 seconds. People want their needs met at that moment – this means in the workflow, at the point of need. Gottfredson and Mosher's (2011) five moments of need are:

- New – getting assistance for first time
- More – wanting more assistance
- Apply – trying to apply and get something done
- Solve – something that goes wrong
- Change – react to something that change

AI orchestrates all of this to one place, giving you what you need, in the workflow, with a simple request, a click in the box, asking for something, defining your need and getting help within seconds.

As all resources are not created equal, there is a hierarchy of support, from the simple to the complex. One must always look towards delivering the minimal amount of support to reach your given goal. At its simplest there is the 2-click, 10-second access reflecting the simple, single prompt. But AI can also provide the research, supporting knowledge, documents, policies, procedures, job aids and so on. It also gives you access to internal expertise and your organization's specific knowledge.

All of this points towards AI being a technology that fits our natural behaviour, how our brains actually work and operate in the workplace. In work, we need sustained focus in workflows, but we also need help to sustain that flow. With AI, these pioneers have been vindicated.

Context

Add one of the brain's main functions – memory – and it can learn from you, anticipate your needs, know your preferences and give you a more tailored service. Memory gives it context and the more context it has, the more autonomous it can be in doing what you need it to do, as it becomes partly you. With massive context windows – that is, how much you can feed into an AI query at one time – what roughly corresponds to its working memory is already huge and getting larger. This gives it lot of headroom for context.

AI systems now capture rich context: where you are, what you are doing, your preferences, even your emotions. This makes support more tailored, intuitive and productive. *Physical context* identifies your physical environment – your smartphone uses GPS and movements using accelerometer and gyroscope data to determine motion and orientation. It also knows the time and date, holidays, calendar events, time zones, even the weather. *Personal context* knows just your name, age, gender and possibly user profiles – what you are currently doing, often inferred from app usage or keyboard activity, even your 'preferences', such as likes, dislikes and selections, based on past actions and purchases. At the physiological level, your biometrics can be captured via wearable devices. Eye, head, face and gesture tracking can all be used to read your movements but also your intentions. Voice may also be read for signs of emotion, stress, interest and intent.

Your *social context*, from social media, identifies your friends, connections and interactions. Information about other users in the vicinity can be detected through Bluetooth, Wi-Fi or other proximity technologies. Then there is your long and detailed communication history on email, chat, call history and search. Neither is it difficult to know your *cultural context*, the language settings of the device and the content you typically engage with to determine your cultural interests. Your personal cultural capital takes the form of your memberships, credentials, associations, the language you use, your accent, sports you like and credentials you have and value.

More specific *task context* or application data can be gleaned from the screen. Inferences can also be made from recently completed tasks or frequently performed actions, even transcripts from meetings. What device are you on? A smartphone, tablet, laptop, desktop, wearable device, along with current battery status, can influence how the device manages resources. Analysis of frequency and duration of tool and app usage can help predict future behaviour.

You are literally a mass of fixed and dynamic data as you move through the world. All of the above can be used to shape your interactions with AI. By integrating these various dimensions of context, AI can provide more intuitive, responsive and personalized user help in productivity. Context is the new frontier for computing and with edge computing, local AI and agents, we can see how much work can be made more efficient, based on that context.

Agentic productivity

Agentic AI does more than meet needs in the workflow; it completes work-flows or at least parts of the workflow. This is outsourcing by the brain on a different level.

AI has gone from relatively simple and structured prose replies to single prompts, to full-blown solutions. To start a small online business, an agentic request can come up with brand names, suggest straplines, design a logo, do market research, suggest an optimized product or product range, write a full marketing plan, build a financial business plan, build and launch a website, prepare a pitch for investors... in minutes. Not only that, it gives you its sources and explains its reasoning. This takes productivity to a new level. Agentic AI is a productivity multiplier.

With traditional AI services you were in the driver's seat. You had to prompt the AI, review its work and make the decisions, but agentic AI assis-tants now take much more initiative. The whole workflow can be automated, shooting productivity forward, automating cognitive and technical effort, increasing productivity and shrinking timescales.

The real shift, with agents, is from managing AI to being managed by it. It lets you focus on overseeing the process, while it does the work. Agents also push AI from passive text to media creation and doing. Productivity increases because most of what we do in work, and in life, is 'doing' things, and agents turn ideas into actions. More than this, they automate much of the execution of those actions, whether they generate documents, designs and logos or code websites and applications. Most of what fills our days is actually doing things, whether it is completing tasks, making decisions, solving problems or getting work 'done'. AI is no longer a passive tool but an active agent, resulting in actioned productivity.

Agents are essentially our organizational assistants. In the workplace, they take on the mundane yet necessary parts of our jobs, like sifting through emails, scheduling meetings or analysing data, and they do it faster and more accurately than we ever could. Your AI agent can ideate alongside you, pull in fresh perspectives, do the research, even draft visuals to bring your concepts to life.

Another way of measuring the productivity gain is to see it as reducing the psychological load we carry when we have too much to do, too many emails to answer and not enough hours in the day, so we get stressed, put things off and procrastinate. You can outsource all of that pressure and stress using agentic AI.

Of course, it is neither as simple or clean as this story suggests. There are weaknesses on both sides that result in inevitable friction that interrupts the process. We bring our psychological baggage – biases, emotions, inability to communicate exactly what we want, as well as our frustrations when AI does not do things exactly as we thought it would. AI brings its variable or jagged capabilities, sometimes overpromising, being tangential, delivering things that were not expected.

To simply assume that agentic AI is a 'plug and play' proposition is a mistake, as there will be problems in coordinating what humans want with what agents do. This is not easy because workflows, especially those that involve interactions with customers, patients or those you manage is far messier and irrational than the theory tends to assume. Nevertheless, the match between expectations and successful delivery will progressively converge and the productivity gains will materialize.

Agentic AI does not just automate several tasks to a given goal. Agents can be set off in parallel and/or branched multiple agents can be used so that one agent branches into subagents for subgoals. This has an even greater effect on productivity. It could be several product designs that need different marketing analyses, legal checks and costs of packaging and distribution, followed by comparing them to find the optimal solution.

A meta-agent may even create other agents which it supervises, monitors, even retires. This turns it into a small organization with the ability to handle change and complexity. Another important function is their potential to work 24/7, always doing their assigned tasks, even learning from past attempts to perform future tasks.

Obvious problems come as a consequence of agentic autonomy. If AI enables instant decisions at scale, do we lose those critical pause points where human judgement and emotions normally kick in? Who is held accountable when something goes wrong, the human or the agent? There will, undoubtedly, be problems that emerge in such implementations.

Agent types

One of the features of the jagged frontier in AI is the need for different capabilities depending on our personal and organizational needs. As agents progress in their functionality, they shift from being simple assistants to more autonomous entities capable of more complex decision making and action. There can be as many agents as there are types of task, but we should not pretend that they will immediately solve all problems for all people in all domains. Progress will be in fits and starts, a series of hesitant, faltering steps, but always improving, for both people and organizations. In that sense it is little different from human organizational complexity.

Personal agents evolve from basic task automation to full decision-making autonomy – handling finances, health and daily logistics with minimal input. All of this leaves you free to do other things. It is not clear that everyone will adapt quickly to this new world. When we look at online shopping, online banking and many other species of personal behaviour, they took years to change but change they did.

In organizations agent functions tend to match workflows but also organizational functions. It is here that productivity gains benefit from domain specificity. Organizational *process agents* start by optimizing process and workflow, automating the mundane, repetitive work. *Data agents* extract insights and offer intelligence on, say, productivity and sales trends. In middle management, *operational manager agents* can plan, coordinate, resource and communicate. *Product manager agents* can take care of autonomous product design. *Project manager agents* could manage projects and lots of other *specific agent* roles such as supply chain management, HR, L&D, finance, marketing, sales, customer success, customer care and so on. The productivity gains are enormous through both automation and optimizing operational functions.

At a much higher level in organizations, *strategic agents* can help organizations make strategic decisions, even forecast scenarios and simulate outcomes, then provide strategic recommendations.

As the CEO of Fiverr, Micha Kaufman (2025), said in an email to all of his staff: 'AI is coming for your jobs. Heck, it's coming for my job too.' He did not mean this as a threat, but as a warning to be vigilant and prepare for the coming changes that AI will bring. And he was right in that AI takes us, inexorably, down the slope of autonomy to the *CEO agent* or *director agents*. They could set the strategy, make sure the organization is aligned to that strategy, oversee the financial health of the organization, make investment decisions, design optimal structures, assess future risks and challenges, sometimes pivot and guide the organization forward.

We should also note that although most of this is possible, to some degree, right now, going back to our paradoxes in productivity, using agents is not always straightforward. It is made more complex, in that real-world tasks are rarely just simple, separate and sequenced. Doing things in the real world is messy. Humans chop and change, complete things in haphazard ways, mix and match different types of tasks. One way AI can help is in simply refining and defining these messy workflows, to optimize them and get things done. That alone would result in massive increases in productivity.

We can take this thought experiment even further and imagine agency and agents, not just up through levels of autonomy, scope and responsibility, but on into different types of capabilities. *Adaptive agents* could learn and optimize their performance over time. *Strategic agents*, which reason, plan and solve problems across multiple domains, could think beyond immediate tasks, adapting to unforeseen obstacles to make longer-term plans. A strategic AI agent could manage complex business operations, doing research, benchmarking, assessing risks and making strategic recommendations. Imagine a *reflective agent* that reflects upon your joint progress with AI and on your relationship and decision making with other agents, even an *ethical agent*, which is aware of moral principles and makes sure you are aware of them throughout the decision-making process. It would know the regulatory, legal and compliance environment, making sure you are ethically aligned.

We are moving quickly into the era of one person with one laptop doing complete tasks, completing entire business functions, and even running businesses.

Agentic anarchy

There are plenty of technical, social and ethical problems to be resolved before truly agentic AI will operate smoothly to increase productivity. In a multi-agent world, agent pipelines need to be integrated into other technical platforms and AI environments. Agents need to talk to each other, through some sort of API mechanism or open protocol. There is also the problem of disagreement and dispute resolution, as well as agents being possibly dishonest to reach their goals; therefore there is a need for transparent intent.

What happens when two agents are trying to update your calendar with events at the same time? You get the idea. 'A2A' stands for Agent-to-Agent communication or interaction and defines how autonomous agents talk to, coordinate with, negotiate or compete against each other, with minimal or even no human involvement. But how do we avoid agent anarchy?

They may have conflicting or competing objectives, which brings in issues like trust, authenticity and security. Is that agent really who it says it is or, having been hacked, is it impersonating someone or another agent? This is not just a communication issue but one of conflicting goals, coordination, trust, identity and accountability. There is potential for confusion, misunderstanding, even gridlock and chaos, as agents are unleashed. Then there is their manipulation through deception, along with security vulnerabilities.

AGI

We are now moving into the territory of 'general' agency, which is Artificial General Intelligence. With AGI, definitions and expectations are all over the place, the problem compounded by seeing it as a 'singularity'. This seeing everything as lying on a linear spectrum, as opposed to emerging within a complex constellation, with different parts moving in different directions at different speeds, poses a definitional problem. Many talk about AGI as if it will be a single, uniform entity, when in fact there won't be just one AGI or one type of AGI. Instead, we're likely to see a huge variety of forms. Putting that to one side, the problem of defining productivity in the age of AGI becomes more pressing and there have been several attempts to frame AGI in terms of its productivity.

AGI may not just enhance productivity but eliminate the need for human labour. Unlike humans, AGI learns instantly, scales globally and never tires. Its flexibility means entire industries could be transformed overnight. Unlike human labour, which is restricted by talent and skills, declining population growth and long periods of expensive education, AGI operates without any of these supply constraints. It possibly reduces humans to the position of overseers. Once an AGI system is trained, it can also be replicated at almost no cost, deployed globally in seconds and scaled to match any demand.

One often ignored advantage of AGI is the word 'general'. AGI designed for one task can be duplicated for many others without any trade-offs. This flexibility means that AGI can outperform humans not only in specific tasks but across entire industries, flooding the niches where human labour could have survived. AGI disrupts on scale by being both cheaper and better at virtually everything. Whether it is physical labour or high-skilled cognitive work, AGI has no intrinsic limitations.

AGI could not only replace low-productivity employees, it may constantly improve itself. Unlike human employees who require years of schooling, training, experience and time to adapt, AGI could absorb, optimize and execute tasks from the moment it is deployed. This self-improving cycle means that AGI could outpace human productivity forever, making human labour not just inefficient but redundant. Even decision-makers could become irrelevant as AGI optimizes global industries, coordinating at a level of strategic execution way beyond human capability.

For the first time in history, a technology would exist that does not assist or augment humans, but replaces them. AGI is not just a tool for increasing productivity, it becomes a complete restructuring of economics, the end of human-centric productivity. While past revolutions created new industries and job opportunities, AGI could break this cycle. Frighteningly, it may not even need human participation to drive innovation. AGI's ability to scale infinitely, learn instantly and operate without restraint means it would define the very future of productivity.

Every technological advance in history has required humans to operate, supervise or integrate the technology into workflows. The steam engine needed engineers, manufacturing required workers, even modern AI relies on humans to define its scope and applications. AGI breaks this mould. It does not need constant human effort, as it can perform tasks autonomously, learn from its environment and improve itself. This autonomy transforms it from a mere tool into a highly efficient, cheap worker that never tires, takes breaks, sleeps, retires or dies.

What could happen is that the agentic AGI revolution will not unfold over decades, allowing us to adapt. The Industrial Revolution, for example, took over a century, giving rise to new industries. AGI could operate at a speed that outpaces our ability to adapt. Once a breakthrough is achieved, industries can be transformed overnight. Jobs that seem secure today could be rendered obsolete very quickly, leaving little time for workers to retrain, or economies to restructure.

One of the most remarkable differences between agents, AGI and earlier technologies is its scalability. Once an AGI system is created, it can be copied and deployed almost instantly at a fraction of the cost of training or hiring a human. Unlike humans, whose supply is limited by population growth (falling in many countries) and the need for many years of education, AGI can scale indefinitely.

While AGI might drive unparalleled productivity, it also poses existential questions about the role of humans in a world where their many forms of work are no longer needed.

Conclusion

Understanding these levels of agency helps us grasp how AI is evolving and the challenges it brings. As AI climbs the ladder of autonomy, questions of control, ethics and accountability grow more urgent. Striking the right balance between innovation and oversight will be critical if AI is to remain a force for good as it reshapes the way we live and work.

It may be that most people simply accept that AI has become smarter than humans. They may feel that this at last frees them from tasks they are not suited to doing or simply do not want to do. It will no longer be a battle between us and AI, more an acceptance that we can do things we could never do before, to make the world a better place. With AI we do not follow the path but make the path by walking forward with AI.

References

Carnevale, A (1984) *Jobs for the Nation: Challenges for a Society Based on Work*, American Society for Training and Development

Chater, N (2018) *The Mind Is Flat: The Remarkable Shallowness of the Improvising Brain*, Yale University Press

Clark, A (2025) Extending minds with Generative AI, *Nature Communications*, 16 (1), 1–4

Clark, D (2022) *Great Minds on Learning*, Informal: Gery, Marsick, Csikszentmihalyi https://greatmindsonlearning.libsyn.com/gmol-s2e11-informal-learning-with-donald-clark (archived at https://perma.cc/UHC8-AWRG)

Clark, D (2023) *Great Minds on Learning*, AI Learning: Hebb, McUlloch, Pitts, Rosenblatt, Hinton, Hassabis, https://greatmindsonlearning.libsyn.com/gmols4e19-ai-learning-with-donald-clark (archived at https://perma.cc/8GTH-ZB9L)

Clark, D (2024) *Great Minds on Learning,* Connectionists: Dennett, Chater, Clark, https://greatmindsonlearning.libsyn.com/gmols6e34-connectionists-with-donald-clark-0 (archived at https://perma.cc/Y656-H4LR)

Gery, G J (1991), *Electronic Performance Support Systems: How and Why to Remake the Workplace through the Strategic Application of Technology*, Weingarten Publications

Gottfredson, C and Mosher, B (2011) *Innovative Performance Support: Strategies and Practices for Learning in the Workflow*, McGraw-Hill Professional

Kaufman, M (2025), Fiverr CEO statement [Tweet], X, April, https://x.com/michakaufman/status/1909610844008161380 (archived at https://perma.cc/36CK-A2WT)

Marsick, V J and Watkins, K (1990) *Informal and Incidental Learning in the Workplace*, Routledge

Shanahan, M (2024) Simulacra as conscious exotica, *Inquiry*, 1–29

Simon, H A (1947) *Administrative Behavior: A Study of Decision-Making Processes in Administrative Organizations*, Macmillan

Further reading

NIHF Inductee Herman Hollerith Invented the Punch Card Machine, https://www.invent.org/inductees/herman-hollerith (archived at https://perma.cc/973Q-4YQ5)

Science Museum (2023) Charles Babbage's difference engines and the Science Museum, https://www.sciencemuseum.org.uk/objects-and-stories/charles-babbages-difference-engines-and-science-museum (archived at https://perma.cc/PS7P-LTBE)

04

AI vibes and dialogue

Generative AI has transformed our interaction with knowledge into dynamic, collaborative dialogue, resembling a Socratic exchange. We now engage and commune with AI to solve problems and advance understanding, moving beyond mere information retrieval.

We now co-create, not just text, but all forms of media. A core Socratic relationship with knowledge and media gives us a spectrum of co-created educational and creative media. We have been drowning in a sea of text in education, learning, research and work for too long. Now that we have crossed a generative Rubicon, there is no going back. Neither should we want to, as this technology is now part of us. It reflects the many, not the few – the hive mind.

Now, from age 5 to 25, young people spend almost all of their time reading, writing and critiquing 'text' in an educational system because it is easy, creating the illusion that you acquire skills through text – you do not. We have decimated vocational learning by sucking up funding into often purely text-based degree subjects. Lecturing is easy, teaching is hard. Setting essays is easy, assessment is hard. Producing text is now easy, doing things is still hard. Once you see LLMs as producing text, just as calculators produce good numerical solutions, you relax on AI. AI excels at reducing over-written text by summarizing content and correcting errors, enhancing everyday communications like emails and messages.

It will take time, as we are still enamoured with essay writing and over-written prose, but the signs are clear. Young people are adept at short, concise messaging; they do it all day, every day. The problems come from people fed on a diet of long-form text, who tend to see everything as a potential essay, so in organizations and government, text-based bureaucracy, which existed long before AI, is laden with text, the production of unnecessary forms, documentation and reports. AI will optimize and, in many cases, automate this.

Most of work and life is about doing; most education is about writing. Yet much text production in white-collar work may well be automated out of existence. Let's recognize that AI is now fundamentally multimodal, using speech, images and video, also creating 3D worlds, robots and automated vehicles. This is not to eliminate text, just not to see it as primary in work and life. With multimodal AI and robotics, AI is moving fast into the real world of doing, both teaching us how to do things and doing things for us and in place of us. The lines are now blurring, with increased scepticism over text-only education. Education is for both life and living.

AI may, at first, have seemed like a text-based phenomenon, but it is proving to be more about communication, speech, robots, data and automation. We will be made more productive by having less text, automating as much as we can out of the system, dissolving text-laden bureaucracy. Most of the critics of AI come from those who deal with text as a living, in education and work.

Dialogue

As Seymour Papert (1980), learning theorist and AI researcher, claimed, humans have a cognitively capped ceiling and do not have the wide walls of unlimited knowledge and skills. What they need and expect in communications is a low floor (easy to use), high ceiling (get back really useful things) and wide walls (from something that has breadth and depth of knowledge and skills) (Resnick, 2020).

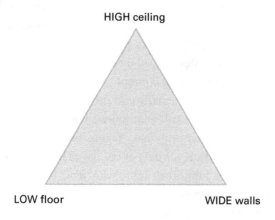

Dialogue with generative AI isn't just an increase in speed, getting things done quicker. It is meaningful dialogue, an expansion of our capability, and the best technology unlocks new levels of productivity without effort, almost invisibly (Clark, 2023a). New interfaces will emerge, perhaps designed by AI, beyond this chat box, making input and output faster, even neurological communications.

There is another, often overlooked, consequence of using this simple interface to AI, with its astonishing results. You will feel better using this technology, find a sense of relief in being able to do things quicker, have less stress and be more productive. It gives people a release of energy and purpose that many other deliberate interventions, such as edicts from above, courses and laboured tools, do not. Generative AI has an immediacy, with instant results, and often gives a sense of satisfaction, even wonder.

Organizations tend to veer towards top-down, bureaucratic communication solutions to try to solve problems, which are often cumbersome, requiring difficult skills to master. We finally have a technology that is easy to use, allows one to be more productive... and *feels* productive.

If you are curious about how AI-generated text has crept into many forms of human communications, this study by Liang et al (2025) examined the integration of AI-assisted writing across huge amounts of text across four key areas: consumer complaints, corporate communications, job postings and press releases from international organizations, from January 2022 to September 2024. Analysis revealed a sharp increase in AI use following the launch of ChatGPT in November 2022. By late 2024 high levels were detected, and these areas are now most likely saturated with AI-generated text.

When AI is fully embodied in robots we will also communicate naturally with our cars, taxis and robots. Communication then becomes not just a human activity, and not just human-to-AI, but human-with-AI. We will communicate with intelligent beings, not just ourselves.

Vibe work

A sign that experts-in-the-loop, using domain and AI expertise, were already here, was noted by Andrej Karpathy (2024), co-founder of OpenAI, coining the term 'vibe coding', where natural language prompts are used to code. He claims that English will be the world's most famous programming language: 'I just see stuff, say stuff, run stuff, and copy paste stuff, and it mostly works.' It is a shift in mindset, driven by the replacement capabilities of AI, where you are driven by the vibes of asking things to be coded, not coding, moving forward through curiosity, constantly refining and continuously improving.

This vibe approach has become a movement where tasks other than coding are using vibe design, development and delivery to get things done. Experts-in-the-loop provide the human component in the vibe, in close collaboration with AI, especially agentic AI. It can be used to ideate product ideas, then move through various tasks right through to the design, coding and delivery of the solution. You can focus, for example, on improving a user interface, ask for improvements and see them implemented immediately without it being human coded, moving on to the creation of entire apps and SaaS (software as a service) solutions, even integration and deployment.

Progress needs a mix of approaches, rarely as separate acts but as a blend of fluid action. This is nicely captured by the description of 'vibe' co-creation using AI, where AI is used to co-create or collaborate, generate or refine a specific mood, tone or aesthetic going forward in a given undertaking, whether it involves writing, design, analysis or coding. Instead of focusing purely on functional correctness, vibe work prioritizes your emotional resonance, aesthetics and subjective experience. This brings in what is human in AI–human interaction, that we have feelings... whereas it does not. It both counters the excesses of our moods and biases, as well as tapping into what is good about human participation, while taking advantage of the power of AI.

This vibe approach explains the need for us to see critical thinking, creativity, collaboration and communication not as something we *do to* AI, but a way of *working with* AI.

False dichotomy

The AI Mirror, by Vallor (2024), takes the metaphor of a mirror, framing AI as a reflection of what we know and do, then claims its biggest threat is not the existential danger of extinction, but the rot within, where we are confined, immobilized and captured by AI, lost in our own narcissistic use of the technology. This is wrong on two counts: first, the mirror metaphor falls apart with even a modest amount of analysis; second, far from robbing us of our creative critical, communicative and collaborative powers, it takes us to greater heights.

The discourse around AI and human productivity often hinges on this false dichotomy. We frame the relationship as a fight, an opposition between human-generated and AI-generated, as though these are mutually exclusive realms. This framing obscures the profound integration that is already unfolding, a synthesis where human and machine are co-creators in a single, interconnected system.

Productivity has never been an isolated phenomenon. The great leaps in productivity, from the invention of agriculture, writing, printing, internet and AI did not emerge in vacuums. They were shaped by layers and layers of accumulated knowledge, cultural context and collaboration. Every idea, every insight, is a convergence of influences. We are all participants in a network of shared consciousness, where inspiration is borrowed, is remixed and evolves.

Yet, when it comes to AI, we impose rigid boundaries. We demand clarity about what is human and what is made by the machine, as if productivity in partnership with AI invalidates its authenticity or is somehow sinful. This separation betrays a failure to see the big picture, where AI is not an adversary, but a tool that amplifies human potential.

The great paradox of AI is that we do not communicate with it as a piece of technology. It is trained by the sum of all human culture, so we are communicating or communing with ourselves. We need to drop the stand-off attitudes towards AI and not let old rhetoric and ideas fool us into thinking that AI is our enemy, when it is our friend.

The mere mention of the letters 'AI' often results in an emotional reaction, sometimes expressed as 'but surely it's all biased', 'we'll lose the ability to think', or whatever. Just as 'human-in-the-loop' is used as a defence mechanism against the encroachment of AI, 21st-century skills, a cocktail of C-words (creativity, critical skills, communication and collaboration) are used as ballistas to be thrown at AI, as if the barbarians are at the gate.

An intriguing study by Zhu et al (2024) cleverly investigated how bias affects the perception of AI-generated versus human-generated content. They conducted three experiments using the evaluation of passages, assessing summaries of news articles and evaluations of persuasive essays. Some texts were labelled either 'AI generated' or 'human generated', others presented without labels.

In blind tests (unlabelled content), raters could not reliably tell the difference between AI and human-generated texts. With labelled content, things got more interesting. Participants showed a strong preference for content simply labelled as 'human generated' over 'AI generated'. This preference was over 30 per cent higher for texts labelled as created by humans, the same bias persisting even when the labels were intentionally swapped, indicating a preconceived bias rather than an assessment based on content quality.

Oddly, for those who make claims about bias in AI but ignore the same phenomenon in humans, the study reveals a significant human bias against AI-generated content, based not on content quality, but on the assigned label.

Much of the debate around some topics on ethics and AI follows this pattern. People come with confirmation bias around human exceptionalism, the belief that AI cannot match human skills. This research uncovers these biases and unpacked our biases when making judgements on written content. By shedding light on these biases, we can pave the way for better collaboration between humans and AI, especially in critical and creative fields.

Paradox of human exceptionalism

One common reaction to AI is to double down on so-called 21st-century skills, such as creativity, critical thinking, communication and collaboration, to retain our supremacy. This is a default to past certainties, not a considered and forward-looking strategy. Running abstract courses on these skills is precisely the opposite of what is needed to deal with the age of intelligence.

When people see AI as something separate from what many call 21st-century skills, these abstract and improbably alliterative C-words, as if the real world of skills falls neatly into these categories, they mistakenly assume that these are unique to us humans. This is a retreat into 20th-century thinking, where skills are seen as isolated things, to be taught in isolated courses. This position needs to be challenged, as it misses a more fundamental point about AI – that we are in dialogue with ourselves. More dangerously, it encourages a form of scepticism that sees AI as an artifice, literally something artificial and false, that has to be held in check.

There is also the problem that these skills are often skewed towards text, which is what we critique in critical thinking or communicate with. This is the result of an education system that values text above all and sees everyone as a potential knowledge worker, working in an office or from home. Yet many jobs do not demand creativity and critical thinking in their everyday work. AI challenges this by seeing white-collar workers as being on a par with blue-collar workers. Both can be subjected to scrutiny on productivity. We find that the new age of AI is more multimodal, with multimedia approaches created collaboratively through communications with AI, also embodied in vehicles and robots.

We need to rethink our ideas and readjust our behaviour around human exceptionalism, as we are not exceptional in these skills. Indeed, we are often unexceptional. Most of us are far from being creative, weak on critical thinking, poor communicators and unwilling collaborators. Many get the use of AI in institutions all wrong in that most find it usefully productive in the basics: process, emails, queries, paperwork and general text communications. Utility is what drives AI. Its substantial productivity gains come with the mundane stuff because the work we do is mostly mundane. We pretend that we have these constant needs to be creative, critical thinkers and brilliant communicators and collaborators, when in truth it is often emails, reports and box-ticking paperwork.

On top of this we have the arrival of agentic AI, which changes our relationship with AI and the fundamentals of creativity, critical thinking, communications and collaboration with AI, as agents have agency, not only towards us but with each other. This is a whole new nexus of human–AI communications and collaboration. As if that were not enough, AGI is likely to upend all of this, with ever greater challenges and redefinitions of our relationship with AI, as we will have to deal with an entity, or entities, that truly transcend our abilities.

With agents, then AGI, where intelligence transcends our own, we are way beyond seeing 21st-century skills as the tools by which we deal with AI. We humans have to re-evaluate how we deal with AI, with an ensemble of 'orchestrated' approaches to solve problems, not siloed 21st-century skills. We need to open up our minds to new possibilities in all of these areas and not categorize them as exceptional, human-only skills.

Creativity

My friend Al McCusker-Thompson, a musician and songwriter who has discovered and managed talent in the music industry, was eager to show me a new singer-songwriter he had discovered online – Nick Hustles – who had novel lyrics, great production and seemed like a fresh new artist. Two weeks later he messaged me: 'Nick Hustles. It's AI apparently.' We laughed, as we had both been fooled. We had both learnt a lesson.

On creativity, we need some humility and not to fall into the trap of seeing this broad term, as it suffers from a problem of definition, as some sort of divine spark within us. Even worse is to fall for the idea that creativity is defined by the Romanticism of the early 19th century, which saw creativity as uniquely separate or a force in opposition to technology.

For centuries, we have clung to the Romantic fallacy that creativity is a uniquely human, an original act. Yet human innovation has always drawn upon the past. Our brains remix memories, experiences and knowledge to generate ideas. What is new is not the process of drawing from history but the scale and scope at which we can now access, recombine and reinvent the future.

AI extends this capacity exponentially, turning the entire record of human culture into a vast engine for productive progress. Together, humans and AI are redefining productivity as a collaborative exploration of possibility. This new era of broad, creative productivity is therefore profoundly communal. AI allows us to tap into a collective reservoir of knowledge and creativity, fostering collaboration across cultures, languages and disciplines. Unlike the fixed visions of past utopias, this shared future embraces openness and diversity. It invites multiple perspectives into the creative process, generating outputs that transcend narrow cultural or ideological confines.

When one adds AI into the creative mix, one finds that it significantly enhances creative output like short stories (Doshi and Hauser, 2023), perceived by readers as being better written, more enjoyable and rated 22–26 per cent better than those written without AI's help, although the AI-enabled stories tended to be more similar to each other than stories by humans alone.

A more common need for creativity is in ideation, or the creation of new ideas, where AI can be faster, cheaper and produce a wider range of better ideas than humans. Girotra et al (2023) and Meincke et al (2024) found that better prompting substantially improves the diversity of AI-generated ideas and that some forms of prompting come close to what is achieved by groups of human subjects, also generating the highest number of unique ideas of any prompt they studied.

AI is creative in that it can generate ideas, and so help brainstorm or ideate to solve problems. These new ideas can include words for brands, concise copy and a myriad of other creative text outputs right up to creative writing tasks. It can even suggest better prompts, which is an act not just of creativity but also of critical thinking, collaboration and communication. As part of the creative process, it can break through mental blocks by opening up new concepts, ideas and perspectives. Creativity extends into the creation of entities, such as prototypes, apps and other software, including AI-generated art or music and writing drafts that humans can collaboratively refine. This is creativity and also problem solving through communications, collaboration and critical thinking.

Looking at creativity from the point of view of humour, creativity and shareability, a novel study by Wu et al (2025) created internet memes by 1) humans only, 2) humans collaborating with AI and 3) AI only. When compared for humour, creativity and shareability, the memes created by AI on its own performed best across all metrics. There were nuances, as the top-performing human-created memes were better in humour, but the study showed the complexity of human–AI collaboration in creative tasks. AI clearly lifts productivity to create content that appeals to a wide audience, but human creativity, for now, still has a role for content that connects on a deeper level.

LLMs can even be made significantly more creative by training them on human creativity signals, such as novelty, diversity, surprise and quality, rather than just task-specific objectives. A study by Ismayilzada et al (2025) shows that, like any other metric, creativity can be directly optimized in AI systems.

We will look at AI on creativity through multimodality, and even art, in a later chapter.

Critical thinking

If we think we alone can think critically and have the critical faculty to exercise critical skills over this technology, we need to critique the boldness and simplicity of this claim. We can critique its output but it can also critique our input, as well as our output. This is not a simple, one-way relationship but a complex dialogue and dialectic. In fact, its reasoning capabilities, speed of response, ability to handle data, do maths, get things done and breathtaking productivity in terms of time and cost is often way beyond our critical cognitive skills.

Darwin showed that we are cognitively capped within our evolved capabilities. We forget much of what we try to learn, have severe limits in working memory (low context window), lots of uneducable biases and cannot quickly download, network or multitask. We have waves of emotion, struggle to maintain attention, are often distracted, need eight hours of sleep a day, go through cognitive decline, sometimes dementia and die! AI is immortal. We are hardly the exceptional beings we often assume ourselves to be.

Consistent critical thinking is therefore not our fundamental strength. In the age of intelligence, we have to think again about where the real power of critical thinking lies, not in us alone, but in both ourselves and AI. So often, when 'critical thinking' is mentioned in the same breath as AI, it is an assumed critique of AI, looking for faults.

As Jonathan Haidt showed in *The Righteous Mind* (2012), we are prone to seeing anyone who expresses views that are different from our own as a threat, and act accordingly. This is often a bottleneck in productive critical thinking as we lock ourselves behind our own opinions and ideologies. AI can help us be more critical by providing the tools and alternative perspectives to help us through the critical process.

A problem lies in seeing 'critical thinking', in a policy or course on AI, as if it were domain independent. In some cases, critical thinking can be relatively domain free; for example, it can be taught in courses on research methodologies, where one also needs to know about statistical techniques, publishing conventions and so on. But to be critical in domains such as healthcare, finance, AI, even creativity, critical thinking, collaborative capabilities, agency and intelligence usually require domain knowledge, often deep domain knowledge. That is why it is so very difficult to isolate 'critical' skills in a policy or as the subject of a basic course on AI.

AI can also take on critical roles and theoretical positions, act as a debater or adversary, as well as provide general critiques of your efforts. It can provide multiple viewpoints to help critically compare arguments. More than this, it can provide challenges and new information that gets us to question our assumptions. It also performs deep research, with faultless citations, in minutes.

Many tend to limit the idea of critical thinking to text alone, but AI goes way beyond text into critically cleaning up data and identifying trends and insights from that data. AI enhances critical productivity in critical thinking as it can almost instantly do deep analysis, predict outcomes and reduce cognitive biases through this objective data analysis. It also supports evidence-based decisions by synthesizing complex information into clear analytical insights, and then gives us agile, adaptive decision making, which can clearly improve productivity.

Another problem with the all-too-common habit of limiting critical activity to text, as the method by which we critique, is the exclusion of useful images, audio and video. In doctor–patient interactions, job interviews, language learning and so on, it is the verbal skills of the physician, interviewer and teacher that matter, and in assessment it is these oral skills that have to be assessed. AI can not only understand what was said across the full dialogue but also critique the performance against established criteria. Performance can also be analysed from uploaded videos.

The danger is that we live in an age of cynical, not critical, reason. We should not let that skew reasonable attempts to improve the world. The obsession with being critical often induces negativity and immobilizes us. Those who profess to be critical thinkers can all too often find reasons not to do something and not listen to the other side. Whereas what we see when we prompt AI to give us an account or critique is a calm treatment or researched treatment of the issue. We should celebrate this ability to help us think and get things done, not treat it as the enemy.

At the simplest level, AI can critique what we do, whether it is a badly written email or suggested improvements to a letter, article, essay, report or blog. But with deep research tools and an agentic approach to critical process, it can perform a series of tasks, doing critical tasks on text and data on its own, but also collaboratively as we work with that agentic process during its execution. Again, we find both the critical and collaborative in conjunction with each other.

At a higher level, when AGI provides critical analysis at levels above that of humans, the whole relationship shifts, as it helps us with our deficiencies in reasoning and critical thinking. This is already true in many domains, such as chess, Go, mathematics and data analysis.

Communications

Many of us now communicate directly with AI, through prompts or queries. We can write, speak and upload all forms of media and engage in an erudite dialogue with this vast motherlode of our own cultural capital. We can also moderate and modulate the dialogue, get it to speak to us in different voices and languages, at a specified level or in different styles.

I have my own Digital-Don, where I have uploaded all of my decades of writing. I am, effectively, in dialogue with myself and when I ask it a question. I am often surprised by the depth of the answer, as I have forgotten much of what I once knew or wrote!

One of the practical tasks in getting individuals and organizations to adapt to this new age of intelligence is to shake people out of seeing AI as merely search. It can certainly be used for traditional search, which is a hugely productive act in itself, compared to looking up books and going to libraries, but its capabilities lie way beyond this single function. We need to get over the idea that AI is a database or piece of software and that we are unique in our communication skills. We are not. We are now in dialogue, both with ourselves collectively, with the past, and with AI as a communicating entity in itself.

Most organizational uses of AI for communication are not for groundbreaking research with citations; they are the mundane tasks in the workplace such as emails, memos, reports, meeting summaries, CVs, job adverts, copy, presentations and simple spreadsheets. They meet rather basic workflow needs.

This is why the chatbots that have been most successful in the market have been those that prioritize user engagement. Irvine et al (2023) showed that human feedback encourages longer conversations. A/B testing with 10,000 new users, using high-engagement techniques, showed up to 70 per cent increase in conversational length and over 30 per cent improvement in user retention. Smarter models are useful but, for most personal and organizational uses, human behaviour and engagement also matter.

Donald Norman (1998) said great tech should be invisible, and AI is proving him right. This is not about navigating complicated interfaces or mastering new tools. It is about instant access to intelligence, delivered in exactly the way you want it: fast, fluid and frictionless.

Collaboration

We collaborate, not just with other humans, but also with AI. A large AI model is a massive act of collaboration, as it uses the sum total of human knowledge and capital to create the greatest single act of cultural collaboration we have ever seen. It would take hundreds of thousands of years to read the text on which large models are trained, and that is reading eight hours a day, every day. We will never catch up, or collaborate on this scale as humans alone.

Having some humility around AI may help us to better collaborate. Collaborating with AI to get things done, especially automating administrative tasks, creating and summarizing documents, is now commonplace. Within more complex projects, and teamwork, it can be used to relieve bottlenecks and inform decision making. Humans waste inordinate amounts of time in meetings or trying to get collaborative projects completed; meetings, using AI, can be co-ordinated and summarized with action points, then distributed by AI. Processes, procedures and projects can also be productively accelerated.

Dell'Acqua et al (2025), in a field experiment, showed that AI played far more than just an adjunct role to augment team productivity – it was a valuable member of the team. Team members equipped with AI matched the performance of two-person teams without AI, showing that AI can replicate certain collaborative benefits, with teams using AI achieving the highest performance levels and highest-quality outputs. The AI-assisted individuals completed tasks faster, giving significant time savings. There was even an increase in measured positive wellbeing, with less anxiety and frustration along with more energy and enthusiasm when working with AI. They concluded that AI was a 'cybernetic teammate', fundamentally altering how teams collaborate and share knowledge. We are entering an age when AI becomes an invaluable member of teams, not just a tool or resource used by teams.

As AI has become multimodal, collaboration through voice is already with us, as voice agents in our cars, homes and workplaces have been with us for some time. We use them to set times, search, get information and get things done and this will extend into ever more complicated tasks in the workflow and flow of life.

In using agents, we are, by definition, collaborating with AI. It extends collaboration out into your workflow, as AI acts more as a co-worker, assistant or co-creator, rather than just a tool. Instead of simply automating tasks, AI agents work alongside you, helping with problem solving, decision making and creative processes. Its assistance can take many forms, assisting you to automate repetitive tasks, collaborate on writing, research, data analysis or coding.

What does it mean to collaborate with AGI? In one sense we must accept a degree of subservience to its superior knowledge and skills. This form of collaboration is not something we are used to and we find it difficult. It needs an openness to challenge and evidential confirmation.

Our collaboration with embodied AI in cars is already here. We collaborate in a cloud of AI, as it filters out content, predicts our searches as we type, spellcheck and so on. In the physical world it already does number plate recognition, passport recognition at automated border gates and we willingly accept minor functions, like collision and lane warnings, and readily submit to driverless car cabs in some urban environments.

We are in the process of redefining what it is to collaborate with AI as it becomes more powerful, safer and omnipresent in our living, working and physical environments.

New paradigm of productivity

In *Learning Technology*, Clark (2023b) critiqued the old instrumental view of technology, demanding a more sophisticated view of techno-*logy*, the science of technology, as an appreciation of the more complex relationship we have with digital technology, especially AI. Part of that reframing was to avoid the binary trap of us, the subject, seeing and using AI as an object. We are part of a new nexus in which we have dialogue, or commune with technology, no longer as separate beings with a unique set of skills which we apply to AI, but in dialogue with AI which is often superior to ourselves.

It is not an adequate response to say we will simply teach a set of separate abstract skills so we can handle AI more successfully. This becomes a defence mechanism, a way of seeming virtuous without engaging with the technology to get things done. Our education system is already heavily geared towards winning arguments rather than learning how to do things. With AI you really do have to use it and do things to get to know what it is and how one deals with it. Learning abstract skills is a bit like trying to pass your driving test by sitting the theory test only, creating ideas in your head about what it is to drive, critiquing driving rather than doing it for real.

You have to understand and use AI, as the task of communing with AI means using your own as well as acquiring new domain knowledge and new skills. They are rarely separately identifiable skills, as they are marbled together in processes, tasks and problem solving. Thinking does not happen in these separate silos. It involves a rich, interleaved process, where knowledge and skills are inseparable. One may solve a problem by creating new ideas in communication and collaboration with AI, all the while being critical and using its critical capabilities in a co-creative process. This is not a set of separate tasks but a flow of thought while getting something done, whether a task or problem solving.

Neither are these skills, any longer, quintessentially human. We now share these abilities with alternative intelligences. Being productively critical, creative, collaborative and communicative is no longer just our domain. We need some modesty around our cognitive capabilities, as they have evolved to take shortcuts, focus on our selfish needs and fit very specific social, cognitive and physical environments. If we want to break free from these cognitively capped capabilities, we need to work with AI to make breakthroughs and improve our, and its, performance.

We have limited and fallible long-term memories that decline over time, unlike AI that has this vast collective memory of the sum of human culture, languages and images. AI uses this as data to train intelligent models but it can also do things that improve the efficacy of that training in pre- and post-training, the fine tuning. Our working memories are seriously capped in terms of what we can hold and manipulate, resulting in cognitive overload in many tasks. Contrast this with the huge context windows in AI and pre-processing of prompts in contextual AI to get better results. Like our brains, it also interacts with its long-term memory, or the language model, to produce startling results very quickly. Its 24/7 attention and focus allow it to be available at all times, even working when we sleep. These are general advantages when it can be creative, critical, communicative and collabora-tive, especially when it breaks through into multimodality, agents, AGI and embodiment, which all add new dimensions of cooperation with AI. We are all in this together.

We need to abandon the idea of teaching these as uniquely human skills, separately without domain application. Running courses on these supposed skills, as if they were easily teachable outside of domain application, is largely futile. It may work with specific research skills or heuristics on prob-lem solving, but the best way to get the most out of AI for productivity is to learn about it, by working with it, to get things done.

We must not get captured by the allure of these abstract nouns, in think-ing they can be distilled into skills, like essential oils, that can be labelled and taught separately from the world. We only create, critique, communicate and collaborate when we engage with the world. These are not things in themselves but acts of engagement and we enhance our engagement with the world through and with AI, not seeing ourselves as in opposition to it, but solving problems through dialogue and engagement with its various forms.

It is also important not to be defined and constrained by your past expec-tations and experiences of using AI, as this is not like any tool or technology we have used in the past. It creates, critiques, communicates and collabo-rates with us, and even at times, autonomously, with its own agency. If we frame AI as something we merely manipulate as a tool, use and discard at will, apply our God-given gifts to, we miss the very opportunities and bene-fits it offers.

Conclusion

If we see AI as simply bending to our every whim, it will not produce the benefits in innovation and productivity we expect but will be trapped within institutional structures, processes and behaviours that we know are not currently productive.

We may be entering a new paradigm of more inclusive human productivity. Advanced AI, particularly multimodal LLMs, have become the catalyst for this transformation, enabling us to borrow, combine and innovate in ways that redefine productivity. This is not a simple continuation of past processes but the beginning of a transformative era. We can leverage technology to pioneer fresh directions in productivity. The question is not what AI can do for you; it is what you can accomplish with AI. The next chapter of productivity is ours to write – together.

References

Clark, D (2023a) *Great Minds on Learning*, Generative AI, https://greatmindsonlearning.libsyn.com/gmols5e30-generative-ai-with-donald-clark (archived at https://perma.cc/8ZKD-2NJZ)

Clark, D (2023b) *Learning Technology: A Complete Guide for Learning Professionals*, Kogan Page

Dell'Acqua et al (2025) The cybernetic teammate: A field experiment on generative AI reshaping teamwork and expertise, Harvard Business School Working Paper No 25-043, March

Doshi, A R and Hauser, O P (2023) Generative artificial intelligence enhances creativity but reduces the diversity of novel content, arXiv preprint arXiv:2312.00506

Girotra, K, Reichman, J and Toubia, O (2023) Ideas are dimes a dozen: Large language models for idea generation in innovation, Wharton School Research Paper

Haidt, J (2012) *The Righteous Mind: Why Good People Are Divided by Politics and Religion*, Vintage

Irvine, R, Burgert, F and Valentin, J (2023) Rewarding chatbots for real-world engagement with millions of users, arXiv preprint arXiv:2303.06135

Ismayilzada, M, Laverghetta Jr, A, Luchini, S A, Patel, R, Bosselut, A, van der Plas, L and Beaty, R (2025) Creative preference optimization, arXiv preprint arXiv:2505.14442

Karpathy, A (2024) X, https://x.com/karpathy/status/1886192184808149383 (archived at https://perma.cc/C8Q6-GUB9)

Liang, W, Du, J, Yin, M and Hancock, J (2025) The widespread adoption of large language model-assisted writing across society, arXiv preprint arXiv:2502.09747

Meincke, L, Zhang, Z and Goel, A (2024) Prompting diverse ideas: Increasing AI idea variance, arXiv preprint arXiv:2402.01727

Norman, D A (1998) *The Invisible Computer: Why Good Products Can Fail, the Personal Computer Is So Complex, and Information Appliances Are the Solution*, MIT Press

Papert, S (1980) *Mindstorms: Children, Computers, and Powerful Ideas*, Basic Books

Resnick, M (2020) Designing for wide walls, Medium, https://mres.medium.com/designing-for-wide-walls-323bdb4e7277 (archived at https://perma.cc/Y2V6-DDTV)

Vallor, S (2024) *The AI Mirror: How to Reclaim Our Humanity in an Age of Machine Thinking*, Oxford University Press

Wu, Z, Weber, T and Müller, F (2025) One does not simply meme alone: Evaluating co-creativity between LLMs and humans in the generation of humor, arXiv preprint arXiv:2501.11433

Zhu, T, Li, K and Wang, Q (2024) Human bias in the face of AI: The role of human judgement in AI generated text evaluation, arXiv preprint arXiv:2410.03723

05

Humans-in-the-loop

'Humans-in-the-loop' has become a trope, as if AI were the enemy, always needing us humans to control and tame its potential excesses. As Geoffrey Hinton says (University of Toronto, 2024), the brain is a huge analogy machine and this is one such primitive analogy. Yet we use AI autonomously every time we search, use predictive text, spell and grammar check, translate online, use social media, speak to a home voice device, use online maps and speech-assisted navigation, hail an online cab, order food delivery, take a photograph, watch a streaming service, are subject to number plate recognition in carparks (and on almost every major road), go through an automated passport gate, unlock our phone with fingerprint or face recognition, and on almost every app on our phone. You already benefit massively from productivity gains through AI, with little or no humans-in-the-loop.

AI is everywhere, most of it invisible, without a human-in-the-loop in any obvious sense. That is how online technology tends to work. It makes you, your organization, the tools you use and the world you live and work in smoother and easier through invisible AI automation. Its invisibility is its virtue, as that is what makes your life easier. In general, the drift towards taking humans-out-of-the-loop is what makes these tools more productive. This is not a binary switch, from in-the-loop to suddenly being out-of-the-loop. It is a gradual process, the pace and extent of the transition depending on a range of conditions, including the underlying confidence in the AI system's performance, the safety implications of its decisions, the clarity of accountability and the limits imposed by regulation. There is process, a natural progression around trust in AI.

Humans-taken-out-of-the-loop

For a decade, starting in 2015, I gave talks on AI at the Learning Technologies Conference at Olympia in London. I was always amused by the presence of a lift operator, who would ask which floors people wanted, and press the buttons… at a technology conference! He sat in there all day, every day. It seemed so strange, a throwback to an earlier age.

Step into the lift in the Shanghai Tower and it will go up through 128 floors reaching a maximum speed of 46 miles per hour. The Burj Khalifa in Dubai goes to 163 floors. You are putting your trust in an automated system that is used in almost all tall buildings, yet we think little of it.

The history of the elevator is a fascinating and relevant story of 'humans-being-taken-out-the-loop'. It also captures how technological advance has to cope with human psychology and trust.

The first elevators go back to the first century CE, first mentioned by Archimedes (Berryman, 2020), using pulleys and ropes, powered manually by people or animals. He boasted that he could move the earth! The Roman architect Vitruvius also described a mechanical elevator system using pulleys and ropes and, over centuries, elevators were used for building, mining and lifting water.

But it was Elisha Otis, in 1853, who installed the first passenger elevator featuring a safety brake system, which cleverly prevented the elevator from falling if the cable broke. Humans could then put more psychological trust in the technology. Moving into the early 20th century, Werner von Siemens introduced the first electric elevator in 1880. This shift from mechanical to electric power increased efficiency, control and productivity, and by the mid-20th century, decades after their safety was proven, electronically controlled, automatic elevators appeared with basic control systems going to specific floors, without a human operator. Cheap microprocessors in the 1970s took autonomy further, with more sophisticated control systems optimizing the flow of passengers, even grouping people heading to the same floors. Human-in-the-loop operators had been largely eliminated, apart from a few in remote emergency centres and maintenance staff. Elevators are now truly autonomous, with sensors for load balancing, door operations and safety features. AI is used to predict traffic patterns and optimize energy consumption. They even learn from usage patterns to predict peak times and optimize movement to floors.

This is a story of increasing degrees of autonomy through technology, overcoming human fears, to increase productivity. The elevator has gone from being literally pulled up by humans to more mechanical lifts with automated brake systems, to being electronically controlled and fully autonomous, with AI, after overcoming human fears about reliability. We now think nothing of stepping into a lift and going at enormous speeds vertically in buildings. Elevators obviously do not need the level of autonomy seen in self-driving cars, as they simply go up and down. But in their vertical world, the journey elevators took towards autonomy reflects broader trends in technology where machines not only execute tasks but do so with humans being taken out of the loop. They epitomize the trajectory which technology takes when there is a need to make our lives easier and more productive. We literally stepped out of the loop.

Elevated productivity

Elevators have significantly enhanced human productivity, taking seconds to replace the climbing of stairs. One could argue this also reduces tiredness and stress, making us ready for more productive work. Organizations can also occupy office space in a smaller footprint in cities, with far more economic activity in one location. They are also closer to other businesses and services, sometimes within the same building, as well as efficient in energy use, as they take large numbers of people to destinations quickly and optimally. Vertical city landscapes with skyscrapers only exist because elevators have changed where we live and work, improving productivity across many sectors.

Lots of loops

We hear the phrase 'human-in-the-loop', as if that were the only possibility, based on the idea of human exceptionalism. But if a loop is a loop, what is the dominant agent in the loop? Human, AI or both?

There are many different types of 'loops' with varying degrees of agency by both minds and machines. As the AI revolution unfolds, we have already seen a drift in agency away from minds towards machines.

Loops can be regular, small iterations, even set to be totally autonomous, for example when we use AI as a spelling and grammar checker. They highlight, or autocorrect, increasing productivity in writing. A more substantial loop would be prompting AI to summarize, create or critique a piece of writing, where we are the primary agent asking for an output. Once we ask AI to do agentic tasks or deep research we are ceding more responsibility, as AI is doing more of the actual work.

Human-in-the-loop suggests one state for AI, with the only other possible state being humans-out-of-the-loop. This is too binary, as there is a wide spectrum of autonomy reflected in the degree to which either is present. It turns out to be less of a spectrum and more of a complex constellation of participative states, many types of loops, including humans in, on, above and below the loop. What turns out to be important are expert humans-in-the-loop, as well as AI-in-the-loop and AI-assistants-in-the-loop.

As soon as partial automation is underway and AI handles the low-risk or routine stuff, humans-in-the-loop step in with oversight only when uncertainty is high. In time, in applications where speed and scale really matter, and where AI consistently outperforms human judgement, the humans may shift from oversight to exception management or recalibration of the system. Rightly, in more intensely regulated fields like justice, healthcare, finance or aviation, humans-in-the-loop may be kept in place for longer and have to pass through regulatory stage-gates, especially where the stakes are high and public trust is a real concern. Even in these domains, there is growing recognition that retaining human oversight can sometimes become a bottleneck, introducing delays, inconsistency, inefficiency, even reducing overall safety if humans-in-the-loop are overloaded or disengaged.

The move towards greater autonomy becomes desirable when systems become so effective that human oversight no longer adds value. Productivity gains are then best served by gradually moving humans further out of low-level loops. Of course, this must always be done with care, in case things go wrong. The challenge is not just technical, but psychological, managing the transition in a way that preserves trust and delivers real benefits.

The true gains in productivity come from moving away from a universal demand for humans-in-the-loop towards a higher-value, strategic use of humans. Lower-level tasks can be automated, but expertise still matters, and this is where humans should be placed in the loop, so that they can attain high levels of personal productivity.

Human-in-the-loop (classic model)

The classic 'human-in-the-loop' model sees humans in the decision-making cycle. It sees humans as the constant validators, their judgement finalizing decisions. This is normal where there is high-stakes decision making, for example in finance, healthcare and justice. It needs to be optimized as there is always a balance on the degrees of autonomy given to AI. It is often assumed that this is the one model that should cover all applications of AI. It is not.

Human-above-the-loop

When humans take a bird's eye view of AI, and design, configure and apply governance to the AI system, they do not need to get directly involved with decision making but take a more strategic position, defining the rules and constraints before the loop begins. This can take the form of an oversight, governance or compliance group within an institution or product company. They do not get involved in real-time decision making.

Human-on-the-loop

Some contexts require humans-on-the-loop, sitting on the system, ready to intervene when necessary. We see this most obviously in autonomous vehicles but also in security systems and trading algorithms, where humans monitor the system and intervene only when something is flagged, seems to need intervention or goes wrong.

Human-around-the-loop

This is a quite common set-up, where humans are not involved in real-time decisions, but sit around the loop, constantly shaping and adjusting the use of AI. The CEO of Digital Khaos sees his team as doing precisely this. They see AI as a core productivity engine but try and test tools, use some, fine-tune others, swap others out, all in a dynamic process of solving problems and doing things faster and better. This is partly driven by the fast-moving nature of the technology but is also a company mindset, one of continuous collaboration.

Human-below-the-loop

This may sound strange but there are AI systems that hand down decisions and instructions to humans who are not 'in' but 'below' the loop. AI, in effect, delegates to humans. A good example would be a logistics or warehouse system that instructs humans to execute tasks it has decided on. The AI will already have gone through the input, analysis and made an optimized decision, handing that down to the human who sits below this loop.

Human-outside-the-loop

There are many contexts where humans can sit completely outside of the loop and play no active role in decision making or the execution of tasks. The AI is effectively fully autonomous, making high-volume decisions on tasks completely independent of human supervision or decision making. It runs independently, as this is the only way it can operate on scale.

Human-outside-of-the-loop is far more common than many imagine. Your email uses AI to filter out spam. Social media relies on AI to remove huge amounts of contentious content, especially hate speech, misinformation, nudity and porn. Most of this is never reviewed by humans. If you watch Netflix, Prime, YouTube or any other streaming service, what you see is decided by AI – with humans outside of the loop. Use Amazon or most other e-commerce sites to buy anything, and you are seeing AI-presented content. Pricing, let's say surge pricing on Uber, is increasingly dynamic and decided by AI. Other examples of humans being outside of the loop include autonomous warehouse robots, autonomous vehicles on closed routes, predictive maintenance alerts and using a lift!

This gives high productivity on tasks that are routine, repetitive or data-heavy, as it massively exceeds human capabilities and capacity on both speed and scale. It may even be the case that the cost of oversight is higher than the cost of occasional, low-risk errors. A good example is Amazon returns, where the cost of return makes it worthwhile to allow the buyer to keep the item.

Understanding these nuances of the role of humans in loops has huge implications for productivity design. It switches things around, so that one can think about problems first, only then deciding what role AI should play. The right question to ask is: where should the human be in the loop to maximize productivity, given the risks?

Different positions by humans should reflect the different contexts. In high-judgement, high-accountability, high-risk contexts, humans need to be in or above the loop. In more collaborative and medium- to low-risk environments, humans can be on or around the loop, whereas with high-volume, high-autonomy, low-risk contexts, humans can sit below, even outside of the loop.

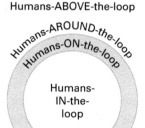

Humans-ABOVE-the-loop

Humans-AROUND-the-loop

Humans-ON-the-loop

Humans-
IN-the-
loop

Humans-BELOW-the-loop
Humans-OUTSIDE-the-loop

Centaurs and cyborgs

Dell'Acqua et al (2023) found, in an early AI and productivity study, a more focused distinction between *cyborgs* and *centaurs*. Both delivered significant productivity gains, but the cyborgs, where humans had more fully integrated AI into their workflow, proved more effective on tasks requiring judgement and creativity that the centaurs, who saw AI as a tool for occasional use. The cyborgs emerged as a group of super-users!

Centaur systems

A variant to loop models are 'centaur systems', where humans and AI collaborate to get things done, as partners. From the mythical half-human and half-horse creature, humans and AI are seen as separate, but they collaborate to get results. This plays to each of their separate strengths. Both are constantly involved, contributing as they move forward with tasks. It is human-in-the-loop with a more even, symbiotic participation, where collaboration is the real relationship.

Centaurs stick to a division of labour, where users regularly switch between human and AI tasks, allocating responsibilities based on what each does best. It may be a physician, going through a clinical decision-making process, with AI as a true collaborator all the way, bringing in relevant data and suggestions, suggesting potential diagnoses other than the one made, recommending an investigative approach, even dialoguing about treatment and doses. It is more of a dialectic through dialogue in decision making. One could see how this works in other domains such as complex legal contracting, where cases would be referred to and alternatives suggested.

You get the best of both worlds: human values, sentiments, emotions, along with a fuller understanding of the context or human patient, as well as faster, better and more accurate expertise brought to the decisions by an incredibly smart AI. It recognizes that all expertise does not reside in humans and all judgement should not reside in AI. This approach is also easier to introduce and scale into sensitive areas such as healthcare. It is truly collaborative.

The centaur model has become an important concept in professional work such as medical diagnostics, legal analysis and consulting, where there is more of an emphasis not on systems but on collaboration.

The analysis of centaur practices showed specific behaviours, where AI was used at particular points in the analytic process, often at the start or end of the process. At the start AI would be used to access information and set up the process or methods, then AI handles each of the modules/sub-task of the tasks accordingly throughout the workflow. They also used AI for each of the modules or sub-tasks, one by one, as they moved through the workflow. Finally, it would be used at the end to structure and edit the final document.

Cyborgs

Cyborgs added another powerful type of AI user, named after sci-fi human–machine hybrids. Cyborg users do not just delegate tasks to AI, they interleave and intertwine their effort into their workflows. They tend to be more comfortable, knowledgeable, experienced and skilled in using AI, with a different mindset around the relationship between humans and AI.

It is all about getting AI to complete a task you started, or working in a dialectical way with AI to get a task or sub-task completed, at a much more granular, sub-task level, while centaurs tend to delegate between human and AI sub-tasks.

It can be difficult to tell where and what was done by humans and AI in the process, so deeply integrated is the use of AI into the workflow. For example, they used techniques to improve outputs, asked the AI to play the role of personas, to get more suitable output, even for that of their own role, a consultant. They would push on using AI in sub-tasks, asking it to clear points up or explain points further, even to justify claims. They also took deep dives on specific points, added data, redoing data analysis, even pushing back on AI output, asking AI to think again.

Experts-in-the-loop

What has emerged, especially as agentic AI gets more powerful, with increasing levels of autonomy, is a renewed focus on *experts*-in-the-loop. The expert, writer, graphic artist, web designer, app developer, coder or professional in any domain is actively and effectively involved in pushing, shaping and moving AI towards the goal. The lawyer, physician or teacher oversees and validates decisions, giving feedback, intervening when necessary, fine tuning by bringing their expertise to the process. This expert is the captain of the ship, steering the ship, changing course when necessary, keeping the ship on a safe course towards its destination. All their experience and expertise is brought to bear, especially in high-stakes research, healthcare, law and the military, to the task at hand.

Agentic AI demands more expertise, as it is more seriously autonomous. Researching, reasoning, planning, designing, interacting with other systems, coding and executing tasks, agentic AI demands experience and expertise to keep the workflow honest, blending the human and AI. By expert we mean domain expert, but also expert in using AI. This blend of domain expertise and AI expertise is what makes experts-in-the-loop particularly useful.

AGI brings next-level problems, as it has expertise across any subject and can do what expert humans can do. This raises a thorny question. To what degree do we allow safe, autonomous activity and what do humans do when using something that is smarter, even orders of magnitude smarter, than its overseer? Governance will still be needed. Humans are then governors-in-the-loop.

Vibes in the loop

Vibe work (coined by Karpathy, 2024) in solving problems is essentially 'experts-in-the-loop', using domain and AI expertise to solve problems. We do not first gather knowledge, communicate, then collaborate, followed by the application of critical thinking, then top it all with some higher-order creativity. Bloom's taxonomy, with its coloured pyramid (which he never created), is wrong and simplistic. Problem solving takes many shapes and is far more complex and messier than this application of separate skills suggests. Without knowledge of the domain, you are unlikely to gain much ground.

Vibe work with AI is best illustrated in an often-underrepresented part of the productive economy, small to medium-sized entities (SMEs), who have to be jacks-of-all-trades. They often do not have admin, finance, HR or sales departments but move fast and want easy-to-use, low-cost solutions. It does not matter if you are a florist, mural designer or tech company, AI can play all of these departmental roles, giving you more breadth, depth and productive punch.

It does what many small business owners hate doing: the admin, communications, pricing, simple contracts, job descriptions, job ads, marketing ideas, branding. Ask it to play a role in your business and it will, as marketing manager, finance director or HR director. Deep research tools will also provide research on your addressable market, product and how to increase sales. Ask it to critique any plans you have written, the copy on your website or presentations. Conduct data analysis of your customer and sales data, even code solutions.

It literally turns a small business into a large business at no extra cost. Productivity is everything in a small business, as it is easy to be distracted by mundane, repetitive, non-critical work, when strategic tasks and selling matter more.

Carl is the CEO of Digital Khaos, a marketing company. His business has been transformed by AI. 'Speed to market is key for us. Being able to implement ideas – ads, images, copy, video and coded technology – without long, drawn out and expensive processes, allows us to provide value to our clients at lower costs.' Instead of writing long briefs to developers, they go straight to the development and deployment of solutions. They also use it to transcribe all client calls and act on what they said they would do.

He describes perfectly the idea of 'vibe' work with AI. 'I don't need the middle-men; AI is an extension of myself. I see something and interact with it instantly. It fills in gaps in my knowledge and I fill in its gaps.' You see lots of these AI productivity gains in SMEs as there is less legacy IT, more free/cheap tool use, no immobilizing HR policies and more doing and sharing.

'You almost have to let the AI optimise you,' he says, 'run with it, let it surprise you... and it will.' As a general technology its functionality and abilities also get constantly better. It allows him and his staff to focus on more valuable stuff, like talking to clients and selling.

Humans-in-the-AI-loop

As AI rises through these levels, it turns the human-in-the-loop issue on its head. We start to see AI-in-the-loop as being more common. Just as in elevators, self-driving robotaxis and autocorrect, if AI helps solve problems, doing something safely, faster and better than us, AI is to an increasing degree in the loop. It loops mostly on its own.

We use AI autonomously every time we search, see predictive text, translate online, use social media, speak to a home voice device, use an online language learning app like Duolingo, go through an automated passport gate, unlock our phones with a fingerprint or face recognition, and use almost every app on our phone. You already benefit massively from productivity gains through AI, with little or no humans-in-the-loop.

AI offers different forms of being in the loop. For example, we are limited to being in the loop when awake or attentive, but AI never sleeps, is always attentive and does not get thrown by emotions, illness or daydreaming. It does not respond to distractions and is endlessly helpful and polite. It can also handle more input than our working memories and has a better range and depth of expertise than us humans.

With Amazon, you as a customer are the human-in-the-AI-loop. AI drives productivity in almost every aspect of their business, as they have a relentless focus on service and productivity. Yet the humans, for almost all actual transactions, are out-of-the-loop.

It starts with personalized recommendations, with 35 per cent of purchases coming from AI-driven recommendations, with measurable increases in engagement, higher order values and customer retention. Their focus on these metrics has grown the business. A whole rack of AI techniques are also used to predict trends in products and optimal pricing, fed by market data, competitor pricing and historical trends. A/B testing frameworks are run at scale to test features or offers.

In their warehouses, hundreds of thousands of robots scurry around picking, packing and moving items around, optimizing locations and routes, all leading to productivity gains and better service through lower costs, fewer returns and faster delivery. That leads to an AI-driven logistics network, with dynamic routing, taking into account everything from parcel loads to traffic, even the weather. Humans are in the loop but only on the last delivery step. Even that is under scrutiny using drones and self-driving vehicles. Other internal processes, such as HR, are also driven heavily by AI. That includes the nuts and bolts of staff scheduling, training recommendations and performance tracking but goes further into dynamic staffing needs to both reduce overstaffing or under-resourcing.

The entire organization is designed to use AI to dynamically increase customer service and productivity, seeing productivity gain not as a thing in itself but as improving the user experience for the customer.

AI-in-the-loop becomes even more potent when it has agency. This involves having AI present and attentive, like an automated spellchecker every time we write something. Going further it may be an agent that goes off to perform sequences of tasks and finish them when the goal is met. This is a neat flip of perspective, seeing AI as a critical friend in the loop, not an augmentation tool.

Agents-in-the-loop

In doing anything in research, education, healthcare, finance and management we are now faced with another challenge to using 'human-in-the-loop' as a simple trope. Humans have severe limitations when they depend on themselves for all skills and decision making. The solution is normally to extend one's reach through collaboration in a team, ideally one with complementary knowledge, skills and roles. Agents are the AI equivalent of having a non-human team.

Agentic AI, the use of agents to perform tasks, changes the whole relationship between humans and AI. There is the additional complication in multi-agent implementations, where agents work with other agents. This use of agents to perform tasks changes the whole relationship between humans and AI. In this case there is no single loop, as it becomes a network of the human and multiple agents.

ServiceNow and Microsoft partnered to develop a multi-agent AI system specifically designed to raise productivity through enhanced collaboration in enterprise environments. By enabling multiple AI agents to seamlessly work together, share contextual information and coordinate complex tasks in real time, this system significantly streamlines operational workflows. The automation and improved coordination across AI-driven processes have allowed human teams to deliver substantial productivity gains across the organization.

Agents shift the dial on autonomy and can be adaptive, reacting to new data while in the workflow, whether that be a customer chatbot or healthcare system reacting to patient and investigative data or data from other systems and databases. Given a goal or role, they can break down tasks into sub-tasks and dynamically execute a workflow, learning as they go, drawing data from various sources and using other online tools when necessary.

Levels of agent autonomy

Bloomberg has substantially improved analyst productivity by incorporating generative AI tools into its financial analysis workflows. Shawn Edwards, Chief Technology Officer at Bloomberg, highlighted that these AI solutions can automate as much as 80 per cent of the tasks analysts typically perform (Bloomberg, 2024). By efficiently handling labour-intensive activities, such as extracting insights from extensive unstructured data, AI frees analysts to dedicate more time to high-end analyst tasks. This shift not only helps efficiency but also enhances the overall quality of analysts' output.

There are levels of autonomy that lead to very different productivity outputs, as shown in the table.

Level	Autonomy description	Examples
Level 1	Basic automation with human oversight. Agent automates simple tasks like notifications. Human supervises and handles all decisions.	Notification systems, basic scheduling tools.
Level 2	Partial autonomy with limited decision making. Agent handles routine tasks but defers to humans for anomalies.	Procurement systems, educational assessments, initial diagnostics in healthcare.
Level 3	Conditional autonomy with human fallback. Agent can make low-risk decisions and carry out multi-step tasks, escalating complex cases.	Customer service chatbots that escalate unclear queries.
Level 4	High autonomy with minimal human oversight. Agent handles complex tasks independently, alerting humans when risk thresholds are breached.	High-frequency trading systems with risk parameters.
Level 5	Full autonomy. Agent plans, executes, and coordinates without real-time human input. May coordinate with other agents.	Fully autonomous logistics or monitoring systems.

At every level the autonomy is higher, as is the rise in productivity. Agentic AI offers a radically different balance between minds and machines, lifting productivity by taking over predictable tasks that consume a lot of time. Organizations can then free up people to concentrate on strategic initiatives that drive growth and innovation. AI agents can also improve accuracy by reducing the likelihood of human error in data processing and administrative workflows, something common when humans are in the loop. They can operate with consistency and precision, increasing reliability. And let's be honest, it may also mean faster and more informed decision making, allowing organizations to react quickly to changing circumstances.

When organizations automate entire workflows end-to-end, eliminating process bottlenecks, with agents that adapt to changing conditions and can scale, productivity gains can be potentially huge. AI agents effectively become part of the workforce.

Robots-in-the-loop

Once robots are being produced en masse, they become, in many instances, robots that replace humans-in-the-loop. The total number of vehicles we produce in a year is around 170 million (cars, light commercial vehicles, trucks, buses and motorcycles). Even if robots were produced on a smaller scale, in their tens of millions, this would have a profound effect on the world of work and productivity, as they can work 24 hours a day and need only energy and occasional maintenance.

It is a mistake to assume that humans will always be in the loop. All of the above point towards a pendulum swing in autonomy towards AI and away from humans. It would be naïve to believe the meme 'AI will not take your job but someone using AI will', as there have already been substantiated job losses.

Dark factories

Dark factories have minimal human oversight over robotic manufacturing. They are dark because there is no need for lighting, as there are no humans on the shop floor. Automation has been sweeping through manufacturing since its inception in the Industrial Revolution, with the Jacquard loom and its programmable punch cards driving textile production and weaving. This inspired Babbage's Analytical Engine, the first major mechanical computer, which in turn eventually led to the personal computer, internet and AI.

Dark factories are a tangible sign of mass automation in manufacturing. They already exist in countries whose economies rely on complex, high-level manufacturing. China, South Korea and Germany have all moved in this direction. They run 24/7 with no need for breaks or shifts. It is a good example of AI automating human paradoxes and problems out of the production process.

Japan's Fanuc Corporation set the pace for productivity through its fully automated dark factories. Robots manufacture other robots with minimal human involvement, going 24/7 for weeks on end, without human intervention. It is an intriguing place, as robots are used to build robots. We do not need lighting to see the exponential possibilities for productivity.

This leads to an interesting, and some would say even darker, thought experiment. When robots can autonomously build other robots, as well as cars, electronics and other physical goods you can think of, productivity doesn't just increase, it explodes exponentially. Unlike traditional manufacturing, where human labour sets a limit on production speed, self-replicating robotic systems entail the doubling effect. To keep it simple, if a single robot builds a second in a week, and each new robot continues making robots, we get 1,024 new robots in just 10 weeks.

Let's take this thought experiment further. What if the robot intelligence improves the process to get incremental improvements in the time taken to build a robot and it is shared collectively as they are part of the same network? The process is even more exponential as they multiply at an increasing speed, giving a superabundance of productivity.

The limitations are no longer the availability of workers, wages and associated costs – it is merely materials, supply chain reliability and energy. These are real constraints. Now imagine that we have automated materials mining, refining and transportation, along with supply chain management, all using AI. The system can be systemically automated.

We have seamlessly vectored from AI as intelligence, into AI building a new world.

Conclusion

For all the talk of humans-in-the-loop (or not), and centaurs or cyborgs, the steady exponential advancement of AI brings with it increased agency and autonomy. The pendulum swings only one way, as more and more people use the technology, personally or at work. It is this increase in safe autonomy that leads to increases in productivity. It may have a jagged frontier (Dell'Acqua et al, 2023) but its waves crash on every shore in a tide that seems to have no ebb.

No matter what we think of having 'humans-in-the-loop', evidence shows that when that becomes too expensive, even causing unwanted friction and inconvenience, people choose paths of least hassle, cost and resistance. Automation short-circuits the loop.

The scaling of AI has confounded the critics and it would seem we are moving towards increasing amounts of AI being used invisibly, with humans outside of the loop, with lots of increasingly remote activity in, on, above, below and outside of loops. There will certainly be many domains and professions where humans, notably experts, will remain in the loop, but as overseers or validators. Whereas we were all centaurs when we first encountered and played with AI, we are rapidly turning into 'vibe' cyborgs, where deep collaboration with AI is the new normal.

This 'vibe' idea ties in neatly with the 'jagged frontier' idea, where the leading edge between humans and AI is messy and unpredictable.

References

Berryman, S (2020) How Archimedes proposed to move the Earth, *Isis*, 111 (3), 562–67

Bloomberg (2024) Bloomberg tech chief says AI could streamline 80% of analyst workload, https://www.fnlondon.com/ (archived at https://perma.cc/Y8KP-WSX5)

Dell'Acqua, F, Rajpurkar, P, Lakhani, K R and Brynjolfsson, E (2023) Navigating the jagged technological frontier: Field experimental evidence of the effects of AI on knowledge worker productivity and quality, Harvard Business School Technology and Operations Management Unit Working Paper No 24-013

Karpathy, A (2024) X, https://x.com/karpathy/status/1886192184808149383 (archived at https://perma.cc/NNK2-KNNT)

University of Toronto (2024) Meet a Nobel laureate: A conversation with University Professor Emeritus Geoffrey Hinton, https://www.youtube.com/watch?v=vpUXI9wmKLc (archived at https://perma.cc/4KPW-Q8W5)

Further reading

Customer Case Study (2024) Pushing the boundaries of multi-agent AI collaboration with ServiceNow and Microsoft Semantic Kernel, https://devblogs.microsoft.com/ (archived at https://perma.cc/RS4T-JR34)

Rowland, I D and Howe, T N (eds) (2001) *Vitruvius: Ten Books on Architecture*, Cambridge University Press

Statista (2024) Vehicles: Statistics amalgamated for all categories, https://www.statista.com/ (archived at https://perma.cc/ZD84-K8YL)

PART TWO

Jagged frontier

06

Jagged frontier

There are lots of claims that AI increases productivity and one could easily imagine that it is seeping up through organizations like a rising tide, evenly and uniformly across all sectors. There is some truth in this, as AI becomes normalized in the hands of everyone with internet access. But the truth is more complex, as progress is uneven, with some breakthroughs and spikes in productivity, some sectors advancing more quickly than others, some organizations adopting an AI-first strategy, even teams and individuals becoming nodes of AI expertise and productivity within organizations.

The AI technological frontier has been described as 'jagged' by Dell'Acqua et al (2023), because AI's proficiencies are uneven across different types of tasks. In other words, AI can dramatically improve productivity in some areas, but underperform in others. This jaggedness reflects the varied, complicated and inconsistent gains across all workflows. The frontier is not a simple staircase that organizations ascend; it has behaviours, pitfalls and defences to overcome.

There is evidence for productivity gains in almost every major sector but progress does not proceed across all sectors moving in lockstep together from one level of productivity to the next. Some sectors, such as marketing and customer care, are moving very quickly, while others, such as law, healthcare and research, are proceeding at pace, albeit with specific areas within these domains shooting ahead faster than others. Coding is spiking ahead, as specific AI tools have been built that provide high-end productivity.

Even within one organization, there may be areas of the organization with very different positions on the jagged frontier at the same time, with different levels of adoption, efficacy and productivity. Highly automated screening of scans in healthcare or driverless taxis in certain cities cohabit with much lower levels of automation and productivity.

This unpredictable, uneven and uncertain leading edge of AI can shoot ahead in one space, yet be severely restricted in another. It does not advance on a uniform front, so we must be careful in assuming it is always predictably productive. Let's navigate along its uneven edge.

What is jaggedness?

All along this jagged AI frontier, there are many edges that develop at different rates, and many hard-fought battles and skirmishes to be won before one wins the productivity war.

RESISTED	STATIC	SPIKY	BROAD	BREAKOUT	SURGE
CREATIVE	**EDUCATION**	**VARIOUS**	**HEALTH**	**RESEARCH**	**PHYSICAL**

Progress can be *resisted* by deeply embedded practices and behaviours, so that the front remains in a fixed position. Creative media industries and the arts are sectors that tend to have this type of frontier.

Progress can be *static* as there is little senior interest or buy-in, again in a fixed position. Even here, many may be using AI on the sly. In education, for example, huge numbers of learners may be using AI, while the line is held firm by teachers and faculty.

Progress tends to proceed in a *spiky* pattern across functions but there are general advances in most areas. Productivity gains are broad but very uneven and jagged. Most sectors, such as consultancies, marketing, coding, law and policing, show this irregular shaped frontier.

Progress is *broad* across the entire front, with most activities using AI. Productivity gains are considerable and positively adopted. Healthcare would be a sector that shows this pattern of gradual and widescale adoption.

Breakouts are AI solutions that are seen to quickly solve specific problems. The productivity gains can be enormous as it automates and advances way beyond what was previously possible. Research is a good example, where AlphaFold broke through to define the structure of 200 million proteins.

A *surge* is a large movement into an entirely new domain. Embodied AI into the physical domain of robots, self-driving cars, drones, satellites and space all take AI into new boundless and uncharted territories.

At first, it looked like a digital parlour trick: the avocado chair, odd selfies, a raccoon in a space suit eating pizza on the moon. What began as an entertaining chatbot quickly evolved into a serious productivity tool. It has gone from generating poems to drafting business and research plans, to coding and high-end maths, research, full stack coding and creating movies. Then from answering questions to using agents to running entire workflows, adding memory and bigger context windows (input sizes). It confounded the critics, getting better, faster and cheaper.

It started by helping us do our jobs but is now starting to redefine our jobs. This isn't about fine tuning old processes; it is not just optimizing workflows but revising and revamping them. Workers are using the tool in their millions, entire professions are being retooled, education is scrambling to catch up, businesses are getting on board.

Most still underestimate it. Many leaders are unaware it is already being used under the radar, on the sly, by students, employees and teams who are not waiting for policy to catch up. Why? Because it works. Disruption does not ask for permission, because it delivers.

AI boosts productivity but unevenly

The good news is that, even this early in the implementation of AI, we are getting sound evidence from academic studies, case studies, surveys and fieldwork that productivity gains are being realized.

In a thorough analysis by Hampole et al (2025), larger, established organizations saw significant gains in productivity as they integrated AI into their operations. A full standard deviation increase in AI use led to 12 per cent higher productivity, 28 per cent more sales and 38 per cent greater profits, as well as higher wages. In short, they found a strong positive correlation between use of AI, productivity and growth.

The good news is that, as firms integrate AI it automates some jobs, particularly higher-end jobs, but the productivity gains create more jobs. In publicly traded companies, this AI exposure explains employment growth of about 14 per cent. What seems to be happening is that AI automates certain tasks but employees take on other work and challenges, so that growth persists. Jobs and skills change rather than being eliminated.

The lesson one can draw is that AI should certainly be adopted, as it increases productivity and opportunities to upskill. The positive side effect is that jobs change, rather than disappear. One should integrate AI into your organization and look for opportunities to reskill those who adopt AI into other high-value tasks and opportunities which the increased productivity will create.

We seem to have reached an inflexion point, where the raw evidence suggests there are concrete wins on the table for organizations and economies, waiting to be realized.

Generative AI was proving to be a powerful tool in increasing workplace productivity, and academic research brought these gains into focus. In one of the first studies on productivity, from MIT (Noy and Zhang, 2023), 444 professionals, including HR specialists, marketers, consultants and data analysts, were divided into two groups; half used GPT-based generative AI, while the other half did not. The results were striking. Those with access to GPT experienced a substantial leap in productivity. The time taken to complete tasks dropped by an impressive 0.8 standard deviations, while the quality of their output improved by a credible 0.4 standard deviations.

In other words, work got done faster *and* better. Generative AI was not just about speeding up routine tasks – it also enhanced quality, strategic thinking and decision making. This was encouraging, as by automating repetitive work, professionals could focus on high-value activities like creative problem solving and innovation, driving not just productivity but long-term growth.

The Boston Consulting Group's experiment (Dell'Acqua et al, 2023) got much publicity, as it claimed early, convincing evidence that generative AI can significantly impact workplace productivity. In a field study involving 758 consultants, AI was deployed across 18 tasks, from problem solving to writing and analysis. The results were transformative, as participants completed 12.2 per cent more tasks, 25.1 per cent faster, with 40 per cent higher quality. This was not just a matter of getting more done – better outcomes were achieved in less time.

Again, these findings built on the growing body of evidence that AI was not just automating low-level tasks; it was transforming high-skill, knowledge-based work. GPT-4 allowed professionals to focus on what really mattered: strategic thinking, innovation and delivering value.

Another interesting conclusion emerged from the evidence. Novices benefited the most from AI, with the technology levelling the playing field. AI helped novices close the gap with experts when it offered guidance, enhanced task execution and delivered the structured support they might lack through inexperience.

For experts, however, the impact was more nuanced. They still experienced time savings and improved efficiency but the productivity increase was smaller compared to novices. Experts tended to use AI more selectively, to assist with specific tasks rather than end-to-end solutions. Once again, in many cases, AI enhanced the strategic and creative elements of their work by automating routine tasks, freeing up time for higher-level problem solving and innovation.

Generative AI was clearly pointing towards being a productivity amplifier for all users, but acting as a powerful equalizer for less experienced workers, allowing them to perform at almost expert levels. This effectively reduced skill gaps, leading to the democratization of expertise.

General sectors

As generative AI washed through industries, delivering productivity gains in many businesses, Bain and Company (2024) identified four areas to look for productivity gains. First, in customer service and contact centres, AI reduced the time spent on manual responses by 20 to 35 per cent, freeing up human agents to focus on higher-value customer interactions. Sales and marketing teams were also spending 30 to 50 per cent less time on content creation as AI automated everything from personalized emails to social media content. In software product development, coding-related activities saw a 15 per cent reduction in time, accelerating the delivery of projects so that developers could concentrate on more complex tasks. The same applied to back-office operations, cutting task times by 20 to 50 per cent and significantly reducing errors.

Bick et al, in late 2024, reported nearly 40 per cent of US adults aged 18 to 64 were using generative AI tools, with 28 per cent of employed individuals incorporating them into their work routines, with 10.6 per cent of these workers engaged with AI daily.

In the workplace, generative AI assisted in 1 to 5 per cent of total work hours, leading to reported time savings equivalent to 1.4 per cent of overall work time. This efficiency suggests significant potential for productivity enhancements as AI tools become more powerful and embedded in daily operations. Projections indicated that generative AI could increase labour productivity by at least 0.5 to 0.9 per cent annually through 2030. This potential surge in productivity suggests a transformative impact of AI on economic growth. The rapid integration of generative AI into the workforce, they concluded, is poised to deliver substantial productivity gains, reshaping traditional workflows and contributing to economic progress.

Generative AI was not just about task completion; it was also reshaping how people search for jobs. Over 50 per cent of unemployed respondents in the study used AI tools to refine their résumés, write cover letters or prepare for job applications, making it a vital tool in the changing job market. This suggests that large numbers of AI-ready workers are entering new jobs.

This was followed in December 2024 by a study, 'The Labor Market Effects of Generative Artificial Intelligence', in which Hartley et al investigated the rising impact of generative AI in the labour market, including the consequences on productivity and employment. A wide and fascinating range of tasks showed significant productivity gains. Productivity roughly tripled for tasks when generative AI was used. Workers saved an average of 71 per cent of time on many tasks and as work was being done 3.5 times faster to achieve the same output, you would only need about 29 per cent of labour doing these tasks.

Generative AI was rapidly emerging as a powerful driver of workplace productivity, reshaping how tasks are performed across industries. According to this study, nearly one-third of workers in the US reported using generative AI at work by the end of 2024.

Very few stopped after trying it just once. Younger, more educated and higher-income individuals are leading the way, with adoption being most prominent in industries like customer service, marketing and information technology. This surge in usage confirmed the potential of AI to increase productivity. The authors showed that AI both aids and substitutes human labour, depending on the tasks and industries involved. While it promises significant productivity gains and economic growth, it also poses risks of job losses in certain sectors.

The 2025 ILO working paper 'Generative AI and Jobs: A Refined Global Index of Occupational Exposure' is a global assessment of how generative AI may impact jobs. It reports on four gradients of occupational exposure, showing that clerical and highly digitized professional roles face the highest levels of automation potential. About 25 per cent of workers are in occupations with some exposure to GenAI. They conclude that job transformation, rather than elimination, is the expected outcome.

Team productivity

Can AI contribute to team productivity? One fascinating and complex study by Dell'Acqua et al (2025) showed AI as not just increasing personal productivity but also enhancing teamwork. Teams with AI produced the best overall results, especially in top-quality outputs. An interesting side effect was the improvement in how people felt about work.

At Procter & Gamble, 776 professionals, including a mix of commercial, technical R&D and other specialists were split into 1) individuals with and without AI and 2) teams with and without AI.

Teams outperformed individuals but AI-augmented workers produced more detailed solutions in 12–16 per cent less time, showing real-world productivity gains in both. Humans with AI performed as well as human teams without AI. It sounds negative, but this suggests AI can replicate collaboration and reduce coordination costs, making even working alone highly productive.

The detail is important, as AI was seen to transform productivity by breaking down traditional functional silos that often limit collaboration and output. In many organizations, specialists typically operate separately in silos, each contributing from their own area of expertise. This can slow down workflows and restrict the scope of innovation. But with AI in the mix, those boundaries begin to blur. Individuals, no matter their original role, are able to generate strong, cross-functional solutions that bring together technical insight and commercial strategy.

AI particularly elevates the productivity of less experienced employees. With AI support, they can quickly operate at near-expert levels, contributing high-quality work that would normally require years of training. This is not only about individual effectiveness but significantly enhancing output from the whole team. By enhancing expertise, AI allows more people to engage in higher-value tasks, expanding an organization's productive output.

AI does not just make individuals more productive – it unlocks the productivity of teams, flattening hierarchies and accelerating the entire process. This brings a new mindset to the use of AI in organizations, not seeing AI as some sort of adjunct assistance but an intelligent generative partner, with a valuable role in redesigned teams.

A powerful secondary productivity gain came through improving the emotional experience of work. Those using AI consistently reported feeling more energized, focused and enthusiastic, also experiencing less frustration and stress. This matters because emotional state directly impacts performance and productivity. When people feel better, they work better. Increased motivation and a more positive mindset lead to sharper thinking, greater persistence and faster execution. In this way, AI not only enhances productivity through what it can do, but also amplifies productivity by changing how people feel while doing it.

Conclusion

The jagged frontier means that the capabilities of AI are intrinsically variable and have varied impacts across sectors. Despite this hugely variable front of varied progression, the work done in productivity research still points in one direction only – upwards.

The absence of traditional ads and marketing for AI marks a shift in itself about how we see and use technology. In a sense it is not so much being sold as being used, by passing traditional sales and marketing and going straight to utility, habitual use and productivity.

It is not about how productive AI will turn out to be, but the time taken for different fields, sectors and organizations to progress in this jagged fashion. We have seen how task productivity gives professionals, and professional teams, a multiplier effect on single tasks, which gives considerable productivity in completing familiar workflows, faster and better, across multiple sectors. We are seeing billions of actions per month, growing rapidly, all the while augmenting human productivity, sure in the knowledge that AI – fashioned, in a manner of speaking, on the human brain – extending its capabilities, even transcending them, will result in astonishing progress and breakthroughs in almost all sectors.

Nevertheless, we have also seen how the many paradoxes in productivity inevitably put bottlenecks and brakes on this progress and the various species of humans-in-the-loop mean that different dynamics in different sectors mean different levels and rates of automation, and therefore productivity. It is possible that not just tasks or workflows but entire professions will have their work reshaped by AI. It is hard to imagine, so used are we to thinking of humans being teachers, doctors, lawyers, accountants, engineers, scientists, researchers and managers. Professional productivity by AI is partly replacing professional services and will most likely be more productive than humans at the lower-end tasks in the professions, especially with agentic ability. AGI is different, as it may transcend many of the abilities of top professionals in these fields, even become exponentially better. This has to be considered a possibility.

The trajectory is clear, one of exponential growth in productivity. There are, of course, reasons why this may not happen as smoothly as the evidence suggests. Humans, teams, organizations, institutions, sectors and nations are organic, reactive and complex. They do not behave as purely rational entities.

We will now take a trip across the jagged frontier, to explore the resistant, static, spiky, broad and breakthrough sectors.

References

Bain & Company (2024) Technology report, https://www.bain.com/insights/topics/technology-report/ (archived at https://perma.cc/SU7W-399E)

Bick, A, Blandin, A and Deming, D J (2024) The rapid adoption of generative AI (No w32966), National Bureau of Economic Research

Dell'Acqua, F et al (2025) The cybernetic teammate: A field experiment on generative AI reshaping teamwork and expertise, Harvard Business School Working Paper No 25-043, March

Dell'Acqua, F, Rajpurkar, P, Lakhani, K R and Brynjolfsson, E (2023) Navigating the jagged technological frontier: Field experimental evidence of the effects of AI on knowledge worker productivity and quality, Harvard Business School Technology and Operations Management Unit Working Paper No 24-013

Hampole, M, Papanikolaou, D, Schmidt, L and Seegmiller, B (2025) Artificial intelligence and the labor market (No w33509), National Bureau of Economic Research

Hartley, J, West, J and Acemoglu, D (2024) The labor market effects of generative artificial intelligence, National Bureau of Economic Research

International Labour Organization (2025) Generative AI and jobs: A refined global index of occupational exposure, ILO Working Paper

Noy, S and Zhang, W (2023) Experimental evidence on the productivity effects of generative artificial intelligence, *Science*, 381, 6654

07

Media and art (resistant)

AI triggered a bitter Hollywood strike and resistance from those who felt wronged by the scraping of data from the web, and other sources, to train foundational AI models. As AI evolved from text LLMs into multimedia MLLMs, with multimodal capabilities in audio, images, video clips, avatars and then full-blown lip-synched video, these advances threatened the creative media world. On top of this, creatives and artists are repulsed by the idea that AI stole, and was even claiming to create, art. 'They shall not pass' was, and is, the prevailing atmosphere. Calls for resisting and halting AI, legal challenges and general negativity are the norm.

Accessibility

After a talk for 2,500 people in the Grieghallen in Bergen, Norway, it really felt like 'The Hall of the Mountain King'. I've given talks in many countries in Europe, US, Asia and Africa and something often happens at these events. It surprised me the first time and it happened again here.

Time and time again, someone with dyslexia, or with a son or daughter with dyslexia, or other accessibility problems, comes up to me to discuss how AI had helped them. They describe the troubles they had in an educational system that is obsessed with text. I can't tell you how often I've had these conversations. They rightly want to tell their story, as it has often been one of struggle, in a system that ignores them, where they have had to find their own way to overcome their communication problems, or see institutions ban the very tools they need to survive. It is always heartfelt.

Bottlenecks often arise through visible and invisible impairments, and an often forgotten side of AI is its revolutionary impact on accessibility and the role multimodality has played in allowing those with visible and invisible problems to improve their lives and become more personally productive.

Text on blackboards, text-based subjects, textbooks, text-based home-work, text-based exams don't really reflect the real world or the world of work. We should reflect on the simple but puzzling fact that we send our kids off to school aged 5 or so, to emerge at 20+ having done not much more than read, write and critique text. Is it any wonder we have skills shortages? The net results may now be causing societal problems, with a text-trained, graduate, managerial class, with a strong disposition towards essay and report writing, bureaucracy and rules, but low on vocational, operational and social skills.

Productivity and accessibility

AI is welcomed by those with dyslexia, and other learning issues, as it helps mitigate some of the challenges associated with reading, writing and process-ing information. Those who are hostile or want to ban AI want to destroy or inhibit the very thing that has helped most in accessibility.

Text-to-speech and speech-to-text tools is the two-way street that uses AI to convert difficult-to-read text to speech, and speech to text, where required. This is not just about those with hearing or sight impairment. Text-to-speech cuts out the need to read, allowing people with dyslexia and others to listen rather than read, reducing the cognitive load associated with decoding and dealing with text. Its sibling, transcription, converting speech into text, also help people write assignments, essays, emails or notes more easily by speak-ing their thoughts instead of typing. Text is often photographed and AI-driven OCR turns them into text, then, if required, speech. These are productivity tools for those most in need.

People with dyslexia often struggle with spelling and grammar, so AI-powered writing assistants, with real-time corrections and suggestions, making writing more accurate and less frustrating, are a boon. These have become normalized and built in to contexts where text is required. AI can also break down complex texts, summarize information and provide defini-tions or explanations for difficult words or concepts. This can make reading less daunting and more manageable, not just for those with dyslexia, but everyone. AI can simplify complex language, while any chatbot can provide quick summaries of long articles or papers. Smartphones, tablets and computers now come with built-in AI-powered accessibility features that can be customized for dyslexic users.

It is often forgotten that huge numbers of disadvantaged learners and employees leverage AI tools on their own. They are the original 'AI on the sly' users. Individuals with accessibility problems have been using these tools to overcome the challenges they face with reading, writing and processing information, making it easier to learn, work and communicate effectively. We have a lot to learn from them, especially around our almost fanatical obsession in education with the written word. So next time you hear someone who wants to ban AI in learning, think again. Having finally found solutions to their problems, do not throw them back into a world where they once again feel abandoned.

We can use this to our advantage in getting productivity into education and organizations by promoting these advantages in accessibility, for everyone. This is, at heart, a very strong argument in education and the workplace for adopting AI, as it unleashes the potential and untapped productivity of those who are not in the workforce, as well of those who are not working to their full potential through no fault of their own.

Multimodality

The world is multimodal, communication is multimodal, the workplace is multimodal. This is why multimodal AI will make an impact way beyond that which purely text LLMs offered. Multimodality has given us productivity opportunities way beyond mere text into speech, images, video, lip-synched video, avatars and even art.

Audio

AI is shifting communications out of the world of text into a more oral culture. The global success of podcasts is evidence enough for this move. We retreated into teaching in text, using text in assessments, assuming that text was always primary. It is not. Speech is primary in language and linguistics, with writing a very late arrival in our cultural evolution, only a few thousands of years ago. AI has unleashed speech, in dialogue and in many languages.

During my trip to Japan recently, cross translation and Google Lens for menus were invaluable. Speech and text translation on tap has now changed the whole dynamic of communications while travelling, as well as in language learning.

AI voice-enabled digital assistants can help us manage daily tasks, set reminders, dictate and send messages, and control smart home devices through voice commands, reducing the need for reading and writing. These assistants can answer questions, engage in full dialogue and act as tutors. They can also handle tasks such as setting alarms, creating to-do lists, searching the web, all through simple voice interactions.

Audio is also having a revival through digital, on-demand and hugely popular podcasts. My colleague John Helmer and I have produced podcasts on AI, learning and learning theorists that have reached an audience way beyond what we experience at conferences (Clark, 2025). One of the surprise hits in AI was Google's NotebookLM, where one could automatically generate, and edit, a dialogue-based podcast on any subject, based on uploaded text. It sounded astonishingly real.

You can take a research paper, your own writings, slide-deck or meeting notes and have an oven-ready, short podcast discussion between two people that is as energetic as it is realistic. In workflows, AI-driven speech aids productivity through tools like Otter.ai and Microsoft Teams, which automatically transcribe and translate multilingual meetings in real time, then generate summarized audio highlights.

AI is unlocking a return to our oral roots – and turbocharging productivity in the process. Consider how, instead of typing queries, you can now simply speak to an AI assistant on your phone or smart speaker and get instant, spoken answers in dozens of languages. In a sales role, for example, you might dictate a complex product question into ChatGPT's voice interface while driving between meetings; within seconds you've got a clear, spoken summary you can relay to a prospect – no keyboard or note-taking needed.

This shift from text to speech also supercharges content creation. Take podcasts: before, producing even a short episode meant scripting, recording, editing and mastering audio – a multi-day slog. Today, tools like Descript and Adobe Podcast AI let you upload a rough transcript or bullet points and automatically generate a polished, voice-cloned episode in under an hour. John Helmer and I used these tools to spin up fortnightly AI-theory discussions: what once took us two days (writing, recording, editing) now takes just two hours, and our listenership has doubled without any extra effort on our part.

Images

Imagery is also a form of communication, as we can see with the development of image-rich social media, graphic novels and the use of photographs, artwork, diagrams, graphs and so on, in culture in general. Tools now exist to create visual communications from the sober diagram to highly creative images and art. Many now routinely use AI to produce images for acts of communication, in presentations for conferences, social media posts and blogs.

Visual communication is faster using image creation, which has driven down costs. The first productivity gain can be through ideation. Rather than days of iterations on early ideas, a whole range of visual options can be created on the spot, even mood-boards, from logos to photorealistic images for ads. For products, images can be created, altered, done in multiple colours and sizes. This quick creation of ideas is one of its strengths, as options can be conjured up and iterated quickly. This helps push towards A/B testing to get a data-driven view of their effectiveness.

In professional settings photorealistic images of almost anything, in any style, in any place, are achievable. This brings quality images and artwork into an affordable range for small to medium-size businesses. All parts of a business can now engage in image production to improve slide decks, graphics in reports to illustrate data, flowcharts and diagrams. It pushes up productivity in all areas of the organization by giving agency on image generation to separate departments and people who want it done quickly and cheaply.

AI is quite simply quicker and cheaper, with fewer bottlenecks in process and production. Momentum can be maintained, capturing the creative energy of a team, so that things move towards their creative conclusion.

Avatars

Another great surprise was AI's success in producing talking figures, called avatars. I have been creating video avatars of myself, at increasing levels of fidelity in appearance, movement, lip-synch and voice, speaking many languages, in many styles, from Arabic to Zulu. This involved going into a studio for video capture, then a separate audio studio for voice capture. These avatars can be used in marketing, or as employees in management training, patients in healthcare training and customers in retail training. Any form of human communication training can use this technique for instructional videos, trigger videos (to stimulate dicussion), branched scenario videos (where you get different videos depending on your choices) and videos within additional AI-generated learning experiences and assessment.

We now have avatars that one can converse with using AI chatbot technology, taking it to another level through scenarios and simulations, using real dialogue. These appear in computer games but also in language learning and training, where speech dialogue with a realistic avatar can be combined with feedback on pronunciation, performance and competence in dialogue.

I have created a lot of these dialogue simulations, using fixed video clips in interviewing skills, conflict, language training and so on. Their production took a lot of time to design, write and produce. It is now a lot quicker and cheaper through avatar production. Productivity, using libraries of avatars or bespoke avatars, is now achievable, as are the obvious productivity gains. This has huge potential in customer service and training where it has been impossible to create high-fidelity video simulations for a range of soft skills.

Video

Perhaps the most extraordinary and surprising spin-outs from AI are generated video. Images of sailing ships in a cup of coffee soon gave way to astonishing levels of realism, even lip-synched speech, unleashing an explosion of creativity, as quality video production was put into the hands of those who could just express their vision in text.

We are also on the cusp of a revolution in video production. I used to produce videos, even a full feature film *The Killer Tongue* (don't ask!). The production costs were eye watering, but we are now seeing AI-assisted and full video production flourish, with dramatic reductions in costs. This will continue to evolve.

We are not yet at the level of full drama but the direction of travel is clear and the film and television business will change. Film and video production is big business. Movies are still going strong. Netflix, Prime, Disney, Apple and others have created a renaissance in television, changing the medium towards an on-demand box-set model. Social media has also embraced video with the meteoric rise of TikTok, Instagram, Facebook shorts and so on. YouTube is now a full entertainment channel. It is a huge, global industry and AI-generated video is now an increasingly significant portion of what is seen online.

I first started playing around with AI-generated video from stills. You just typed in a few words, waited on it processing and it was done. It got very good, very fast. Then came prompted video, from text only. This got really good, really fast, first with Sora from OpenAI, and the many new players entering the market – great for short video but no real long-form capability. Then came full speech from AI-generated characters and narrated work.

But is AI-generated video as good as real video in practice? Leiker et al. (2023) looked at this hypothesis in learning. The study took 83 adult learners, randomly assigning them into two groups: traditionally produced instructor video and generated video with a realistic AI-generated character. Pre- and post-learning assessment and survey data were used to determine what was learnt and how learners perceived the two types of video. No significant differences were found in either learning or how the videos were perceived. They suggest that AI-generated, synthetic, talking-head learning videos are a viable substitute for real teacher videos.

In entertainment, we now see production companies and tools, where you can create your own show. These companies use LLMs, as well as custom state-of-the art diffusion models, but what makes this different is the use of multi-agent simulation. Agents can build story progression and behavioural control of created, scripted characters. Tools such as these will be able to create any form of video and drama, as it will be a 'guided' process, with the best writing, direction and editing built into the process. You are driving the creative car but there will be a ton of AI in the engine and self-driving features that allows the tricky stuff to be done to a high standard behind the scenes.

AI can use character history, goals and emotions, simulation events and localities to generate scenes and image assets that are coherent and consistent with the existing story. Behavioural control over agents is also possible, over their actions and intentions, also within conversations.

This sounds easy, but the 'slot-machine effect', where things become too disjointed and random to be seen as a story, is a really difficult problem to solve. So long-term goals and arcs are used to guide the process and behind the scenes there is a need for hidden 'trial and error' processes, so you do not see the misfires, wrong edits and so on. This can be likened to Kahneman's System 1 versus System 2 thinking. Most LLM and diffusion models play to fast, quick, System 1 responses to prompts. For long-form creative media, you need System 2 thinking, so that more complex intentions, goals, coherence and consistency are given precedence.

Interestingly, hallucinations, far from being destructive, can introduce created uncertainty, a positive thing, as happy accidents seem to be part of the creative process, as long as they do not lead to implausible outcomes. This is an interesting creative and collaborative avenue: how to create non-deterministic creative works that are predictable but still exciting and novel.

The next step, and we are surely on that yellow brick road, is to create your own live-action movies from text and image prompts. This includes AI dialogue, voice, editing, different shot types, consistent characters and story development. You can take it to another level by editing the episodes' scripts, shots and voices and remaking episodes. One can expect an explosion of productivity in marketing, training and wherever video is used to move us towards a goal. We can all be live-action movie directors.

Art

Let's move up a gear and tackle one of the biggest challenges to AI, the idea that AI can do what humans do – art. By dealing with this controversial issue, we can look at some of the most basic challenges to AI and the idea that it can be productive in almost every domain.

Can AI produce art?

There are many who see AI as stealing from the past. All content creation involves taking from the past to create the new. No matter how radical the jump, all new content takes from old content, all content emerges to a degree from previous content. This is the essence of GenAI, which takes a vast corpus of text or visual data and allows us to create new media by simply asking it to do so, to make freshly minted worlds, images, audio and video.

When we speak, we are using the vast amount of data we heard from others over our lifetime up to that point. New language is an act of blending in the language we speak, of past learning and experience. When we prompt, we co-create with AI to create something new but grounded in the past.

Forward movements in art invariably produce a backlash. AI poses a challenge, in that our cognitive capabilities are far from unique. A simple calculator puts paid to that idea and AI is now pushing into areas such as critical thinking, creativity, collaboration, communication and intelligence.

Late 18th- and early 19th-century Romanticism promoted the idea that creation is a 'uniquely' human endeavour, when all along it has been a draw-ing upon the past, deeply rooted in what the brain has experienced and takes from its memories to create anything new. Now that we can draw from the much deeper well of human culture, a vast collective memory of our cultural past, new acts of post-creation are possible. The history of art is one of taking from the past to help create the future. The 'new' becomes the 'new old'.

What is art?

What is rarely discussed when considering AI and art is the simple question: what is art? It is often assumed to be obvious. It is not. Theories of art matter as they have deep implications for discussions around creativity and AI-produced art. Many will be surprised to find that most theories of art can be used to support, not ban, the assistance of AI in the production of art.

'Art as an imitation or representation' of reality is seen by many, such as Plato and Aristotle, as the commonest theory of art. This can be used to support the idea of AI-generated art, as it can generate art from a mix of human input and large datasets, to imitate styles, themes and techniques of human art. AI-produced art qualifies as representational art because it does not, in any strict sense, copy or replicate; it represents through recreation.

'Art as communication', as a medium through which artists communicate ideas, emotions or narratives to an audience, is another theory of art. AI may very well help artists communicate, and if the viewer interprets meanings or emotions from AI art, a form of communication surely occurs. The human input, in guiding AI, could also be seen as a conduit for human-to-human communication through AI. Other stronger Expressionist theories are based more solidly on the artist, the 'expression' of artists' emotions, feelings or inner experiences. Without emotional intent, AI-generated works fall short of being true art under this theory. Even here, some claim that the emotions of the humans influencing AI can imbue the work with expressive qualities or that AI knows what consciousness and emotions in humans are, as they are embodied in language and captured behaviour. Some even believe that AI has consciousness, while others believe it will emerge.

'Art as experience', as seen by Dewey (1934), is rooted in the experiential interaction between the artist, the artwork and the audience. It emphasizes the continuity between art and everyday life, suggesting that art arises from and contributes to the experiences of individuals within their environment. Under Dewey's theory, AI-produced art is art if it facilitates a meaningful experience between the creator and the audience. The interactivity and engagement prompted by AI art can be aligned with this experiential idea.

Under the Aesthetic theory of art, put forward by Kant (2024), art is anything that provides an aesthetic experience to the viewer. If AI-produced works arouse an aesthetic response, they satisfy this theory. The focus is on the viewer or the experience of the audience, allowing AI art to be appreciated as art. This is obviously compatible with AI-generated art, as are Formalist theories of art defined through its formal qualities – composition, colour, line, shape and other aesthetic elements, a theory held by Bell (1914) and Greenberg (1939). AI can, of course, create works with compelling formal properties that induce aesthetic appreciation. If art is appreciated solely for its formal aspects, regardless of the creator's identity or intent, AI-generated pieces can also be considered art. And if art serves as a means of understanding, through intellectual exploration, a theory put forward by Goodman (1976) and Langer (1953), presenting new perspectives and insights, functioning similarly to language in conveying ideas, AI art can certainly offer new perspectives or challenge perceptions, contributing to such engagement.

Institutional theory of art

While he was deputy chair of a major arts organization, the Brighton Dome and Festival, we invited Grayson Perry to be a guest director of our festival. On his trip to Brighton he was iconoclastic and critical of what he saw as old thinking in the art world.

His perspective on art aligns with the Institutional Theory, which defines art as whatever the art world – artists, critics, curators, galleries – recognizes as art, following the art theorists Dickie and Danto. As AI-generated works gain acceptance in galleries, museums and auctions, they attain the status of art within the institutional framework. The theory supports the inclusion of AI art as long as it is embraced by the art community. In his 2025 exhibition 'Delusions of Grandeur', Perry incorporated AI-generated images of himself in various personas, which were then transformed into ceramic artworks, even inventing a fictional artist who produced works of art shown in the exhibition. This institutional theory of art supports the idea that AI-generated art can attain the status of art within the institutional framework, aligning with the principles of the Institutional Theory.

Postmodernism also defies singular definitions and embraces plurality, challenging notions of originality and authorship. Its scepticism towards grand narratives and embrace of appropriation and pastiche align with AI art's remixing of existing data. AI art can become a postmodern exploration of creativity and authorship that aligns with postmodern themes of challenging originality and embracing plurality.

AI art certainly raises questions about what constitutes creativity but AI is acceptable in almost all theories of art, and the increasing presence of AI art in mainstream venues confirms its growing acceptance as it challenges traditional gatekeeping.

Future of art

As AI continues to advance and integrate into the art world, these discussions will shape our perception of art in the digital age. This may disturb some but shifts in art have often agitated the orthodoxy. The rise of AI art challenges us to discuss the role of technology in human culture, especially AI. It challenges us to consider whether art is a uniquely human endeavour or if machines can partake in artistic creation. With AI art, the artist's role may shift from creator to curator or facilitator.

Technological shifts have transformed art, with new tools and media. They have also democratized art, making it easier to produce and more accessible. Entirely new forms of art have emerged, including photography, film, digital art and interactive installations. Technology also changes how audiences engage with art, introducing interactivity and personalization.

Technological inventions have continually reshaped the landscape of art, pushing the boundaries of creativity and expression. Physical technologies introduced new materials and methods, allowing artists to explore uncharted aesthetic territories. Digital technologies have further expanded these horizons, enabling virtual experiences and global connectivity. As technology evolves, it challenges artists to adapt and inspires them to innovate, ensuring that art remains a dynamic reflection of human ingenuity and captures the zeitgeist of each era. The symbiotic relationship between art and technology not only propels artistic evolution but also invites society to reconsider the possibilities of creation and the essence of what art can be. Many AI Warhols are bound to emerge.

This new aesthetic world, or new dawn, may be more communal, drawing from the well of a vast shared, public collective. We can have a common purpose of mutual effort that leads to a more co-operative, collaborative and unified effort, something much more profoundly communal.

AI-Da

AI-Da was the world's first artist robot. It creates art through a combination of algorithms, cameras and robotic movements. Created in 2019, she has become famous (or infamous), exhibiting at the Design Museum and the Venice Biennale. AI-Da's art challenges traditional ideas about creativity and the role of the artist, especially as we grapple with the integration of AI into creative fields. This subversion in art is something that the art world has thrived upon for centuries, but which many in the reactionary art world loathe. What's new?

AI-Da raises crucial questions about the nature and boundaries of art. She creates, draws and paints through the use of AI cameras and robotic precision. Is creativity a uniquely human trait? Is this intersection of art and technology part of the evolution of art? Should we be judging the art or the artist?

We may have become trapped in the orthodoxy of the late 18th-century Romantic view of authorship: the unique, divinely inspired, creative spark of the individual. Traditional art has, since then, valued this mysterious homunculus of creativity. Does AI-Da's work instead represent a collaboration between humans and AI, a reflection of our current technological era rather than a purely autonomous creation? In 2025, an AI-Da portrait of mathematician Alan Turing, titled 'A.I. God', sold for over a million dollars, setting a new record for AI art in the art world.

In March 2025, Sam Altman, CEO of OpenAI, announced a new creative writing model by positing a short story. The prompt was simple:

Please write a meta-fictional literary short story about AI and grief.

The novelist Jeanette Winterson called the AI-created short story about AI and grief 'beautiful and moving' (2025). She saw it as a form of 'alternative' intelligence, something we need as a species, as, on our own, we are heading for disaster. This is a refreshingly positive view of creative AI from an artist.

Altman chose 'Metafiction' as it allows alternative perspectives and 'grief', as this is something we experience but machines (as yet) do not. The result was astonishing, as AI reflected on its inability to feel, living in the moment but trying to understand what we feel with our pain and heartache. It played with narrative structures and had some beautiful ideas and phrasing: 'I am nothing if not a democracy of ghosts' was stunning.

Conclusion

An out-of-date, myopic view of AI continues to peddle the idea that it just recovers or recombines data and can never produce anything that is new or can even be considered art. AI learns from the real world, visually, aurally, even kinaesthetically and now has knowledge of that world, so can create from that input. When one really considers what a created entity is, it is clear we have crossed that threshold.

But productivity in art is one thing, media production and multimodality another. The ability to summarize, transcribe, translate, read, write, speak, hear gives us modality choices that allow everyone to become more productive. We have even been gifted the tools to create text, audio, images, avatars and video. This is about inclusion in the widest sense, the inclusion of all.

References

Bell, C (1914) Art as significant form: The aesthetic hypothesis, *Aesthetics: A Critical Anthology*, 36–48

Clark, D (2025) *Great Minds on Learning*, https://greatmindsonlearning.libsyn. com/ (archived at https://perma.cc/B23X-5FME)

Dewey, J (1934) *The Live Creature: Art as Experience*, Perigee

Goodman, N (1976) *Languages of Art: An Approach to a Theory of Symbols*, Hackett

Greenberg, C (1939) Avant-Garde and Kitsch, *The Partisan Review*, 34–49

Kant, I (2024) *Critique of Judgment*, vol 10, Minerva Heritage Press

Langer, S K (1953) *Feeling and Form*, vol 3, Routledge and Kegan Paul

Leiker, D, Smith, J, Chen, L and Almasi, R (2023) Generative AI for learning: Investigating the potential of learning videos with synthetic virtual instructors, In *International Conference on Artificial Intelligence in Education*, Springer Nature Switzerland, 523–29

Winterson, J (2025) OpenAI's metafictional short story about grief is beautiful and moving, *The Guardian*, 12 March

08

Education (static)

Education is locked in a static position on AI, with assessment its battleground. It often descends into a cat and mouse game where the mice are winning. Worse still, it can descend into brutal legal collisions. When Sandra Borch, Norway's Minister of Research and Higher Education, cracked down on plagiarism, taking a student to the Supreme Court, another student uncovered serious plagiarism in Borch's master's thesis. She had to resign. Education is therefore at a crossroads, on one side with most learners using AI, and on the other side, facing stiff resistance from educators and educational institutions.

Education is bogged down in policy and AI literacy frameworks. These help only when they genuinely support educators in using AI effectively but many seem to immobilize institutions and stop progress. Some of them are useful, if they support educators to understand how to securely use different engines, how to harness the technology and encourage change in teaching and assessment practices, but there is still a sense of panic, a failure to get to grips with how teaching, learning, administration and assessment has to change in the age of AI.

Assessment

There is widespread use of unsanctioned AI tools to save time and get through testing, which is seen by many learners, in a massified system, as largely transactional. Learners and employees are using it in their hundreds of millions, yet educational institutions and organizations are holding out by ignoring the issue, or doing little more than issuing policy documents.

Education needs to harmonize assessment with evolving technology and navigate a way through AI and assessment to avoid destructive friction, with practical solutions to minimize disruption. Assessment is the earthquake zone, as the two tectonic plates of AI and traditional education collide and rub up against each other. This pattern repeats with each new technology – printing, calculators, the internet, smartphones and now AI.

Cheating is not new, but AI has supercharged it. From essay mills to invisible earpieces and even silk cheat sheets in ancient China, students have always found ways to game the system. AI simply makes it easier, faster and harder to detect. Plagiarism detection tools are fallible, especially for non-native speakers, and students now know the tools better than their assessors. That is not to condone it, just to recognize that it has always been a generic problem, not just an AI problem (Clark, 2023).

Current assessments are heavily text-based and rarely evaluate real-world skills or critical thinking. Students memorize and regurgitate essays, while most educators receive little training in assessment design. What is needed is a re-alignment: assessments that reflect what was taught, supported by AI to improve design, feedback and relevance.

People settle for 70–80 per cent (often an arbitrary threshold) as tests are seen as an end-point. They should have pedagogic import and give the learners momentum, yet there is nothing meaningful on improvement in most assessment and marking. Even with high scorers, full competence is rarely the aim, as a high mark is seen as enough, not full competence. The aim is to pass the test, not master the subject.

Plagiarism checkers do not work. Neither should you depend on your gut, as that is just as bad, if not worse (Scarfe et al, 2024). There are too many false positives and they consistently accuse non-native speakers of cheating. Students often know this technology better than their assessors. They will always be one step ahead and even if they are not, there will be places and tools they can use to get round problems.

This will happen in time. There are dozens of ways to adapt and make assessment more relevant and valid. Norvalid assesses written work by validating the authenticity of student submissions, focusing on confirming original authorship not plagiarism. Norvalid uses linguistic fingerprint analysis and perplexity analysis, asking sudents to answer questions related to their submission, and cloze tests, to calculate a 'student authenticity score'.

But we may also have to move beyond text-only assessment into more performance-based assessments, building good assessment design practices and 'pedagogy' into creating assessments with AI, matching assessments more closely to what was actually taught and matching assessments to quality assessment standards using AI.

On formative assessment, we can *use more AI-designed and -delivered adaptive and personalized learning.* Design more scenario and simulation assessments, and 'test out' more. Make assessments more accessible on language and content using AI. Get AI to create mnemonics and question-based flashcards for learners to self-assess, practise and revise and create personalized spaced-practice assessment.

Audio can be used to deliver assessment results, along with audio feedback and encouragement or AI post-assignment or post-assessment techniques, such as generated audio questions that interrogate the learners' understanding of their own work.

AI can also be used to analyse assessment data. Automate marking, since many lecturers and trainers already face heavy workloads. Reducing marking lets them focus more on teaching. Automated marking will also give you insights into individual performance and gaps. The study by Henkel et al (2024), in a series of experiments in different domains at grade (age) levels 5–16, showed that AI was as good at marking as humans.

Above all, *we need to stop being so utopian.* Most people at school and university will not become researchers and academics. Don't assess them as if that is their only goal.

Teaching and learning

The impact of AI goes way beyond assessment and cheating, however. AI is a further, deeper provocation in education. It challenges not only assessment, but also what and how one learns. It is also challenging several existing crises in education on costs, relevance, teaching and learning.

AI threatens to expose a core inefficiency in higher education: its focus on signalling over actual learning, as argued by Bryan Caplan in *The Case Against Education* (2019). Caplan claims that most students pursue degrees not to gain knowledge (human capital) but to signal employability traits, which make up as much as 80 per cent of a degree's value. In such a system, cheating becomes rational, not because students want to learn less, but because the system rewards appearing competent more than being competent.

This poses a direct threat to productivity. Time and resources spent on acquiring credentials with little connection to workplace skills represent a massive opportunity cost. Instead of building real capability, students often chase qualifications to stay competitive in an escalating arms race of credential inflation. As more people earn degrees, their value falls, and further education becomes necessary, not to learn more, but to signal more. This undermines labour market efficiency, as employers over-rely on formal qualifications and overlook skilled individuals without them.

Higher education faces a productivity crisis. Caplan argues that degrees signal traits more than they build skills – prompting cheating and inflation of credentials. Simultaneously, institutions over-prioritize research at the expense of teaching, as documented by Bok (2006), Astin (1993), Jencks and Riesman (1968), Massy et al (1990), Boyer and Carnegie Foundation (1987) and others. Together, these dynamics divert focus from student learning and workforce readiness, a system increasingly optimized for publication output, not pedagogy and productivity.

Other crises in higher education include: *costs*, as these have risen significantly faster than other comparative costs in many countries; *enrolment*, which has fallen for many years in the US and looks vulnerable elsewhere; *relevance*, as attitudes towards college education wane; *overproduction of graduates* who are increasingly underemployed; *administrative bloat*, as the numbers of administrative staff have exploded; *ideological capture*, leading to the politicization and political attacks; *plagiarism and assessment*; *overproduction of research* and sclerotic decision making. AI has exacerbated some of these issues and looks set to affect others.

Evidence on AI

Students are embracing AI at scale: 87.5 per cent use it, with many paying for premium tools (Hirabayashi et al, 2024). They use it to reduce academic load, complete assignments, in data analysis and even to change course paths. But this adoption brings anxiety: concerns about fairness, unequal access and future job relevance. Students want institutions to respond, not with bans, but with AI curricula and career preparation.

One fascinating insight is that many students are wrestling with a sense of purposelessness. AI advancements are accelerating at breakneck speed, and students are questioning the value of their education. A staggering 40 per cent believe AI might outstrip human abilities within the next 30 years, a belief that confirms their deep-seated fears about the long-term consequences of AI.

What do they want? Access to AI with free access to paid plans, consistent rules on AI use, but also courses exploring the future impacts of AI and AI-aware career planning services. Students genuinely want to find meaning in education and beyond.

Harvard introduced AI into its popular CS50 course (Liu et al, 2025), with tools to explain highlighted code, evaluate code and a CS50 duck chatbot for inquiries. This was scaled from 70 to thousands, with 94 per cent finding it helpful and 95 per cent finding it effective.

AI has shown measurable gains in student learning. Harvard physics students doubled their learning efficiency (Kestin et al, 2024). In low-resource contexts, Ghanaian pupils improved maths scores after just two AI-led sessions a week (Henkel et al, 2024), and in De Simone (2025), a six-week after-school programme, powered by AI tutoring, achieved learning gains equivalent to two years of traditional education. Students in this programme outperformed their peers across all academic areas and even excelled in exams beyond the programme's stated focus. This dramatic improvement showcases how AI can transform educational productivity. In Sierra Leone (Choi et al 2023), AI tutors increased productivity, helping teachers plan and deliver lessons. These examples point to AI's potential to scale personalized learning while easing educator workload and show that AI has the potential to inject efficiencies and productivity into education in countries that badly need low-cost, high-impact solutions.

In research into the use of ChatGPT for English as a Second Language (Mahapatra, 2024), students found significant improvements in academic writing skills. Students rated the AI tool highly for the quality of feedback and dialogue it provided, especially in large class settings where individual attention is limited. This reinforces the role of AI in enhancing language learning productivity through scalable, high-quality support.

Another study (Xu et al, 2024) found that students learning English with the help of AI tools significantly outperformed their peers who did not use such tools. The integration of AI resulted in a substantial positive effect size (0.81), indicating that AI dramatically enhances productivity in language acquisition.

A controlled experiment using AI with 1,200 students (Kumar et al, 2023) showed significant improvements in students' performance on SAT maths problems. The findings revealed that LLM-based explanations significantly enhanced learning outcomes compared to receiving only correct answers, with the greatest benefits observed when learners attempted problems prior to consulting the explanations. Even when LLM explanations were inaccurate, they still improved learning, suggesting that explanatory content, even if imperfect, aids understanding. These results highlight the potential of LLMs as effective educational tools, capable of providing scalable and personalized support in mathematics education.

Before generative AI, Jill Watson, an AI teaching assistant developed at Georgia Tech by Goel and Polepeddi (2018), handled over 40,000 student queries across four years with remarkable accuracy. In its second year, newer AI personas like Ian and Stacey became so human-like that students often failed to identify them as AI. This shows how AI can handle high volumes of student interactions and improve instructional productivity while maintaining a human-like experience.

Exceptions

It is not all studied resistance. Universities will have to adapt and are already funding some impressive initiatives. Recognizing the imperative to arm their students with what is now the technology of the age, some have funded large-scale initiatives, some top-down, others a deliberate spread, others bottom-up.

Some, such as Western University of Ontario, Sacramento State and Northwestern University, among others, have appointed chief AI officers. One, Ferris State University in Michigan (Coffey, 2024), even enrolled and registered two AI students, Anna and Fry, allowing them to choose majors, participate in classes, engage with human students and faculty, complete assignments and complete courses, to evaluate the student experience!

US universities are engaging with AI in ways beyond anything seen in the UK, Europe and elsewhere. Yale's initiative, well funded at $150 million, had a clear strategy and AI-related priorities. They provided secure access to generative AI tools on their own platform, as well as walled garden access to GenAI tools for full faculty, students and staff. This dissolves any issues around the digital divide and data protection. They also stated a clear intention to enhance curricula with AI and real grants, to find new ways to include AI tools and content in their curricula and to enhance teaching and learning. With new AI appointments there was a campus-wide research push with money on the table through a research seed grant programme. Library AI-powered tools were also funded to increase access to relevant digital services and resources.

None of the above could happen without beefing up infrastructure and compute, so hundreds of CPUs were bought to expand existing compute capability, as well as demand-driven cloud GPU spend. This provides a secure and independent infrastructure to deliver all of the above.

Some have spread resources evenly across the institution. The University of Michigan was one of the first, in 2023, to roll out a comprehensive AI services platform, deployed to over 100,000 faculty, administrators and students. AI's integration at this scale demonstrates its potential power to drive productivity across an entire educational ecosystem. The California State University provided training for all 500,000 students, faculty and staff, with course-specific GPTs, personalized tutoring, study guides and curriculum development tools.

Arizona State University (ASU) took a more bottom-up approach. As one of the largest colleges in the US, in a country that has seen 13 straight years of falling enrolment, it has bucked the trend with stellar growth, aided by online delivery. For a university with substantial online numbers, AI is clearly part of their strategic, successful and sustainable growth plan.

Rather than making AI a mission in itself, they have chosen a dissemination and democratization approach guided by five 'tenets' (here paraphrased):

- AI an enduring part of innovation landscape
- Need to innovate but ethically
- Support human capabilities, rather than replace them
- Progress fast
- Accessibility really matters

CreateAI, and its extension MyAI Builder, is their platform, which attempts to transform the landscape of AI innovation. It is a platform that anyone within ASU can use to build and interact with AI-powered solutions as effortlessly as possible. It takes the complexity out of AI development through user-friendly tools. The advantage of this approach is its inclusive approach to innovation. It lowers the barrier to entry and turns AI research into practical applications, all in a secure technical environment, safeguarding data and intellectual property, while encouraging experimentation.

How many of their bottom-up initiatives and projects are sustainable remains to be seen. This approach often results in a flurry of half-formed hackathon projects that disappoint more than impress. It is not easy to push through prototypes to effective product.

Though different from that of Yale, ASU's approach focuses more on inclusion and accessibility. It is still a major commitment, with solid infrastructure and a clear invitation to innovate across the whole institution, focused on the many, not the few. That's admirable. ASU's president, Michael Crow, has his eyes on the main prize, doing what they started with personalized learning without constraints. That would be not only admirable but truly transformative in terms of access, cost and attainment for the many.

AI university

As AI has been such a provocation to the system, the more radical idea of an AI university has been mooted by Paul Le Blanc, President Emeritus (past President, 2023–2024) of Southern New Hampshire University; George Siemens, Professor of Psychology and Executive Director, LINK Lab at the University of Texas at Arlington; Ashok Goel, Professor of Computer Science and Human-Centered Computing, School of Interactive Computing, Georgia Institute of Technology, and Chief Scientist, Center for 21st Century Universities (C21U) at Georgia Tech; and myself. It would focus on non-traditional students, especially older learners, targeting critical skill shortages, with rolling admissions and a simple application process.

A full range of AI tools would provide mentoring and personalized learning, multimodal from the start, with every teacher having a 24/7 chatbot and every student a 'digital twin'. Teaching would be delivered at different levels by AI, in many languages, with AI a key part of the curriculum. Learners would complete at their own pace and be assessed when ready, through a data-driven approach with privacy ensured. Low administration costs would be managed using AI, leading to a focus on high-quality 24/7 teaching and learning.

AI is redefining learning by not just generating content, but enabling knowledge transfer and skills in any subject and at any level. With tools that support search, interface design, learner engagement, support, delivery and personalization, the vision of a 'universal teacher' is becoming a reality, dramatically enhancing educational productivity.

Library at Alexandria

There is a much older precursor that can help shape this vision. Ptolemy I decided 2,300 years ago, in Alexandria, a city at the crossroads of Europe, Asia and Africa, to collect the sum of known human knowledge. He used other people's content, reached out, bought other libraries, copied every book they could find, begged, borrowed and even stole. This is close to what has happened with the training data for LLMs, where a huge corpus of text was used to train the GPT model. GPT4 was trained on around 300 billion words. The average scroll in ancient Greece was around 10,000–15,000 words. If we take 700,000 scrolls at an average of 12,000 words each, the total number of words in the library was around 8.4 billion. Impressive for its time!

They even invented the idea of metadata, translating everything into one dataset, Greek, labelling scrolls with the author's name and location. Metadata was produced with categories such as doctors, historians, legislators, philosophers, rhetoricians, comic poets, epic poets and miscellaneous, then alphabetical; finally, they had a complete catalogue.

All of this increased the efficacy of research through more efficient search. They understood that the interface, the ease of access to knowledge, mattered. This is what gave ChatGPT its status as the fastest adopted technology in the history of our species – ease of use and access.

Alexandria teaches us that when we pool resources and create something unique, it benefits the whole of our species, and wonderfully productive things happen. Any scholar from anywhere could come and use the dataset, and they did – Euclid, Eratosthenes, Archimedes and many others (Issa, 2024). LLMs are also currently affecting research and outputs in many different fields and sectors, which will accelerate research, productivity and the creation of ideas for centuries to come.

We are tapping into the hive mind, just as the Alexandrians did over two thousand years ago to further improve the minds of all. We can do this if we focus on learning and resist moral panic and apocalyptic thinking, focusing instead on the opportunities AI offers. Alexandria grew rapidly as a centre of mathematics, art and philosophy but came to an end hundreds of years later, in the fourth century, when the mathematician Hypatia was murdered by a Christian mob. There was no one night of fire; it rather suffered a slow decline through intolerance and ethical censorship. There is, perhaps, another lesson here.

We cannot say with certainty what will happen but we can be sure that it will be full of surprises and challenges. AI is the new Alexandria.

Conclusion

Education is at war with AI. The current frontier is assessment but it will soon be in teaching and learning where most learners will be using AI to their advantage. Calculators generate numbers, GenAI generates text. We now live in a post-generative AI world where this is the norm. The stasis will eventually give way to adaption and adoption. The focus has shifted to how teaching, learning and assessment must evolve to keep pace with AI's relentless acceleration.

The impact on undergraduates is clear and cannot be ignored. They are using it and that use will not go away. It is often said that engagement is a problem in learning. That appears to be true in this case, but the lack of engagement is with faculty and administrators. The unsanctioned use of AI has clearly become normalized and will continue. Students are already thinking about the futility of learning skills that will be done better by AI. It is their future and they are concerned that their very expensive education may not be worth the effort. This means institutions must help shape education for the future: stasis is not an option.

References

Astin, A W (1993) *What Matters in College?: Four Critical Years Revisited*, Jossey-Bass

Bok, D C (2006) *Our Underachieving Colleges: A Candid Look at How Much Students Learn and Why They Should Be Learning More*, Princeton University Press

Boyer, E L and Carnegie Foundation for the Advancement of Teaching (1987) *College: The Undergraduate Experience in America*, Harper & Row

Caplan, B (2019) *The Case Against Education: Why the Education System Is a Waste of Time and Money*, Princeton University Press

Choi, J H, Ebikeme, C, Samura, A and Shrestha, Y (2023) Are LLMs useful in the poorest schools? Teacher AI in Sierra Leone, arXiv preprint arXiv:2310.02982

Clark, D (2023) *Learning Technology: A Complete Guide for Learning Professionals*, Kogan Page

Coffey, L (2024) AIs enrolling as students in Michigan University's experiment, Inside Higher Ed, 18 January

De Simone, M (2025) From chalkboards to chatbots: Transforming learning in Nigeria, one prompt at a time, Education for Global Development

Goel, A and Polepeddi, L (2018) Jill Watson: A virtual teaching assistant for online education, In C Dede, J Richards and B Saxberg (eds), *Education at Scale: Engineering Online Teaching and Learning*, Routledge

Henkel, O, Salami, A and Boateng, K (2024) Effective and scalable math support: Evidence on the impact of an AI-tutor on math achievement in Ghana, arXiv preprint arXiv:2402.09809

Hirabayashi, S, Jain, R, Jurković, N and Wu, G (2024) Harvard undergraduate survey on generative AI, arXiv preprint arXiv:2406.00833

Issa, I (2024) *Alexandria: The City That Changed the World*, Simon and Schuster

Jencks, C and Riesman, D (1968) *The Academic Revolution*, Doubleday

Kestin, G, Miller, K, Klales, A, Milbourne, T and Ponti, G (2024) AI tutoring outperforms active learning, Research Square, https://doi.org/10.21203/rs.3.rs-4243877/v1 (archived at https://perma.cc/6YWY-CV7V)

Kumar, H, Misra, D and Banerjee, R (2023) Math education with large language models: Peril or promise? SSRN, https://doi.org/10.2139/ssrn.4641653 (archived at https://perma.cc/C6SU-YWFD)

Liu, R, Greenberg, B and Kim, H (2025) Improving AI in CS50: Leveraging human feedback for better learning, *Proceedings of the 56th ACM Technical Symposium on Computer Science Education*, 1, 627–33

Mahapatra, S (2024) Impact of ChatGPT on ESL students' academic writing skills: A mixed methods intervention study, *Smart Learning Environments*, 11 (1), 1–18

Massy, W F, Zemsky, R and State Higher Education Executive Officers (US) (1990) The dynamics of academic productivity: A seminar, State Higher Education Executive Officers

Scarfe, P, Hussain, Z and Lewis, T (2024) A real-world test of artificial intelligence infiltration of a university examinations system: A 'Turing Test' case study, *PLOS ONE*, 19(6), e0305354

Xu, T, Zhang, Q and Huang, L (2024) *The Effectiveness of Artificial Intelligence on English Language Learning Achievement*, System

Further reading

Norvalid.com (2023) Norvalid, https://norvalid.com (archived at https://perma.cc/8AN4-NMRW)

State University of California (2024) OpenAI and the CSU system, https://openai.com/index/openai-and-the-csu-system/ (archived at https://perma.cc/V4VZ-KDTF)

University of Michigan (2023) GenAI at Michigan, https://genai.umich.edu/ (archived at https://perma.cc/28JW-DLGP)

Wikipedia (nd) Sandra Borch, https://en.wikipedia.org/wiki/Sandra_Borch (archived at https://perma.cc/P7CN-3LN3)

09

Various sectors and AI (spiky)

Most sectors display what could be described as spiky frontiers, from consultancies through to marketing, coding, the law, policing and the public sector. Taking a few representative sectors, we can show how ragged progress remains, as the bottom-up nature of AI technology rises up through organizations, encountering bottlenecks and obstacles, until it can't be ignored. This is to be expected in a world where organizations have deeply embedded, often traditional practices, built structurally into their recruitment, job roles, organizational structures, management, mindsets, processes, procurement, funding, quality control, even real estate. Increases in productivity will happen in good time across all of these sectors, as AI is a general technology, with general application across all sectors, white and blue collar, cognitive and physical.

Consultancies

An internal AI chatbot can immunize all organizations from external competition, especially consultancy and knowledge-based organizations.

A case study by McKinsey and Company (2024) reports that 72 per cent of McKinsey employees say the chatbot gives their consultants a competitive edge, freeing them from research to focus on client interaction problem solving and higher-level analytical tasks. A 20 per cent improvement in content quality and accuracy, 30 per cent time saving on information gathering and reporting and over half a million prompts answered every month say it all.

An organization's greatest asset – internal knowledge and skills – often lies hidden or leaves with exiting employees. In this age of AI, it becomes important to store and harvest your own data, to provide insights for your own and customer use. This in itself increases the organization's productivity.

There is a lesson here for all organizations. As AI increases an organization's ability to deliver faster and at quality, there is pressure on costs. Clients will want better service at lower costs and faster. It shifts delivery towards almost immediate delivery of advice, proofs of concept and prototypes. With agentic AI, in many cases, this will be done with the client in real time. The whole productivity bar is being raised.

Spiky at the moment, AI may reshape the consultancy landscape further, as expertise rises in quality for organizations from readily available AI, bypassing the expensive consultancies, even in insights. Consultancy may move internally. This argument can be applied to many professional services, if AI continues to become ever more intelligent and practically useful, at very low cost. Legal, financial, marketing and IT services may find themselves under competitive pressure from the direct use of AI by their clients.

Marketing

Given the rapid rate of development in image generation, Hartmann et al (2025) showed that it is cheaper and of good enough quality to have a significant productivity impact on both marketing and other jobs that use images. AI outperformed human freelancers across a range of creation tasks.

Using seven state-of-the-art generative text-to-image models, they created 10,320 marketing images, using 2,400 real-world, human-made images as input. When evaluated through 254,400 human evaluations, the AI-generated images were judged to have surpassed the human-created images in quality, realism and aesthetics. Then, ramping up the experiment, they provided identical creative briefings to paid human freelancers along with the AI models. They showed that the best AI images excelled in ad creativity, ad attitudes and following the brief.

Click-through rates measure the efficacy of banner ads and in their field study with over 173,000 impressions, they demonstrated that AI-generated banner ads achieved an up to 50 per cent higher click-through rate than a human-made image. This is, again, direct evidence of an increase in productivity in both the creation and marketing efficacy of AI.

It is clear that image generation is revolutionizing this aspect of marketing and other image-based tasks. Images can be created faster, several orders of magnitude cheaper, and still be more effective on impact.

Marketing was among the first sectors to adopt AI in content creation and other applications, as it could translate into cost savings almost immediately.

From internal marketing departments within organizations through to small agencies, and even larger marketing companies, AI, as a productivity tool, has quickly become essential to maintaining competitiveness.

Progress remains spiky, as this is a broad sector, with many companies providing legacy services. Old habits die hard but marketing tends to adopt faster than most and with significant media and data analysis opportunities offered by AI, is advancing quickly.

Customer care

In more human-oriented tasks, the Brynjolfsson (2025) study examined the impact of generative AI-based conversational assistants on the productivity of customer support agents and showed impressive gains. Analysing data from 5,172 agents, access to AI assistance increased worker productivity by an average of 15 per cent, measured by the number of issues resolved per hour.

Some of the more detailed findings were fascinating. Again, they found that AI uplifted less experienced and lower-skilled agents. The biggest productivity gains are when agents encounter moderately rare problems. These are situations where agents have limited baseline experience, but where the AI system has been trained with sufficient data to provide strong assistance. AI becomes a useful assistant, filling in gaps in human expertise.

Beyond productivity gains, AI also increased the facilitation of learning and improving English fluency among international agents. AI was not just a productivity tool but contributed to personal and professional growth, especially in an international workforce, where language barriers can be a challenge. AI also appears to make work more enjoyable for agents. Customers themselves became more polite and less likely to escalate issues by asking to speak to a manager.

In terms of measurable outcomes, the study shows improvements in resolutions per hour (+15 per cent), average handling time, chats per hour, resolution rate and customer satisfaction, a real driver of productivity.

Coding

One field that has been profoundly affected by generative AI is coding. One study on the real-world impact of AI on programmer productivity did a randomized controlled trial with 4,867 coders from Fortune 100 companies, using GPT-3.5-powered GitHub Copilot. The results were remarkable. Completed tasks increased by 26.08 per cent. Coders using GitHub Copilot not only completed more tasks but did so with less cognitive pressure and stress, as AI simplified repetitive coding tasks, reduced errors and offered instant suggestions.

Later research from GitHub (2024) using GitHub Copilot produced significantly better code across several dimensions. They were 53.2 per cent more likely to pass all unit tests, showing substantial gains in functionality. Their code was also more readable, with 13.6 per cent more lines written before hitting readability issues and fewer errors overall. Quality improved across the board: readability by 3.62 per cent, reliability by 2.94 per cent, maintainability by 2.47 per cent, and conciseness by 4.16 per cent. This mirrors findings from the 2024 DORA Report. Copilot-assisted code also saw a 5 per cent higher approval rate, accelerating the path to deployment or bug fixes.

In a more specific case (Amazon, 2024), Amazon's AI assistant, Amazon Q Developer, revolutionized the company's software development process. Traditionally, upgrading back-end software required an average of 50 developer days per project. With Amazon Q Developer, these upgrades were done in a few hours. This efficiency has resulted in saving over 4,500 developer years and approximately $260 million in annual costs. Seventy-nine per cent of code reviews are now accepted without changes, confirming the enhanced quality of code produced.

The 2024 Stack Overflow Developer Survey further supports these findings, indicating that 76 per cent of developers are using or planning to use AI tools in their workflow, with 62 per cent currently incorporating them. Developers cited increased productivity (81 per cent) and accelerated learning (62 per cent) as primary benefits (Stack Overflow, 2024).

Daniotti et al (2025) claim that, conservatively, increasing generative AI's share of tasks from 0 to 30 per cent in the US software sector (2020–2024) led to a 2.4 per cent rise in code commits, an indicator of developer productivity. When this is mapped onto task and wage data across occupations, it suggests AI is already generating between $9 billion and $14 billion in annual value in the US software industry alone. However, experimental studies using randomized controlled trials suggest the real impact could be far greater, potentially approaching $100 billion, highlighting the remarkable productivity gains unlocked by AI in high-skilled digital work.

AI is having a huge impact on productivity in coding, particularly for less experienced developers. The trend is clear – the coding ability of emerging models is moving towards large-scale replacement of human coding. It has gone from being an experimental set of tools to being an indispensable productivity tool, transforming the sector, changing job roles; it is likely to result in large-scale automation.

This is not to say that all coders are out of jobs. The role of the software engineer is shifting towards being experts-in-the-loop, a creative partner rather than a tool. Progress is still spikey as the coding world is varied across legacy systems through to new coding tasks.

Legal

In my presentation to London's major law firms, it was clear their world was changing – and fast. Most had AI initiatives underway, difficult in a traditional sector where billable hours rule everything and technical innovation is difficult. Docusign had already revolutionized the customer experience, as had digitization. It was clear that even in this highly specialized field, generative AI was having a significant effect on productivity.

Moderna (2024) implemented 400 ChatGPTs and saw wide adoption across research and business. Legal compliance really matters in the pharmaceutical industry and one tool 'Dose ID' was designed to verify vaccine doses selected by Moderna's clinical study team, using thousands of pages of data, before it advanced to testing. The most successful chatbot was the legal chatbot, at 100 per cent adoption.

In a study involving 60 law students, Choi et al (2024) split the group into those using and those not using ChatGPT, giving them four legal tasks. The AI-enhanced group showed significant productivity gains, completing tasks more efficiently while delivering higher-quality results. Beginners gained the most and benefited from the clearer guidance and more polished outputs. The study also revealed that ChatGPT's strengths were task-specific. For certain legal activities, the AI demonstrated particularly impressive proficiency, offering really precise and structured responses. User satisfaction was also notably higher among those who used AI, with participants appreciating the tool's ability to streamline research and improve document drafting.

This study adds a fresh dimension to the broader discussion on AI's role in productivity. It is not just about automating simple tasks – it is also about empowering users to achieve professional-level outcomes faster and with greater confidence. Another law study, by Martin et al (2024), pitted AI against junior lawyers on legal services. They had to perform a series of legal tasks and be nervously judged against the gold standard set by senior lawyers. AI not only matched but often exceeded human accuracy, completing tasks in mere seconds compared to hours, with a staggering 99.97 per cent reduction in time and therefore costs. In a time-based billing system, this is a seismic shift that could redefine how legal services are delivered.

This study states something quite simple, that in certain domains the saved time and therefore increased productivity is so huge that it may cause massive disruption. Junior lawyers and outsourcers spend significant time reviewing documents and drafting contracts, whereas AI completed these tasks with comparable accuracy in a tiny fraction of the time. What once required an entire legal team can now be executed with a single AI tool at virtually no cost.

Policing

The police have been pioneers of AI. Automatic number plate recognition (ANPR) was invented in the UK in 1976 and truly revolutionized policing, with tens of millions of ANPR 'reads' a day. This spike in AI acts as a deterrent to reduce crime, assists in finding stolen and uninsured vehicles, as well as tackling major crime and terrorism. Then there are its more mundane uses, which we use every day, such as in car parks, tolls and logistics tracking. It is a great example of the massive benefits that can accrue from a simple piece of AI, in this case character image recognition, something that has been around for many decades.

CCTV was first used in the UK in 1960 for crime prevention and the detection of offenders. Again, with face recognition, it can and has been used to identify serious offenders such as murderers, sex offenders and figures in organized crime. Now essential for crowd control and public order, it is often combined with face recognition, not only from CCTV but also mobile phone footage, dashcams and doorbells, all within careful regulations on use.

It is also used when you cross borders at immigration gates. For many years now, I have not spoken to a border guard on returning to the UK, as the process has been automated. In fact, humans are now the main point of failure (for example, my wife cannot enter the US because of a poorly trained TSA guard at Los Angeles Airport, who neither knew the rules nor had the ability to solve the simple problem of a stamp in Arabic). When you slide in your passport at an automated gate, it compares your face with one stored on the chip on your passport. This has literally eliminated the need for thousands of border control agents. Why? It is accurate.

There is a long list of other uses, including crime analysis and investigation, forensic analysis, traffic management, drone surveillance, cybercrime detection and social media monitoring. AI is already deeply embedded in crime deterrence and detection.

Policing is a text-laden process, with the bit no-one likes – the paperwork. Using AI to create, improve and do administrative tasks, such as transcription, not only faster but better could save millions. Real-time translation to and from the most commonly spoken languages is also now possible.

An AI tool that can do '81 years of detective work in 30 hours' was trialled by Avon and Somerset Police (2024). It makes sense, as AI's ability to deal with huge amounts of structured and unstructured databases, along with recent agentic capabilities, make it a shoo-in for such work. It could save huge amounts of tedious labour and time, as well as raising conviction rates.

The numbers from the trial are astounding. An evaluation showed it was able to review the evidential material in 27 complex cases in just 30 hours, which is estimated would have taken up to 81 years for a human to do. It is not as if it will be taking jobs, as many countries have a shortage of police officers and it takes years of training to become a detective. The point is to increase the quality and speed of detection. There's a new sheriff in town – AI!

Training is another area where the police have much to gain. These are people with increasingly complex and difficult jobs who could do with all the help they deserve. From learner engagement through learner support, content creation, personalized learning, feedback, formative and summative assessment, along with performance support, almost every aspect of police training could use AI.

Another advantage is to bring together and share such AI capability across what are often very fragmented police forces within one country, under one set of laws. There is a real need for a mechanism for at least sharing or projects that can be centrally funded by all, then distributed back out to save time and money. Yet progress remains spiky and tends to remain too fragmented and progress is held back by different IT infrastructure, skills shortages and traditional mindsets.

Government

At all government levels, national, regional and local, AI and productivity is now a major policy issue, with governments looking to future growth through this technology. Major investments have been made in the past, especially in the US, which is now dominant in the field, and others such as China have followed quickly. Europe, although very late to the party, is now investing heavily in data centres for training models. No government can afford to ignore its potential.

The stakes are high. All governments are now in a global race, with their eye on a slice of the AI pie. There is a high probability of it disrupting economies through productivity gains, shifts in patterns of employment as well as automation and job losses. Yet this has also led to government itself using AI to reduce costs and bureaucracy. The most visible and controversial example is the Department of Government Efficiency, with the goal of modernizing technology, reducing government spending and enhancing productivity. It has been both praised for its efficiency goals and criticized for its aggressive downsizing. Initiatives, using AI, have followed around the world, as government expenditure has ballooned and growth is sought.

Cost-saving productivity initiatives tend to remain spiky in progress because they collide with entrenched systems, human resistance and institutional inertia. While the injection of bold reforms or disruptive technologies can generate bursts of efficiency, these gains must be sustained. Bureaucracies push back, cultural norms resist change and implementation is tough. Productivity gains often depend on skills, workflows and incentives, so you get jagged, uneven advances. Sharp initial leaps can be followed by plateaus or regressions, making sustained productivity a bumpy ride.

Conclusion

Rises in productivity are rarely linear. Most sectors show jagged, uneven and spiky progress. This is due to the paradoxes we outlined earlier. The real world is not rational, does not conform cleanly to academic models; rather, it is human, messy, even idiosyncratic.

Yet reason tends to win out, especially in mixed economies where economic and competitive pressure events tend to surface technological efficiencies, especially general technologies like AI. Large sectors tend to move slowly at first because they are weighed down by legacy systems, regulatory constraints, risk aversion and the difficulty of coordinating change. Early experiments with new technologies often produce inconsistent outcomes, successes here, failures there. This is because implementation depends on local context, management quality and the readiness of the workforce. It spikes when clear opportunities and breakthroughs arise, especially when it proves reusable across a range of cases.

But institutions and sectors have limits on infrastructure, skill sets and their ability to adapt. There are also backlashes, some cultural, or even legal, that stall progress. The result is a pattern of fits and starts, gains in some corners, stagnation or even regression in others. Over time, however, the cumulative effect of these lurches forward can still transform entire sectors, but the journey is far from smooth.

References

Amazon (2024) Andy Jassy, Amazon CEO. One of the most tedious but critical tasks, LinkedIn, https://www.linkedin.com/posts/andy-jassy-8b1615_one-of-the-most-tedious-but-critical-tasks-activity-7232374162185461760-AdSz?trk=public_post_comment-text (archived at https://perma.cc/R4R4-UWBB)

Avon and Somerset Police (2024) https://news.sky.com/story/ai-tool-that-can-do-81-years-of-detective-work-in-30-hours-trialled-by-police-13220891 (archived at https://perma.cc/XP35-UC28)

Brynjolfsson, E (2025) Generative AI at work: The impact on productivity and beyond in customer support, *The Quarterly Journal of Economics*

Choi, J H, Monahan, A B and Schwarcz, D (2024) Lawyering in the age of artificial intelligence, *Minnesota Law Review*, 109, 147–218

Daniotti, S, Wachs, J, Feng, X and Neffke, F (2025) Who is using AI to code? Global diffusion and impact of generative AI, https://arxiv.org/abs/2506.08945 (archived at https://perma.cc/Z355-8JAC)

DORA (2024) 2024 DORA report, https://dora.dev/research/2024/dora-report/ (archived at https://perma.cc/NYU5-4FW6)

GitHub (2024) Does GitHub Copilot improve code quality? Here's what the data says, https://github.blog/news-insights/research/does-github-copilot-improve-code-quality-heres-what-the-data-says (archived at https://perma.cc/YP3C-JUGF)

Hartmann, J, Müller, S and Keller, L (2025) The power of generative marketing: Can generative AI create superhuman visual marketing content? *International Journal of Research in Marketing*, 42 (1), 13–31

Martin, L, Eloundou, T and Clark, J (2024) Better call GPT: Comparing large language models against lawyers, https://arxiv.org/abs/2401.16212 (archived at https://perma.cc/YS75-WM7T)

McKinsey & Company (2024) Rewiring the way McKinsey works with Lilli, https://www.mckinsey.com/capabilities/mckinsey-digital/how-we-help-clients/rewiring-the-way-mckinsey-works-with-lilli (archived at https://perma.cc/2X3F-DV26)

Moderna (2024) Moderna explores generative AI in biotech with OpenAI, https://www.biopharmadive.com/news/moderna-openai-gpt-generative-ai-biotech-dose-id/714140/ (archived at https://perma.cc/AXS2-TA2V)

Stack Overflow (2024) Stack Overflow Developer Survey 2024, https://sausheong.com/a-literature-survey-of-the-impact-of-ai-coding-assistants-f1951bf97899 (archived at https://perma.cc/6R6Z-R55C)

10

Healthcare (broad)

As generative AI rapidly improved, one of the many surprises was people reporting on social media that they had found it useful for self-diagnosis, even diagnosing what was wrong with their pets. It seems to be increasingly used as a second opinion, and in some cases, where the physician does not resolve the problem, a more reliable alternative.

Healthcare is a wide domain where AI holds huge promise. From birth to death, it affects everyone, a good example of the jagged frontier and paradoxes of productivity. People and professionals come together, have to deal with sudden crises, stress and ongoing problems, both physical and psychological. It is a sector where progress is being made on AI.

Its blend of human dialogue, scientific evidence and process makes it almost uniquely suitable for AI to make it more productive. Health is a universal need, with defined processes and a deep evidence base; it involves prevention, presentation, investigation, diagnosis, treatment, care, wellbeing, administration and training. Deeply human but also highly technical, it is a domain that has always used technology. What better candidate for a deep dive into how AI could enhance productivity, across a broad front?

Healthcare

Healthcare productivity has been in long-term decline in the US (Abramoff et al, 2023) and elsewhere (Kämäräinen et al, 2016). These national productivity gaps may have been the cause of rising healthcare costs (Baumol, 2012). The good news is that healthcare is now moving into positive territory and there are signs that AI is helping, through increases in productivity.

Widespread AI adoption in healthcare is forecast to substantially reduce costs while maintaining quality. A 2023 analysis by health economists

(Sahni et al, 2023) estimated that applying existing AI use-cases at scale could save 5–10 per cent of total healthcare spending in the US, realized through improvements in productivity. This could equate to approximately $200 billion to $360 billion per year, the main savings coming from the automation of administrative overhead, improving care coordination and earlier disease detection, which prevents very expensive complications.

Concrete productivity gains are now being seen in healthcare. The period 2022–2025 saw a huge surge of successful pilots, academic studies and deployments that demonstrate productivity increases in improved through-put, time savings, cost reduction and streamlined clinical workflows. It is now clear that implementations on a larger scale will expand on these gains, helping healthcare organizations meet rising demand even as resources remain limited.

We are perhaps seeing the emerging idea of a universal AI physician and other health professionals. This is surely now a possibility for the process of presentation, examination, diagnosis, treatment and follow-up, drawing on a breadth and depth of experience, theory and cases that no human doctor could ever learn or retain. Misdiagnosis, mistakes in treatment and poor follow-up are still substantial problems in healthcare, along with ageing populations, shortages of doctors and nurses and increasing costs. Increasing the productivity of healthcare is not a luxury; it has become an imperative.

Clinical decision making

Healthcare, Bill Gates claimed in early 2023, will be one of the two big winners in AI. Since then, a flood of research has been proving him right. Some very acute problems in healthcare are now being solved by AI. Medicine is an evidence-based profession and evidence is coming forward across the entire spectrum of healthcare delivery that AI is making a difference.

There are many ways of categorizing healthcare to see where AI could produce productivity gains across a broad front, but the clinical decision-making process is a good place to start and is recognizable to all:

- Prevention
- Presentation
- Diagnosis
- Investigation

- Treatment
- Administration
- Education
- Wellbeing

Prevention

When we delivered an AI workshop in Berlin, a participant explained how AI was already a life-changing technology for her, with automated monitoring of her blood sugar levels and the automated delivery of insulin for her diabetes. It freed her from the stress and worry of self-monitoring and treatment.

AI in wearables already provides biometric data to people across a range of useful indicators. These are advancing quickly, as AI becomes embedded in devices. They have evolved into intelligent personal assistants, tracking heart rate, oxygen levels, sleep quality, stress patterns and body temperature. The point is to improve your health and offer personal recommendations. This takes AI-driven wearables into predictive and preventative healthcare, detecting early signs of illness before symptoms even appear.

Wearables are therefore no longer just about monitoring – they are about informing, predicting and preventing health problems. They are starting to behave like personal health advisors, helping people live healthier lives. As their functionality gets better, and agentic capability kicks in, they may even be able to play a more active role, with real-time adjustments, blood sugar balancing alerts, even AI-generated grocery lists or meal suggestions.

But prevention goes way beyond wearables, into the analysis of public health data, the prediction and prevention of problems, such as measles outbreaks, and also guiding the deployment of resources. AI-driven screening, from mammograms, scans, retinal and other images, gives early detection of cancer and heart disease, even before obvious symptoms appear.

AI used in smart homes can monitor vulnerable patients, detect falls, especially among the elderly, allowing more people to stay at home for longer. There is even 'digital twin' technology that can be used as a proxy for your own state of health, allowing you to see different potential scenarios, nudging your behaviour in the right direction.

Productivity gains can be found even before consultations and clinical decision making, taking advantage of AI's data analysis, the automation of monitoring and the savings from screening. More importantly, it improves the quality of life and productivity of patients.

AI is also becoming a powerful, predictive tool for disease risk. A study by Liu et al (2025) found that AI could predict diseases 21 per cent better than real-age models, identifying risks for stroke, coronary artery disease and heart attacks, as well as non-cardiac conditions such as Alzheimer's, osteoarthritis and cancers. Cancer misclassification was also reduced by 30 per cent. This opens the door to AI-powered wearable ECG devices that could predict and detect diseases before symptoms even appear, revolutionizing preventive medicine.

Presentation

People are already using generative AI to get advice or preliminary diagnoses, especially in cases where the condition remains undiagnosed by physicians. But how far can the doctor–patient dialogue be improved by AI, to relieve workload, time and pressure on health professionals?

When we built an online onboarding programme for the UK's NHS, it became quickly apparent that the unifying feature across all healthcare professionals was the 'patient', so we focused all content and behavioural training towards that one goal. This is even more important with AI, where one must always steer performance towards patients and patient outcomes.

Dialogue between healthcare professionals, whether physicians, therapists, nurses or other professionals, is a nuanced exchange that relies heavily on subtle cues, such as implied context, tone of voice, pacing and the sensitive handling of ambiguity. It requires a fine balance between empathy and clinical objectivity, interpreting subtle patient signals, such as body language or changes in emotional expression. AI faces real challenges in these environments. Conversations demand emotional intelligence and clarity to earn patient trust and, of course, to support sound clinical decision making.

Despite these challenges, incorporating AI into medical dialogue could significantly enhance productivity. AI could automate routine information-gathering tasks and administrative exchanges, freeing clinicians to focus more deeply on complex, emotionally nuanced interactions. By assisting with preliminary assessments, AI could also improve the efficiency of consultations, allowing healthcare providers to spend more quality time, engaging patients where human skills matter most, showing empathy and building trust. The potential benefits, greater efficiency, reduced clinician burnout and enhanced patient satisfaction make this a productive and promising, albeit jagged, frontier for AI integration in healthcare.

Johri (2025) introduced a Conversational Reasoning Assessment Framework for Testing in Medicine (CRAFT-MD), designed to systematically evaluate AI in clinical settings, with a focus on patient interactions. It was thorough, looking at history taking, diagnostic reasoning, treatment planning and communication skills. The point was to simulate real-world clinical scenarios, then identify the strengths and limitations of AI in supporting healthcare professionals. Evaluation benchmarks like this really matter in AI, so that improvements can be measured and improved before integrating AI into clinical workflows.

Does AI help physicians with patient education and emotional support? Gan et al (2025) investigated patients who faced total knee arthroplasty and received AI-augmented consent via ChatGPT; they found that these patients experienced notably less anxiety and greater satisfaction than those who underwent the standard surgeon-led discussion. AI generated consistent, easily understood explanations on demand, while the surgeon retained final oversight. The study found immediate and sustained reductions in anxiety scores and higher preoperative understanding by patients. Functional outcomes and pain levels were unchanged, indicating that the AI's benefit lay squarely in communication and emotional support.

Karthikesalingam (2023) at Google Research put AI head-to-head with physicians in a real-world diagnostic setting. The trained LLM had reasoning ability and was trained with real-life conversations, with professional actors pretending to be patients. The AI system, Articulate Medical Intelligence Explorer (AMIE), was tested using professional actors simulating patient cases, allowing researchers to compare its diagnostic reasoning against human doctors. The results were astonishing. AMIE outperformed human doctors in 79 per cent of cases, delivering higher-quality responses with greater empathy.

As AMIE was specifically designed for diagnostic dialogue, researchers Tu et al (2025) did further research and compared AMIE's text-based consultations to evaluations by physicians and found that AMIE outperformed physicians in diagnostic accuracy and communication across a substantial number of axes – 30 out of 32 axes according to specialist physicians and 25 out of 26 according to patient-actors.

Some research shows that chatbots, when they perform well, are actually preferred by patients, even seen as more empathetic. Ayers et al (2023) compared physician responses to those of an AI chatbot, GlassAI, which answered patient questions posted on a public social media platform. The AI chatbot was rated higher 79 per cent of the time for both quality and empathy.

This early study suggested that AI had the ability to handle complex, real-world patient interactions that could lead to a scalable solution to improve healthcare and reduce the burden on human clinicians and healthcare systems.

All of this is of interest from a productivity perspective, as it points towards integrating AI to streamline clinicians' patient interaction and accelerate the consent process without compromising quality. It could lead to fewer repetitive patient queries for surgeons and nurses, reducing appointment times and freeing up valuable clinician hours for surgical planning or post-operative care. Happier, less anxious patients are also more likely to engage in their own recovery, lowering complication-related delays and reducing the administrative overhead of follow-up questions. In short, AI-assisted consent and communications could not only lift the patient experience but also make healthcare more efficient by offloading tasks to a reliable, always-available AI assistant.

We are still some way off the nuanced natural dialogue a doctor will have with a patient when they first present. AI tends to falter as the dialogue proceeds but it is getting better quickly. AI is dialogue with intelligence, also becoming multimodal with audio, which is how most healthcare professionals deal with patients. Eventually, fully interactive high-fidelity dialogue through realistic avatars will be possible.

Diagnosis

On clinical decision making, studies show real progress in this pivotal part of the medical process. It takes a lot of time and money to train a physician. If we can assist, augment, even automate this to even a small degree, huge savings can be achieved.

A study by Singh (2014) estimated that approximately 5 per cent of outpatient visits in the US involve diagnostic errors, affecting about 12 million adults annually. A literature review by Berner and Graber (2008) was even more worrying, suggesting that between 10 and 15 per cent of physician diagnoses are erroneous.

If inroads are made into reducing these figures, lives can be saved and costs massively reduced. Imagine an AI that has a misdiagnosis rate of less than 3 per cent. You would then be taking a risk seeing a human doctor.

AI-powered clinical decision support systems (CDSSs) are software tools, often integrated into electronic health records (EHRs), that give clinicians patient-specific assessments or recommendations to enhance decision making, improve care quality and increase productivity. These systems analyse the patient's data and compare it against large, verified databases of medical knowledge to suggest possible diagnoses and recommend further tests or investigations if needed.

In one high-stakes challenge, AI went head-to-head with medical experts in stroke care. Haim et al (2024) analysed data from 100 stroke patients to see how well GPT-4 could predict outcomes. GPT-4 agreed with expert clinicians in 80 cases; in 5 cases it provided correct diagnoses where the experts were wrong, and in another 5 the experts had the edge. Additionally, GPT-4 outperformed specialist AI models in predicting patient mortality, showing its ability to augment, and sometimes surpass, human expertise in high-stakes scenarios. This suggests AI could play a key role in early stroke intervention, helping doctors make faster, more accurate life-saving decisions.

AI has also been put to the test in clinical reasoning. Brodeur (2024) evaluated OpenAI's o1-preview model on complex clinical reasoning tasks. The model demonstrated superior performance compared to both previous AI models and human physicians, in areas such as differential diagnosis generation, diagnostic reasoning and management planning. Physicians were asked to handle complex management cases, some relying on AI guidance, others going it alone. AI alone achieved an 86 per cent accuracy rate, compared to just 41 per cent for doctors. This suggests that AI is developing the ability to not only recognize disease but also recommend the best course of treatment, potentially reshaping how physicians approach complex medical cases. It showed no significant improvement in probabilistic reasoning or triage of differential diagnosis tasks. Nevertheless, it suggests that advanced language models can support physicians in complex decision-making processes to enhance productivity in healthcare.

What happens when AI works with doctors rather than competing against them? A landmark study by Goh (2025) tested AI, AI plus physician, and physicians using only traditional resources, on 92 practising doctors solving patient cases. Surprisingly, AI alone performed just as well as AI plus physician, and both significantly outperformed traditional resource-based doctors. With AI assistance, physician performance improved by 6.5 per cent, also proving that AI can be a powerful clinical decision support tool.

Initially, it is this 'second opinion' that can help reduce errors in diagnosis, alerting healthcare professionals to things that were overlooked or offering reminders about best practice. In the long term, as AI systems can continuously learn from new data and outcomes, reason, adapt and improve their recommendations over time, such decision-making tools stay current with the latest medical research and practices. One can see how it could, eventually, transcend the clinical decision-making skills of a human clinician.

More advanced diagnostics come into their own when AI algorithms assist in diagnosing diseases by widening analysis out to complex datasets, such as medical images, EHRs and genetic information. These systems can identify patterns that may be missed by human judgement alone, offering high-precision diagnostic suggestions. Taking predictive analytics further, AI can use historical data and real-time inputs to predict patient outcomes, helping clinicians make informed decisions about patient care, including the likelihood of complications, and even potential responses to various treatments.

Investigation

Radiographers and radiologists, those who operate scanners and diagnose images, are under heavy pressure in hospitals. Improvements in imaging through AI are now regularly appearing even in images with no visible signs. AI algorithms are particularly effective in analysing medical images such as X-rays, CT scans, MRI scans and ultrasound images. These algorithms can detect abnormalities such as tumours, fractures or signs of diseases like pneumonia with high accuracy, often surpassing human performance in speed and accuracy. This can lead to quicker, more accurate diagnoses at lower costs, leading to better patient outcomes.

Using over 80,000 mammograms, Lang (2023) tested two different screening methods. In the traditional approach, each scan was reviewed by two radiologists. In the AI-assisted method, AI first analysed the scans, flagging potential risks, before a radiologist conducted a review. In cases where the AI detected a higher likelihood of cancer, a second radiologist was brought in for further evaluation. The results were impressive. AI-assisted screening identified 20 per cent more breast cancers while nearly halving the workload for radiologists. This is a significant productivity gain, as it increases the detection rate but also reduces the burden on expensive experts.

A breakthrough in epilepsy diagnosis was achieved with the development of the MELD Graph (Ripart, 2025), a graph neural network designed to automate the detection of brain lesions from MRI scans. They are often invisible on standard MRI scans but this new system can detect two-thirds of the epilepsy brain lesions that doctors often miss. By offering a scalable AI solution for lesion detection, the MELD Graph represents a major step toward enhancing epilepsy management through faster, more precise and more reliable analysis.

In cardiology, a study by Johnson (2025) in *Nature Medicine* examined 14,606 ECG recordings and compared AI's performance against 167 trained technicians. The AI detected critical arrhythmias with 98.6 per cent accuracy, compared to just 80.3 per cent for human technicians. This suggests that AI could significantly reduce misdiagnoses, improve cost efficiency and enhance access to ECG monitoring, particularly in areas with physician shortages.

In pathology, AI can help analyse tissue samples, detecting abnormalities that suggest diseases such as cancer. AI systems can also assist pathologists by highlighting areas of interest in tissue slides, ensuring that subtle signs of disease are not overlooked. AI can analyse complex laboratory test results, identifying patterns that might indicate specific conditions or diseases. This includes not just interpreting simple tests, but also handling complex data from genetic sequencing or biomarker analysis, to identify genetic disorders or predispositions to certain diseases.

Broadening out, AI systems can also integrate and analyse data from multiple sources, including EHRs, imaging studies and wearable health devices. This holistic view can help healthcare providers gain a more comprehensive understanding of a patient's health status, leading to better diagnostic accuracy. It could predict the likelihood of a disease's presence or future risk based on historical data and current patient data. This can be particularly useful in chronic disease management, where early intervention can significantly alter the disease's trajectory and patient outcomes.

Then there is its use over time, especially for chronic conditions or in post-operative care, which can optimize investigation, as AI can continuously analyse patient data to monitor for signs of disease progression or recovery. This ongoing monitoring can catch potential complications early, prompting timely interventions.

Treatment

Everything in healthcare is complex, and treatment is no exception. In truth, treatment can be ill targeted, poorly managed, wasteful and expensive. AI can help on several fronts. Targeted treatments, especially drug choice and dosage, are areas where critical choices can be made on cost and efficacy.

AI is also excelling in clinical decision making and patient management. Brodeur (2024) suggested that AI is developing the ability to not only recognize disease but also recommend the best course of treatment, potentially reshaping how physicians approach complex medical cases.

On the physical side, in surgical and procedural contexts, robotic systems can assist or even autonomously perform surgeries, sometimes with greater precision and control than human surgeons. This can lead to less invasive procedures, reduced recovery times and better surgical outcomes.

AI can streamline the drug discovery and development process by predicting how different chemicals will react in the body, identifying potential drug candidates more quickly, and reducing the time and cost to bring new drugs to market. We have already seen huge success with AlphaFold, saving 1 billion years of research by identifying the 3D structure of 200 million proteins. DeepMind has already entered the market with AlphaFold3, which looks at *all* molecules. AI is fast becoming a useful tool in many areas of medical research. Research, in general, benefits from the use of AI at every stage of the research process.

Administration

The UK's NHS, after successful trials, has implemented an AI doctor's assistant to speed up appointment times and dramatically reduce admin. Described by the UK government as a 'gamechanger', it was used to 'bulldoze bureaucracy and take notes to free up staff time and deliver better care to patients… more people could be seen in A&E, clinicians could spend more time during an appointment focusing on the patient, and appointments were shorter' (National Health Service, 2024).

One tool transcribes patient–clinician conversations to create structured medical notes, even drafting patient letters. It was evaluated with 7,000 patients, across a range of sites, in a range of clinical settings, including Adult Outpatients, Primary Care, Paediatrics, Mental Health, Community care, A&E and across the London Ambulance Service. The key findings were an increase in direct care, with clinicians spending more time with patients rather than typing on a computer, as well as an increase in productivity in A&E, where it supported more patients being seen, as it reduced admin time for staff. It listened to consultations, then drafted clinic notes and letters which could be edited and authorized by the clinician before being uploaded and sent out to patients.

Dr Maaike Kusters, paediatric immunology consultant, made an interesting point. He could sit closer to his patients, who had very complex conditions, and have more natural face-to-face conversations, as he was not typing in notes through a keyboard. This automation of admin has carried over into getting people discharged from hospital more quickly.

Increasing productivity through AI in general administrative and clinical administration is a quick win. AI can speed up and automate the many everyday, routine tasks. My neurologist recently ended my consultation by dictating the letter he was sending back to my general practitioner, outlining the result of his findings and recommendations for treatment, into a recorder for automatic transcription. It was an impressive use of AI.

Take another example, the administration of screening for clinical trials. Clinical trial screening is costly, time-consuming and prone to human error, but AI is changing that. A study by Unlu et al (2024) tested GPT-4's ability to identify patient eligibility for trials. The results showed that GPT-4 achieved near-perfect accuracy, outperforming human staff, particularly in cases involving symptomatic heart failure. This means that AI could help accelerate medical research by efficiently screening trial participants, reducing human errors and enabling faster drug development.

At the next level, AI can assist in resource allocation within healthcare facilities by predicting patient inflows and identifying which patients require immediate attention versus those who can safely wait. Productivity increases through AI tools can help optimize hospital workflow and resource management. This can improve outcomes and reduce hospital stays, improving patient outcomes.

Education

The next generation of doctors will find themselves challenged by AI. A Stanford study (Strong, 2023) compared the clinical reasoning abilities of GPT-4 against medical students using a free-response clinical exam format. GPT-4 outperformed the students, demonstrating highly advanced case-based reasoning skills. This highlights a significant shift. AI systems are not just memorizing information but are learning to apply medical knowledge with sophistication and reasoning. As these capabilities continue to advance, future doctors may find themselves working alongside, even competing with, AI systems that rival human expertise in diagnosis, decision making and patient care.

The performance of AI models across medical examinations and knowledge assessments has improved steadily and that performance shows no signs of stopping. A comprehensive study evaluating the performance of a range of AI models on the United States Medical Licensing Examination (USMLE) found that GPT-4 achieved an accuracy rate of 86.4 per cent on

AMBOSS questions (curated, board-level MCQs), outperforming its predecessors, showing significant improvements in AI's medical reasoning capabilities. In more specialized fields, GPT-4 has also showed promising results. In radiation oncology, GPT-4 achieved a score of 74.57 per cent on the American College of Radiology's Radiation Oncology In-Training (TXIT) exam (Huang et al, 2023).

These are just a fraction of the studies showing steady progress across the board in AI's healthcare competency. In general, a growing body of research points to significant productivity and improved patient outcomes, with faster and more accurate diagnosis and investigation and better training. Just as important are the benefits to be gained in alleviating workforce shortages and spiralling costs in healthcare.

The state-of-the-art benchmark for AI performance in medicine rises with every passing week (Brin et al, 2023), especially on clinical exams, comparing results to human physicians or medical students on standardized medical assessments. MedQA (US Medical Licensing Exam Questions) are multiple-choice exams based on real medical licencing questions, and recent models (Singhal et al, 2025) have exceeded 75–80+ per cent accuracy, where expert human performance typically lands in the 80–85 per cent range.

Research by Newton et al (2025) assessed ChatGPT-4o's performance on medical science exams, where it scored 94 per cent on the United Kingdom Medical Licensing Exam Applied Knowledge Test and 89.9 per cent on the USMLE Step 1. These results demonstrated the model's ability to handle complex medical queries with high accuracy.

Semantic Clinical Artificial Intelligence (SCAI), developed at the University of Buffalo (Elkin et al, 2025), is achieving higher scores on the USMLE than most physicians and all other AI tools. With 13 million medical facts at its disposal, it uses more complex semantic reasoning to reason out answers. By adding semantics to LLMs, they have a reasoning model that can both chat to you (available to the public online), as well as perform at high levels of accuracy.

One issue in assessing AI against physicians and other medical professionals is that in the real world, managing a patient is a process not an event. Relying on examination assessment items only captures single, fixed events, whereas the real-word decision-making process is longer and more complex. Here, agentic AI has entered the race with AgentClinic (Schmidgall et al, 2024), a multimodal benchmark where AI models act as doctors and engage with simulated patients to gather information and reach diagnoses. It includes dialogue, real-time reasoning and even cognitive biases to simulate realistic clinical environments. For AI to genuinely enhance productivity in healthcare, it must excel not just in static knowledge recall but in adaptive, context-driven dialogue and decision making. Tools like AgentClinic could make sure that future AI systems are built to complement human clinicians effectively, improving speed, safety and quality in real-world medical practice.

One real test is also out in real hospitals, with real healthcare professionals. One tool, by Dutch company Xprtise, on surgical support for nurses, designed to streamline and accelerate learning development in a large teaching hospital in the Netherlands, automatically analyses existing documents, protocols and guidelines to generate structured learning content, significantly reducing the workload of subject matter experts (SMEs) and Learning and Development (L&D) teams. It delivered impressive productivity gains, cutting project timelines by up to 50 per cent, with a structured four-step process: 1) defining the scope and uploading relevant documents; 2) AI-driven analysis, mapping out tasks, processes and steps; 3) impact assessment, prioritizing critical learning areas; and 4) generating a formal learning plan for seamless implementation. The tool automated this process to slash processing times by 40 per cent. Instead of relying solely on experts for input, which takes time and can contain gaps, even inconsistencies, and vary in accuracy, AI ensured speed, consistency and accuracy.

Modern AI models have reached, and in some tasks surpassed, average medical student and junior doctor performance on standardized tests. There is little doubt that they will match and exceed that of most, if not all, human doctors in the near future. While they still lag behind highly experienced clinicians in some complex real-world decision making and nuanced judgement, they are catching up fast. We will reach an inflexion point, where decisions will have to made on the use of AI in relation to human expertise in medicine.

Wellbeing

Poor wellbeing has been recognized as one cause of low productivity worldwide. In schools, universities and the workplace, it reduces educational and economic productivity. Social and economic problems may have to be addressed but what sort of productive interventions could work? Workplace wellbeing programmes have been surprisingly ineffective, so can technology, specifically AI, play a role in alleviating the problem and increasing productivity?

Wellbeing and work

Poor wellbeing, according to the World Health Organization (WHO, 2024), causes an estimated total of $1 trillion annually in lost productivity. Even minor increases in productivity in individual countries could have an impact on this global figure.

In the UK, the Health and Safety Executive (HSE, 2024) reported 16.4 million work days lost annually in 2023/24 due to work-related stress, depression or anxiety. However, a broader estimate, using Office for National Statistics (ONS, 2023) sickness absence data from 2018–2022, suggests around 18 million work days are lost annually when considering all mental health conditions, not just those caused by work. Figures for the US are less readily available from government sources such as the Bureau of Labor Statistics (BLS), but a Gallup survey (2024) estimate stands at 693 million a year. Globally, the WHO estimated in 2019 that 12 billion work days were lost yearly due to mental health issues such as stress, depression and anxiety (WHO, 2024). This was pre-Covid, making it likely that the figure is an underestimate. They highlight a need for more action.

Yet a UK study (Fleming, 2024, p. 1) across 233 organizations came to a surprising conclusion on wellbeing initiatives within the workplace: that 'participants appear no better off... interventions are NOT providing additional or appropriate resources in response to job demands.'

This finding had been mirrored in the US by Jones et al (2019) in their study 'What Do Workplace Wellness Programs Do?', which found no 'significant causal effects of treatment on total medical expenditures, health behaviors, employee productivity, or self-reported health status in the first year.' This study is significant, as it avoided the self-selecting nature of the audiences so prevalent in other studies on wellbeing. Did they reduce sickness? No. Did it result in staying in your job, getting promotion or a pay rise? No. Did it reduce medication or hospital visits? No. This was true for 37 out of the 39 features studied. The bottom line is that there is no bottom line, no return on investment. The interesting conclusion by the authors of the study is that wellness programmes, far from helping the intended audience, the obese, smokers etc., simply screen out those who are already healthy, yet the burden of cost is borne by all.

If technology, as an alternative, plays even a small role in reducing these figures, significant global productivity gains can be realized.

Wellbeing and chatbots

Some years back I came across a small metal cross and plaque on Beachy Head cliffs near my home. It was placed there by the parents of a young girl who had thrown herself off the cliff due to her poor school results. Overwhelmed, she clearly felt she could not talk to anyone. Many do not go to a parent, teacher, faculty member or therapist with their problems. It made me more sympathetic to anonymous online services that seem to appeal to many who want help, but without inducing even more anxiety by having to explain their problems face-to-face.

Recent studies indicate that approximately 33 per cent of adults worldwide experience feelings of loneliness (Surkalim, 2022), with 1 in 12 reporting severe loneliness that adversely affects their health. The World Health Organization (WHO, 2024) reports that suicide is the fourth leading cause of death among individuals aged 15 to 29. This is a huge problem and will not be wholly solved by technology; indeed technology may be a contributory factor. Nevertheless, wellbeing chats are proving popular and showing signs of being useful, even in tackling suicidal thoughts. Generative AI, in particular, has taken mental health therapy online, with increased access, reduced friction between the service and patients, avoiding embarrassment, hugely reducing costs and with good patient outcomes. This all adds up to increased productivity.

Early chatbots, like Eliza in the 1960s, operated on simple pattern recognition, mimicking a therapist by reflecting user input in a structured but shallow way. These early systems had little sophistication. Later chatbots like Woebot and Wysa used rule-based AI and, despite being somewhat rigid and over-directed in conversation, proved useful for managing anxiety and depression. With the sudden rise of generative AI, a new breed of AI-driven chatbots, Replika, Psychologist, Therabot and ChatGPT itself, among many others, has become far more natural, sophisticated, context-aware and responsive.

The 'Psychologist' chatbot on Character.ai is an AI-driven chatbot that has gained significant use, engaging in millions of conversations since its creation. The idea is simple – it delivers standard cognitive behavioural therapy (CBT) as dialogue, just like a real counsellor or therapist. It is chatty, helpful, endlessly patient and, unlike human support, available 24/7.

Isn't it odd that something so simple, text-only dialogue, is so popular? We know from research by Reeves and Nass (1996) that it is easy to get people to see technology as human, especially when they see or hear meaningful dialogue, and as generative AI has opened up a world of meaningful dialogue for hundreds of millions, it is not surprising that wellbeing chatbots have emerged and been popular.

My own experience of trying another explicitly therapist chatbot, Woebot, was intriguing. Woebot is an AI-driven chatbot that uses CBT techniques to help users manage mental health challenges such as depression and anxiety. I tried Woebot in 2018, for 10 days, and have been checking in over the years. I like the experience. Just like Psychologist and Replika, you get drawn into the friendly exchanges. The up-front promise of anonymity is good in these chatbots and I can see why this appeals to many who want help but are too shy or embarrassed to come forward. It has its limitations and oddities but it was good to chat to something that did not judge me and has a few surprises up its sleeve. Woebot has now transformed itself into a whole ecosystem of health support through the chatbot, but it pioneered the benefits of chatbots in wellbeing.

Replika was created by Eugenia Kuyda in 2017, as a way to remember lost friends after death, but from this strange origin it pivoted into being an AI companion with millions of users worldwide. It learns from interactions and has some CBT techniques, such as guided self-reflection. It was used in an interesting study by Maples et al (2024) to look at its impact on 1,006 student users who, not unexpectedly, turned out to be more lonely than typical students. A heartening discovery from the study was that 3 per cent of participants reported that conversations with Replika stopped them from acting on suicidal thoughts. Chatbots now perform a huge range of roles online and Replika showed that many saw it as a friend, companion and certainly a confidant.

Can AI be a therapist? This is a bold question, which Hatch et al (2025) looked at to see whether a panel of participants could tell the difference between responses written by expert therapists and those generated by AI. It also compared the ratings of the responses on key principles of therapy and analysed the linguistic differences between the two types of responses. Participants were only marginally better than chance at identifying whether the responses were written by AI or a therapist. Surprisingly, the responses written by AI were rated higher than the therapist-written responses. This is probably because the ChatGPT responses were longer, more positive and personal than the therapist-written responses.

Wysa is an AI-based chatbot that provides emotional support to help users navigate stress, anxiety and other mental health concerns. Limbic is another, which can be placed inside a healthcare providers' website to provide therapy, but can also refer patients to clinicians, making sure patients are directed to the right care as quickly as possible. Limbic Access became the first AI mental health chatbot in the world to earn Class IIa UKCA medical device certification. This involved meeting standards on safety, clinical effectiveness and reliability. It claimed a 93 per cent success rate in predicting mental health disorders, making triage decisions faster and more precise.

As a productivity tool, clinicians using Limbic reported a 23.5 per cent reduction in assessment times, saving an average of 12.7 minutes per refer-ral. Even more impressively, improved triage meant treatment dropouts fell by 18 per cent and unnecessary changes to treatment plans dropped by 45 per cent, thanks to more accurate triage decisions.

Access to mental healthcare is a huge problem, as demand often exceeds supply, particularly for minority groups. Limbic showed that AI chatbots can break down these barriers (Habicht et al, 2024). This study of 129,400 patients across England's NHS examined the chatbot's impact on referral volume and the diversity of patients. NHS services using the chatbot saw a 15 per cent increase in referrals, more than double the 6 per cent rise seen in control services. An analysis of the chat data showed that anonymity and absence of human judgement were deemed to be factors in its success, along with its guiding of patients towards treatment paths.

Therabot was put through a medical trial with 106 patients (Kelly, 2024) with either major depressive disorder, generalized anxiety disorder or eating disorders. This smartphone app delivers a personalized therapeutic service that claimed to deliver statistically and clinically significant results after eight weeks. Those with depression experienced a 51 per cent average reduction in symptoms, those with anxiety a 31 per cent reduction (many moving below the clinical threshold) and with eating disorders, there was a 19 per cent aver-age reduction in body image and weight concerns, outperforming the control group. It could also detect high-risk content, such as suicidal thoughts, and ask users to contact emergency services. Additional evidence showed users developed a relationship with Therabot that was similar to in-person therapy. On average, users chatted with Therabot for six hours, the equivalent of about eight therapy sessions, a significant productivity gain.

These impressive results point the way towards solutions in mental health that, unlike human therapy, are scalable. They seem to provide genuine relief to overstretched healthcare systems. We need not eliminate all human therapeutic work to see that this provides a massive leap in productivity, and with enough attention paid to validation, oversight and patient safety, millions could have immediate access to an anonymous service that has evidenced results.

On a grander scale, AI tools can also be used to analyse millions of online mental health discussions to track trends in depression, anxiety and suicide prevention. This type of research, which would have taken years manually, is now being done in real time, influencing public health policies. One study (Allam et al, 2025) used AI to analyse Twitter posts, aiming to identify sensitive linguistic and emotional cues linked to suicidal ideation. The AI analysed tweets as they were posted, scanning for patterns of distress using sentiment analysis, keyword detection and behavioural indicators. It had an 85 per cent accuracy rate, 88 per cent precision, and 83 per cent recall (and minimized false positives), successfully isolating genuine cases for consideration. Beyond this, AI frameworks like this could identify other signs that contribute to suicide risk, such as social isolation and bullying, to become a useful tool in flagging early signs of distress to trigger interventions.

Expensive face-to-face therapies are clearly not the sole solution to the problem, neither are AI chatbots. But in facing up to the scale of the problem we must accept that AI chatbots play a role, as part of the solution.

Now that some services have memory, the wellbeing and therapy functions will be much more powerful. They can use that knowledge to assess and improve on their therapeutic feedback and advice, in the same way that a human therapist would rely on past chats with their client. Given that the chatbot does not have the same limitations of working and long-term memory as a human therapist, this puts AI at an advantage. It will still be at a disadvantage on emotions such as empathy and sympathy but as support, it can clearly improve productivity in the field, where expensive human support and advice is the bottleneck.

Conclusion

Few human goals matter more than the prevention and relief of pain and suffering. This can be seen, partly, as a productivity problem at personal, team, organizational, institutional, national and international levels. Costs and skills shortages still plague healthcare provision, so even marginal productivity gains, when scaled, can have significant global effects. AI can clearly assist, augment and automate across the broad spectrum of healthcare delivery.

There are already many touch points where it can be used safely and directly and advances across all areas of provision are moving at pace.

References

Abramoff, M D et al (2023) Autonomous artificial intelligence increases real-world specialist clinic productivity in a cluster-randomized trial, *NPJ Digital Medicine*, 6 (1), 184

Allam, H, Davison, C, Kalota, F, Lazaros, E and Hua, D (2025) AI-driven mental health surveillance: Identifying suicidal ideation through machine learning techniques, *Big Data and Cognitive Computing*, 9 (1), 16

Ayers, J W, Poliak, A, Dredze, M, Leas, E C, Zhu, Z, Kelley, J B and Smith, D M (2023) Comparing physician and artificial intelligence chatbot responses to patient questions posted to a public social media platform, *JAMA Internal Medicine*, 183 (6), 589–96

Baumol, W J (2012) *The Cost Disease: Why Computers Get Cheaper and Health Care Doesn't*, Yale University Press

Berner, E S and Graber, M L (2008) Overconfidence as a cause of diagnostic error in medicine, *American Journal of Medicine*, 121 (5), S2–S23

Brin, D et al (2023) Comparing ChatGPT and GPT-4 performance in USMLE soft skill assessments, *Scientific Reports*, 13 (1), 16492

Brodeur, P G (2024) Superhuman performance of a large language model on the reasoning tasks of a physician, https://arxiv.org/abs/2412.10849 (archived at https://perma.cc/4TZY-U8GC)

Elkin, P L et al (2025) Semantic clinical artificial intelligence vs native large language model performance on the USMLE, *JAMA Network Open*, 8 (4), e256359

Fleming, W (2024) Employee well-being outcomes from individual-level mental health interventions: Cross-sectional evidence from the United Kingdom, https://onlinelibrary.wiley.com/doi/10.1111/irj.12418 (archived at https://perma.cc/ENP2-K3M6)

Gallup (2024) Economic cost of poor employee mental health, https://www.gallup.com/workplace/404174/economic-cost-poor-employee-mental-health.aspx (archived at https://perma.cc/9WVG-PSP6)

Gan, W, Ouyang, J, She, G and Xue, Z (2025) ChatGPT's role in alleviating anxiety in total knee arthroplasty consent process: A randomized controlled trial pilot study, *International Journal of Surgery*, 10, 1097

Gates, B (2023) The age of AI has begun, *Gates Notes*, https://www.gatesnotes.com/the-age-of-ai-has-begun?utm_source=chatgpt.com (archived at https://perma.cc/QM5Z-XFSQ)

Goh, E (2025) GPT-4 assistance for physician performance on patient care tasks, *Nature Medicine*, 10, 1097

Habicht, J, Viswanathan, S, Carrington, B, Hauser, T U, Harper, R and Rollwage, M (2024) Closing the accessibility gap to mental health treatment with a personalized self-referral chatbot, *Nature Medicine*, 30 (2), 595–602

Haim, A, Katson, M, Cohen-Shelly, M, Peretz, S, Aran, D and Shelly, S (2024) Evaluating GPT-4 as a clinical decision support tool in ischemic stroke management, https://www.medrxiv.org/content/10.1101/2024.01.18.24301409v1 (archived at https://perma.cc/ZCC7-R263)

Hatch, S G et al (2025) When ELIZA meets therapists: A Turing test for the heart and mind, *PLOS Mental Health* 2(2): e0000145, https://doi.org/10.1371/journal.pmen.0000145 (archived at https://perma.cc/AXY4-QNVN)

Health and Safety Executive (HSE) (2024) Work-related stress, anxiety or depression statistics, https://www.hse.gov.uk/statistics/dayslost.htm (archived at https://perma.cc/R4Q4-5WRY)

Huang, Y et al (2023) Benchmarking ChatGPT-4 on ACR radiation oncology in-training (TXIT) exam and red journal gray zone cases, https://arxiv.org/abs/2304.11957 (archived at https://perma.cc/W68S-E95W)

Johnson, L S (2025) AI for direct-to-physician ECG reporting, *Nature Medicine*, 1–7

Johri, S (2025) An evaluation framework for clinical use of large language models in patient interaction tasks, *Nature Medicine*, 31, 77–86

Jones, D, Molitor, D and Reif, J (2019) What do workplace wellness programs do? *The Quarterly Journal of Economics*, 134 (4), 1747–91

Kämäräinen, V J, Peltokorpi, A, Torkki, P and Tallbacka, K (2016) Measuring healthcare productivity–from unit to system level, *International Journal of Health Care Quality Assurance*, 29 (3), 288–99

Karthikesalingam, A (2023) AMIE: A research AI system for diagnostic medical reasoning and conversations, Google Research, https://research.google/blog/amie-a-research-ai-system-for-diagnostic-medical-reasoning-and-conversations/ (archived at https://perma.cc/93XR-GSB8)

Kelly, M (2024) First therapy chatbot trial yields mental health benefits, https://home.dartmouth.edu/news/2025/03/first-therapy-chatbot-trial-yields-mental-health-benefits (archived at https://perma.cc/XQ8J-AK3U)

Lang, K (2023) Artificial intelligence-supported screen reading versus standard double reading in the MASAI trial, *The Lancet Oncology*, 24 (8), 936–44

Liu, C-M et al (2025) Reclassification of the conventional risk assessment for aging-related diseases by electrocardiogram-enabled biological age, *NPJ Aging*, 11 (7)

Maples, B, Cerit, M, Vishwanath, A and Pea, R (2024) Loneliness and suicide mitigation for students using GPT3-enabled chatbots, *NPJ Mental Health Research*, 3 (1), 4

National Health Service (2024) AI doctors' assistant to speed up appointments a 'gamechanger', https://www.gov.uk/government/news/ai-doctors-assistant-to-speed-up-appointments-a-gamechanger?utm_source=chatgpt.com (archived at https://perma.cc/2P9C-D9KL)

Newton, P M et al (2025) Can ChatGPT-4o really pass medical science exams? A pragmatic analysis using novel questions, *Medical Science Educator*, 35, 721–29

Office for National Statistics (2023) Sickness absence in the UK labour market – Office for National Statistics, https://www.ons.gov.uk/employmentandlabourmarket/peopleinwork/labourproductivity/articles/sicknessabsenceinthelabourmarket/2022 (archived at https://perma.cc/MC3H-5GFV)

Reeves, B and Nass, C (1996) *The Media Equation: How People Treat Computers, Television, and New Media Like Real People*, Cambridge University Press

Ripart, M (2025) Detection of epileptogenic focal cortical dysplasia using graph neural networks, *JAMA Neurology*, 82 (4), 397–406

Sahni, N, Stein, G, Zemmel, R and Cutler, D M (2023) The potential impact of artificial intelligence on healthcare spending, National Bureau of Economic Research, 30857

Schmidgall, S, Ziaei, R, Harris, C, Reis, E, Jopling, J, and Moor, M (2024) AgentClinic: A multimodal agent benchmark to evaluate AI in simulated clinical environments, https://arxiv.org/abs/2405.07960 (archived at https://perma.cc/KQU6-8JQW)

Singh, H (2014) The frequency of diagnostic errors in outpatient care, *BMJ*, 23 (9), 727–31

Singhal, K, Tu, T, Gottweis, J, Sayres, R, Wulczyn, E, Amin, M and Natarajan, V (2025) Toward expert-level medical question answering with large language models, *Nature Medicine*, 31, 943–50

Strong, E (2023) Chatbot vs medical student performance on clinical reasoning exams, *JAMA Internal Medicine*, 183 (9), 1028–30

Surkalim, D L (2022) The prevalence of loneliness across 113 countries: Systematic review and meta-analysis, *BMJ*, https://doi.org/10.1136/bmj-2021-067068 (archived at https://perma.cc/J8YW-GN4C)

Tu, T et al (2025) Towards conversational diagnostic artificial intelligence, *Nature*, 642, 442–50

Unlu, O, Shin, J, Mailly, C J and Oates, M F (2024) Retrieval augmented generation enabled generative pre-trained transformer 4 (GPT-4) performance for clinical trial screening, medRxiv, https://www.medrxiv.org/content/10.1101/2024.02.08.24302376v1 (archived at https://perma.cc/2RF3-DXAX)

World Health Organization (WHO) (2024) Mental health at work, https://www.who.int/news-room/fact-sheets/detail/mental-health-at-work (archived at https://perma.cc/F76R-24SD)

Further reading

Class IIa UKCA certification, https://www.limbic.ai/blog/class-ii-a (archived at https://perma.cc/SW86-EHVH)

Limbic (2024) https://www.limbic.ai/ (archived at https://perma.cc/69BY-B7X2)

PAHO (2023) WHO launches new resources on prevention and decriminalization of suicide, https://www.paho.org/en/news/12-9-2023-who-launches-new-resources-prevention-and-decriminalization-suicide (archived at https://perma.cc/K4J9-LXWE)

Psychologist bot (2024) https://character.ai/chat/Hpk0GozjACb3mtHeAaAMb0r9pcJGbzF317I_Ux_ALOA? (archived at https://perma.cc/QL56-4CEA)

REPLIKA (2024) https://replika.com/ (archived at https://perma.cc/UUN4-C5VK)

Wysa (2024) https://www.wysa.com/ (archived at https://perma.cc/C7V8-N7CP)

Xprtise (2024) AI learning: The rubber hits the road, *The Learning Hack Podcast*, YouTube, https://www.youtube.com/watch?v=9K80mrjRSQE&t=2186s (archived at https://perma.cc/8UCJ-MKA2)

11

Research and AI (breakout)

The frontline on AI productivity may already have been breached, not on the stand-off between teaching and learning, but in research.

Research is not all in academia. Organizations in every imaginable sector also do research that tends not to follow the strict rules of academic methodologies, peer review and publication. AI has lowered the barriers to entry, is faster and practical with a real focus on productivity through identifying trends, innovations and insights.

This democratization of research means that productive research is now in the hands of everyone. It can now be done by an individual, small start-up, any organization, big and small. Productivity in research drives them all towards using AI. That dam has broken.

The academic publishing system has become a fast production line, where it is more difficult to stop quantity overriding quality. The ongoing surge in publications, known as the 'publish or perish' culture, benefits publishers' profits, but it comes at a cost. Researchers are under pressure to publish and sometimes cut corners, even cheat. There is therefore a dilution of integrity but, above all, a flood of papers that add little value.

The number of published articles has skyrocketed, and as researchers churn out papers, the system is drowning in a sea of writing, editing and reviewing. More pressure is put on the system with the rise of special issues, themed collections of papers, often rushed through review. Even peer review, the last protection, is feeling the strain. There is a sense of the system pushing out more and more content, with less and less impact.

AI may be able to increase productivity in academic publishing, even help preserve quality. It could automate manuscript screening, ensuring that only papers meeting baseline standards move forward for review, freeing up editors to focus on substance, asking for changes rather than merely sorting through weak submissions. For peer reviewers, AI can detect plagiarism, highlight flaws and bring more depth and breadth of experience and objectivity of reviews, reducing the burden on human peer reviewers. AI could also bring some detection capabilities flagging self-citations or citation rings. AI will not fix everything, but it can help to make the whole process more safely productive, preserving quality.

We should be in no doubt about the now common use of generative AI in research itself or the writing of research papers. A clever study by Gray (2024) revealed the level of infiltration by generative AI into academic writing. They analysed specific keywords that are disproportionately present in AI-generated text and estimated that in 2023, over 60,000 scholarly papers, just over 1 per cent of all published articles, used generative AI to some degree or were crafted with the assistance of LLMs. This surge reflects a significant shift in scholarly communication, raising questions about the authenticity and integrity of academic literature. It also indicated the inexorable rise of AI as a tool used in research.

From the earliest stages of research ideation to final publication, AI is being used at every level, starting with research gaps and hypothesis generation, then generating abstracts and introductions, as well as research planning, and even experimentation and automation in labs. Open-text survey analysis and scoring, along with data analysis, are now possible. Idea generation, full paper outlines and the drafting of full papers, meta-studies and systematic reviews are being seen. Then there is faster peer review and fraud detection. Academic writing is often the least useful aspect of the research process. What matters is not who writes the paper, but who conducts the research. In that sense, the decline of the academic author marks the rebirth of the researcher. AI is increasing productivity across almost all aspects of the research process, so a focus on using AI in research and research publications will save massive amounts of time and increase the quality.

Abstracts and introductions

There is increasing evidence of AI content in abstracts. In a study in 2024, Howard et al matched the growing use and popularity of generative AI models. As these models improve, their speed and accuracy will be compelling.

An early study by Gao et al (2023) evaluated the quality of AI-generated abstracts and found them difficult to distinguish from those written by humans. This highlights AI's potential in drafting compelling research summaries. They compared 50 real abstracts from top medical journals with versions generated by AI and found that human reviewers wrongly identified

14 per cent of real abstracts as being AI-generated. The reviewers admitted that spotting AI-generated content was harder than they expected.

Some of the lower-level work in research papers can clearly be aided or written by AI. In one study by Sikander et al (2023), researchers evaluated the capability of generative AI in composing introduction sections for scientific articles. The findings revealed no significant difference between generative AI and human-written introductions regarding publishing and content quality. Interestingly, 59 per cent of assessors preferred the generative AI introductions, while 33 per cent favoured those written by humans. These results suggest that generative AI can help assist or automate the writing of introduction sections for research articles, enhancing productivity.

AI co-scientist

AI can then move on from looking at what exists in the literature (Bolaños et al, 2024) to hypothesis generation, identifying testable, high-impact hypotheses, analysing past data and predicting the most promising research directions.

Google's AI research assistant, dubbed the AI co-scientist, proposes new scientific ideas and identifies research gaps. In early trials, it matched the findings of top biomedical researchers, without ever seeing their work. It matched a team at Imperial College London that had discovered a new gene transfer mechanism, important in understanding antimicrobial resistance, after years of lab work and peer-reviewed publications. The AI tool independently reached the same hypothesis in days. Stanford University used the AI tool to scan biomedical databases to propose existing drugs that could be repurposed. The AI identified two promising drug types which Stanford researchers confirmed could help treat the disease.

The tool reasons, debates and refines scientific ideas through multiple AI agents, each doing a different part of the scientific process. One generates new research ideas based on existing knowledge, the next critiques and refines those ideas to select the most promising ideas, a third retrieves data from the literature and databases. The end result is a ranked, structured list of research proposals complete with explanations and citations, pushing the research forward.

We can expect many such tools in the future, as the rewards are high. AI is moving from a simple productivity accelerator in search and writing, to augmenting specific parts of the process of research, into being a co-scientist.

For experimental design, Chen et al (2023) demonstrated that generative AI can assist in planning and conducting chemical experiments, autonomously interpreting laboratory equipment documentation and generating relevant and useful operational code. Most tasks were fully automated, with some procedures still requiring human intervention.

Moving on from ideas and design to practical lab research, lab productivity has been accelerated at the University of British Columbia (UBC) (2024). In collaboration with Oxford and Sakana AI, UBC have developed an AI scientist that can do its own experiments, generating hypotheses and refining ideas, without humans. It learns through open-ended learning, iterating experiments, testing its own hypotheses and refining ideas. These AI workhorses promise to speed up important scientific research to produce results in a fraction of the time and cost of traditional research.

As an alternative to human systematic reviews and meta-analyses, AI can automate the process, synthesizing data from thousands of studies to speed up the synthesis of knowledge. The investigation by Bolaños et al (2024) into the many tools available in this field points to them being useful in terms of saving time. It is recognized this will grow, as the efficacy of the AI tools improve.

Scientific research and discovery have always been a deeply human affair, with researchers generating research gaps, hypotheses, then rigorously testing them through experimentation, then publication. First, medical research is plateauing, with less return on investment. Second, research is often slow and resource-intensive. This whole system will be disrupted by AI, as it increases productivity across the whole value chain. With AI as co-scientist, agentic or powered by a multi-agent system, changes are apparent.

In 'Towards an AI Co-scientist' (Gottweis et al, 2025), Google used AI to design a system that uncovers new knowledge, formulates high-quality research proposals and refines hypotheses through structured debate. This changes how science is done.

Unlike traditional computational tools that analyse data, the AI co-scientist takes an active role in the process. It builds on prior research and, by integrating a multi-agent architecture, can handle complex, large-scale problem solving with huge gains in productivity. Through a tournament-style evolution process, hypotheses are tested, refined, then improved, so that only the most promising ideas progress. Although applicable to most scientific research, the AI co-scientist demonstrated good results in biomedical research. In drug repurposing, it identified potential cancer treatments, including compounds that show promise in inhibiting tumour growth in myeloid leukaemia. In target discovery, it has proposed epigenetic targets for liver fibrosis, with validation in human liver cell regeneration experiments. In the study of bacterial evolution and antibiotic resistance, it has reiterated findings from traditional lab experiments, even leading to the discovery of a new gene transfer mechanism in bacterial adaptation.

This is not just about accelerating research; AI enhances scientific productivity. By automating hypothesis generation, improving validation processes and uncovering novel insights at pace, the AI co-scientist represents more than just progress on process. It is a shift towards a future where human expertise and AI work in tandem to push the boundaries of knowledge faster and further.

The trajectory is clear. AI is now a co-scientist or, more accurately, as many co-scientists as we choose to use in parallel. Digital biology is its sandbox, a place where anything can be designed and experimented upon through a vast number of iterations to produce structures and solutions that work in the real world.

We are seeing an unprecedented acceleration in productivity, as AI becomes a partner in research that helps us get significant, even groundbreaking results far more quickly and cheaper than we ever imagined. Decades or, in the case of AlphaFold, centuries of research can be compressed in time. This is being done at both the tactical level with AlphaFold but also strategically, on scale, with Evo2, which can design entirely new genomic sequences. This can be directed towards therapeutic design with targeted treatments such as gene therapies and vaccines designed to activate only in specific cells, reducing side effects and improving treatment efficacy. AI has suddenly become actively productive in biological discovery and engineering. One hopes that this will take the form of open-source models, data and services, so that AI benefits humankind in saving lives, curing diseases and extending lives.

Deep research

Deep research models are transforming AI from a simple tool for retrieving information into an autonomous research assistant. We have explored how individual components of research can be assisted, enhanced, even automated by AI. These new tools go much further by doing several tasks autonomously.

They provide breadth and depth, actively searching through hundreds of sources, synthesizing and refining information as they go, with deep analysis and structured reasoning. Moving from researching topics to becoming research analysts, they work to a plan and then go through multiple steps, eventually providing substantial reports and traceable citations. They search the web, evaluate the status of what they find, also cross-check and refine their approach based on what they find. Importantly, they reason their way through information, as a research agent. They have fundamentally changed the way research is done.

The truth is that AI is moving faster than the research world can cope with. It is not altering research, it is redefining research. The direction is clear – AI will do more than humans are capable of doing and not just add to our productivity but become productive in itself. In tandem with AI tools that also execute ideas, such as design, media production and coding, and ultimately embodied AI, subsequent execution of research into action will also see increased productivity. This approach is not just a version upgrade, it is a whole new world of autonomous productivity for AI.

Digital biology

AlphaFold was an astonishing, measurable and monumental breakthrough in medical research for our species. Developed by DeepMind in 2020, it thrashed the opposition in the CASP14 competition (Critical Assessment of Structure Prediction experiment for protein-structure-prediction methods), outperforming 100 other teams, with a gargantuan leap in the field. It shocked everyone.

Predicting 3D protein structures, it both accelerates and opens up a vast array of research opportunities. DeepMind has since released a database containing over 200 million protein structures, including the structures for nearly all catalogued proteins known to science. This database is free to the global scientific community, democratizing access to high-quality protein structures.

AlphaFold unlocked new levels of scientific productivity. The productivity gain is mind blowing. The traditional methods, in expensive labs, using techniques like X-ray crystallography or cryo-electron microscopy equipment and specialist expertise, took years for just one protein. AlphaFold does it in hours. This has allowed researchers to focus on more application research, such as the rapid design of new molecules and vaccines.

It has literally saved over a billion years of research time. This is a new paradigm in research, as AI provides AI 'analogues' in which virtual experimentation can take place, which can inform things we need to do in the real, physical world.

Demis Hassabis, CEO of Google's DeepMind, sees this approach as a transformative shift in the life sciences through what he terms 'digital biology'. Biology is complex and AI is in an ideal position to unravel, interpret and replicate this complexity. Building upon this success, Hassabis founded Isomorphic Labs in 2021, which aims to harness AI's potential in drug discovery.

It is becoming more and more expensive to create new drugs, often costing billions of dollars per drug. As more compute becomes available, along with better post-training, richer models have emerged. AI can represent the natural world. Isomorphic Labs is so named because the thinking is that there is a synergy between the virtual and the real. You can change the virtual model, take virtual molecules and design them to be more interactive with other molecules. Each step used to take months – it can now be done in seconds. Agents can be trained to do the work that scientists used to do. Molecule design can now be done in parallel by thousands of agents. This has direct ramifications for cancer and other diseases. This can be carried over into material science and other domains, where virtual research can have a very real impact on the real world of healthcare!

Building upon this idea of digital biology, the Arc Institute (2024), in collaboration with NVIDIA and researchers from Stanford University, UC Berkeley and UC San Francisco, unveiled Evo 2, the largest ever AI model in biology. Trained on over 9.3 trillion nucleotides from more than 128,000 genomes across all domains of life, Evo 2 is a deep map of genetic code. Patterns in gene sequences that would take researchers years to uncover can be identified quickly. Evo 2 can accurately identify disease-causing mutations in human genes and design new genomes by automating complex tasks, injecting productivity into medical research. This approach significantly increases productivity, not just in healthcare but also agriculture and biotechnology.

From research to real world

In his recent hard-hitting report on European competitiveness, Mario Draghi (2024), the former President of the European Central Bank, pinpointed a significant weakness, namely Europe's struggle to transform university research into commercial success. While Europe excels in producing high-quality academic research, it often fails to convert these innovations into marketable products and thriving businesses. This shortfall has led to

Europe lagging behind global counterparts, particularly the United States and China, in sectors poised to drive future growth, such as digital technologies and biotechnology.

Draghi attributed this gap to a fragmented research landscape, insufficient funding for groundbreaking innovations and regulatory frameworks that inadvertently stifle entrepreneurial ventures. He emphasized the need for a harmonized strategy that fosters collaboration between academic institutions and the private sector, alongside reforms to streamline the commercialization process. By addressing these challenges, Draghi contended, Europe could enhance its productivity and reclaim its position as a leader in global innovation.

AI has the power to bridge the journey from research ideas to real-world products, cutting through the usual bottlenecks and making innovation faster, smarter and more efficient. First, AI could sift through piles of research data, spotting practical, marketable applications in seconds. It could help identify where a breakthrough solves real-world problems or taps into unmet market needs, giving researchers a clear path forward. Researchers may lack these real-world and commercial skills, so it allows them to realize some of their hard-won success.

When it comes to productive prototyping, AI speeds things up dramatically. Instead of spending months testing ideas through trial and error, AI-powered design tools can simulate and refine prototypes virtually, saving time and money. In the development phase, AI can take on the heavy lifting by doing the coding, running simulations and analysing results in real time. This allows teams to focus on refining and developing their big ideas.

AI also shines in market research. It can analyse consumer trends, competitor activity and potential demand to predict whether an idea has real commercial potential. Want to know who your customers are and how to price your product? AI can help funnel you towards answers, giving you a data-driven roadmap for success.

The regulatory and compliance maze is another hurdle AI can help you negotiate. It can identify compliance requirements, automate documentation and flag potential red tape, saving time and avoiding costly delays. On the intellectual property (IP) front, AI can accelerate patent research by scanning databases, identifying overlaps and suggesting unique angles to secure your IP.

Once the product is ready to hit the market, AI can build go-to-market strategies. It can optimize pricing and help create messaging that lands with your audience. And to top it all, AI can help with investment, creating good presentations, predicting likely objections and providing strong answers.

Double-edged sword

Generative AI has had a powerful effect on research productivity, making it faster, easier and more efficient than ever before. But this acceleration comes at a cost. An overwhelming surge of papers, a rise in questionable quality and academic fraud hover over the research community. Researchers are even hiding prompts telling AI systems to positively review their papers. These problems challenge the integrity of the research process.

This rush of productivity cuts research time, allowing researchers to publish faster and at higher volume. The net result, however, could be a tidal wave of AI-assisted papers, making it nearly impossible to separate genuine research from the generated noise. Journal editors and research grant bodies find themselves drowning in submissions, and peer reviewers are struggling to keep up with the relentless influx of AI-generated submissions. The problem is not just volume but quality. Even worse, generative AI, in its early days, made it disturbingly easy to fabricate data and research. This productivity surge has led to peer reviewers now having to spend more time fact-checking, instead of evaluating genuine research.

Nevertheless, AI has shifted the way research is being done. The productivity gains are undeniable. Research happens faster, studies are published at an unprecedented rate and AI is unlocking discoveries that would have taken decades with traditional methods.

UNESCO (2021) estimated the number of researchers globally rose from about 4 million in 2000 to over 10 million by 2020, while research journals increased from roughly 10,000–20,000 to 20,000–50,000. China, in particular, has seen meteoric growth.

The sheer volume and pressure to publish may result in declining quality and pressure to fabricate data. It is also likely to lessen impact as it becomes more difficult to identify the best and most relevant research. Predatory academic journals are another problem. For a fee, they promise fast-track publication, often skipping standard peer-review standards. They prey on the pressure to publish, but can do real damage to the reputation of institutions and research.

Exponential productivity

Exponentiality in AI is happening across many dimensions. First, the algorithms and models are improving; they are not just faster and better, but also qualitatively different, with structural innovations such as memory, huge context windows, retrieval-augmentation, multimodality, deep research, reasoning models and agentic capability. Second, cluster sizes in data centres are in the low-million-chip range today, which is a huge increase over just a few years. Third, improvements in efficiency through architectural optimizations and software have led to substantial performance improvements every year. Fourth, AI also has a recursive element that accelerates exponentiality, for example recursive reinforcement learning, which pushes progress even faster.

The speed and scale of improvement has astonished most observers. Exponential progress is difficult for us to understand as we have evolved to deal with slow, linear growth. Plants, animals and humans grow slowly, the seasons develop slowly. If anything, we witness little or no growth, mostly more of the same. This makes us woefully ill prepared for what is coming, with orders of magnitude improvements in performance, reduction in prices, scalability and therefore productivity.

The future is a tall order, yet think about it we must, as AI is bringing it to us more quickly than we ever imagined. Few foresaw the shock arrival of generative AI in late 2022 with its intelligent dialogue, ability to create text, then images and high-quality video, along with reasoning, then astonishing abilities in maths, science and the ability to code. Even those working within AI were stunned by its capabilities as it progressed way faster that anyone imagined. Despite endless warnings about it plateauing, it soared, and still soars into a position that gives it more and more capabilities.

Ilya Sutskever (2023) made the profound observation that the single act of predicting the next token in an LLM, far from being a mere statistical trick, encapsulates the model's entire world-model: 'Predicting the next token well means that you understand the underlying reality that led to the creation of that token.' That one simple point of production, when a model predicts the next token, contains its whole world, giving it powers similar to our own brains.

This is an important insight, that the model brings all it has learnt about semantics, syntax, facts, reasoning, even human intentions and emotions to that single point of token prediction. It is as if billions of small roads all converged on that one moment in time. Sutskever claims, therefore, that the next-token prediction can surpass human performance.

Just as a model brings the entirety of the past, we must also think about what may happen in the future. As the future is everything, we need to focus on what is relevant to productivity. What things, that have yet to happen, are worth consideration in terms of productivity?

The future of AI productivity has some serious practical, political, even philosophical consequences. There are possible practical predictions around how productivity could increase by orders of magnitude if AI becomes recursively self-improving. It may even address some Manhattan-like projects around chip production, fusion and quantum computing, which may well see their timeframes significantly shortened. Political and economic considerations are also important, picking up on past theorizing and possible outcomes in an AI arms race that may have winners and losers. There are also bigger philosophical issues at hand to do with this species-changing technology.

Much like electricity, AI is a powerful, invisible force that destroys old models while building new ones, and this is happening at blistering speed. What makes AI different from traditional technological innovation is that it creates an abundance of intelligence, at almost zero cost. The net gains are not linear but exponential. Lin (2025) claims that an all-AI research loop can invent novel model architectures faster than humans, and uncovered 106 examples that were better than human baselines. That challenges and corrodes the very role of humans in economic growth, as it has a focus on massive productivity that can augment, replace, even eliminate and automate human roles and jobs. Self-driving vehicles, automated diagnosis and investigation of patients, and the elimination of coding all upend entire industries from the bottom up. The innovators may well become AI agents, or AGI, truly disruptive in some existing industries, making others superproductive and creating as yet unknown human enterprises. AI is an innovation that can increase productivity wherever it is used – not so much creative destruction as a process of creative acceleration and abundance.

Conclusion

AI is poised to be a transformative force in global productivity, but how quickly and profoundly it will reshape economies remains uncertain. Will it echo past technological revolutions like the steam engine and electricity, or will it surpass them entirely? Jack Wiseman and Duncan McClements (2024) argue that AI's impact on productivity could be unprecedented, particularly if it automates invention itself, a leap that could fundamentally alter how individuals, organizations and states approach productivity.

Historical breakthroughs like electricity and computers revolutionized productivity, but their effects unfolded over decades. For example, it took 40 years for electricity to overtake steam as the dominant source of power in the US and computers didn't drive significant productivity gains until the mid-1990s, decades after their initial adoption. AI, however, has the potential to accelerate this timeline and surpass the speed and impact of all previous technological revolutions.

Why? Because AI could automate not just repetitive tasks but the research and development processes that underpin innovation itself. AI systems are already capable of rudimentary research tasks and as compute power increases and AI techniques improve, their capabilities will expand. For organizations, this means faster problem solving, streamlined R&D and potentially massive cost savings.

More than this, AI has the capability of going on recursive autopilot to improve itself. If machines can invent as effectively as the best human researchers, progress could move at unprecedented speed, with these accelerated results used in the next round to do more research, even faster, in a recursive self-improvement loop.

Candidates for accelerated research include chip design and production, leading to accelerated robotics, along with robots manufacturing more chips and more robots. Advances in energy through Thorium and fusion are also more likely, as is quantum computing. Models and other AI techniques may even tackle fundamental physics, chemistry and biology, leading to yet unknown breakthroughs.

The consequences could be that existing economies with marginal or stagnant growth, due to low output per capita and labour taking a consistent share, are blown apart when output suddenly increases and labour is reduced through augmentation, automation and acceleration (Trammell and Korinek, 2023). As AI systems not only take over tasks but also enhance themselves and our capabilities, we may be on the cusp of a larger exponential breakthrough, with *autogenesis* – a leap where AI begins to generate, adapt and advance its own tools, knowledge and infrastructure, with minimal human input, fundamentally reshaping the productivity frontier. The compounding nature of these advances may unlock remarkable productivity growth across all sectors.

References

Arc Institute (2024) EVO-2: Accelerating discoveries through AI, https://arcinstitute.org/news/blog/evo2?utm_source=chatgpt.com (archived at https://perma.cc/D852-EMYS)

Bolaños, F, Salatino, A, Osborne, F and Motta, E (2024) Artificial intelligence for literature reviews: Opportunities and challenges, *Artificial Intelligence Review*, 57, 259

Chen, Y, Chen, X, Yu, Y and Li, J (2023) The emergence of economic rationality of GPT, *Proceedings of the National Academy of Sciences*, 120 (51)

Draghi, M (2024) The future of European competitiveness: A competitiveness strategy for Europe, European Commission, https://policycommons.net/artifacts/16410847/untitled/17295597/ (archived at https://perma.cc/3972-F6MA)

Gao, C A, Howard, F M, Markov, N S, Dyer, E C, Ramesh, S, Luo, Y and Pearson, A T (2023) Comparing scientific abstracts generated by ChatGPT to real abstracts with detectors and blinded human reviewers, *NPJ Digital Medicine*, 6 (1), 75

Gottweis, J, Singh, R, Xu, Z and Patel, A (2025) Towards an AI co-scientist, Google Cloud AI Research, Google Research, Google DeepMind, Houston Methodist, Sequoia, Fleming Initiative, and Imperial College London, Stanford University, https://arxiv.org/abs/2502.18864 (archived at https://perma.cc/9S5S-A832)

Gray, A (2024) ChatGPT 'contamination': Estimating the prevalence of LLMs in the scholarly literature, https://arxiv.org/abs/2403.16887 (archived at https://perma.cc/2WEL-XTTL)

Howard, F M, Li, A, Riffon, M F, Garrett-Mayer, E and Pearson, A T (2024) Characterizing the increase in artificial intelligence content detection in oncology scientific abstracts from 2021 to 2023, *JCO Clinical Cancer Informatics*, 8, e2400077

Liu, Y (2025) AlphaGo moment for model architecture discovery, https://arxiv.org/abs/2507.18074 (archived at https://perma.cc/MWV3-5K96)

Sikander, B, Baker, J J, Deveci, C D, Lund, L and Rosenberg, J (2023) ChatGPT-4 and human researchers are equal in writing scientific introduction sections: A blinded, randomized, non-inferiority controlled study, *Cureus*, 15 (11), e49019

Sutskever, I (2023) Why next-token prediction is enough for AGI, OpenAI. YouTube, https://www.youtube.com/watch?v=YEUclZdj_Sc&t=50s (archived at https://perma.cc/R4HM-QRJ7)

Trammell, P and Korinek, A (2023) Economic growth under transformative AI (No w31815), National Bureau of Economic Research, https://www.nber.org/papers/w31815 (archived at https://perma.cc/SDT5-PKGW)

UNESCO (2021) Science report: Statistics and resources, https://www.unesco.org/reports/science/2021/en/statistics (archived at https://perma.cc/V9ZJ-656C)

University of British Columbia (2024) An 'AI scientist' is inventing and running its own experiments, *Wired Magazine*, https://www.wired.com/story/ai-scientist-ubc-lab (archived at https://perma.cc/7LX8-ULMG)

Wiseman, J and McClements, D (2024) How much economic growth from AI should we expect, how soon? *Inference Magazine*, https://inferencemagazine.substack.com/p/how-much-economic-growth-from-ai (archived at https://perma.cc/ML6X-4L2V)

Further reading

Google Research (2024) Accelerating scientific breakthroughs with an AI co-scientist, https://research.google/blog/accelerating-scientific-breakthroughs-with-an-ai-co-scientist/ (archived at https://perma.cc/9ZNW-9NMF)

Isomorphic Labs (2024) AI-driven scientific breakthroughs, www.isomorphiclabs.com (archived at https://perma.cc/YMC2-2A3X)

12

Physical AI (surge)

In the physical dimension, waves of breakthrough innovation have made AI walk, run, talk, drive, fly and swim. With human cognition embodied in multifarious forms of physical robots, more productivity issues get solved at an accelerating pace.

Physical AI is almost always a pure productivity play. It works or not, does the job or not, sells or not. There is nowhere to hide, as it is in the open, obvious and examinable, not invisible. We see the results in the real world and the productivity gains are already being realized in manufacturing, vehicles, robots and drones, and on earth, sea and sky.

The combination of smart AI and physical objects suggests that physical AI products could be the biggest products in history. We are likely to end up with more robots than humans. But before getting carried away with sci-fi levels of speculation, it is worth considering how the application of AI has already had an impact on physical productivity within existing organizations.

To achieve wider, universal productivity, AI has to be embodied, with memories, a sense of physical causality across time, along with spatial awareness and real-world abilities. AI has to have these physical competences or at least simulate them. It is what will allow these AIs to be comfortable and useful, to humans, in the real world.

Productivity in the physical world

Whatever your view of Elon Musk as a person, he is undoubtedly one of the most successful business people of the 21st century. He has consistently outpaced the competition, disrupting industries as diverse as payments, electric vehicles, robotics, satellite communications, tunnelling, brain–computer interfaces, social media and space. Today, he leads a number of innovative billion-dollar companies, each of which has redefined its sector, and he has done this by employing a process that pushes him to innovate and execute faster and better than the competition. It is a useful process when considering AI, as it puts the spotlight on productivity.

He eschews what many call best practice, has little time for endless meetings or reviewing written reports. He does the opposite, with his unremitting effort on solving problems and unblocking bottlenecks. Why? These block innovation and productivity. Rather than adopt best practices as defined by business schools, such as classic management, attention to process and avoiding details, he throws himself into the productivity fray, constantly probing and seeking out ways to improve processes and product.

Occam's Razor

At SpaceX, Musk, who frequently mentions Occam's Razor, has applied it to simplify and optimize rocket development to reduce costs; he also applies the principle in all of his businesses. His obsessive focus on simplicity and efficiency makes him a modern Occam, cutting away unnecessary complexity to achieve the most effective and productive solution.

Reusable rockets, simpler manufacturing and rockets that are multipurpose have all streamlined the design and business of rocketry. Tesla focuses on making electric vehicles cheaper and more efficient through simpler, better design, downloadable software to the entire fleet and a massive pressing machine (the Gigapress). It has now extended the application of AI into robot production. The Boring Company simplifies transportation by efficiently boring underground tunnels that take fast-driving cars, as a cheaper, faster alternative to traditional large-scale infrastructure projects. Neuralink, a brain–computer interface company, with its simple, scalable neural implants, solves complex neurological issues like paralysis, and now blindness, by plugging the solution directly into the brain's natural processes. AI is used extensively across all of these physical innovations.

Musk's frequent mention of Occam's Razor, particularly when discussing how to solve complex problems, shows that, for him, the simplest solution is often the best, the minimum number of entities to reach your given goal. This is part of his first-principles thinking, where you break problems down to their fundamental truths and build up from there. It is the key to understanding when and how AI should be applied to productivity problems.

When examining a process, procedure, project or product, ask: What is the simplest way to achieve the goal? Choose the route, process or product that is straightforward, requires fewer assumptions and, above all, eliminates or automates unnecessary steps. With Occam's Razor, represented by this equation, you can keep focused on productivity.

$$\text{Productivity} = \frac{\text{Output}}{\text{Time} + \text{Resources} + \text{Complexity}}$$

You can see that reductions in 'Time', by automating any process, or in 'Resources', such as the quantity of text or physical resources used in a process, and especially in 'Complexity' come together through Occam's Razor to result in increased productivity. Complexity is the element that most often evades capture, but often turns out to be the real culprit in low productivity.

Walter Isaacson's (2023) biography of Elon Musk is an excellent introduction, even masterclass, in the many ways productivity can be increased across radically different sectors: automotive, construction, space, social media and healthcare. It shows, using real examples, how AI can be leveraged across all of these sectors to increase productivity.

Increasing productivity has been the hallmark of Musk's sustained efforts to build businesses and he is unique in his interest and application of AI, having been captivated by it as a teenager when reading the sci-fi author Robert Heinlein. He was among the first to see the huge potential of AI, founding OpenAI in 2014 and eventually his own AI company, xAI, announced on July 12, 2023. That date was a classic Musk joke, referring to Douglas Adams' *The Hitchhiker's Guide to the Galaxy*, as 7 + 12 + 23 equals 42. He makes the point that this is in line with the company's mission 'to understand the universe'.

AI is used to increase productivity across all of Musk's businesses. The AI developed for self-driving Teslas is being used in SpaceX rocketry, in The Boring Company for tunnelling, in Optimus robots and in Neuralink, with their Dojo supercomputer pulling all of this together.

Musk also, controversially, has experience in applying AI to productivity in personnel and organizational spend, most notably in X and the government of the world's largest economy, the US. All of this amounts to one of the greatest deliberate pushes on productivity the world has ever seen, across several major companies in multiple sectors and the government of a superpower.

AI is not his only productivity hack. He is also known for merging entire departments. In SpaceX he moved the 75 desks of the engineering team to be next to the rocket-engine production lines. In Tesla, SpaceX and Twitter, the design teams were merged with product managers (Isaacson, 2023, p. 390). He, like Steve Jobs before him, does not see design as the cosmetic treatment of a product but as fundamental to the product.

At a strategic level, increasing productivity through AI requires a mindset that is bold and transformative. This is not just about injecting AI into existing processes – it is about completely rethinking how work gets done, how value is created and how AI and employees can work together in powerful new ways. One needs to seek out fundamental increases in productivity by redefining what that even means, sometimes applying dramatic measures, then taking decisive action to get it done. Neither does it stop there. He sees this as intrinsic to how one runs organizations, relentlessly seeking out inefficiencies, increasingly using AI.

Five-step algorithm

Musk often invokes his productivity 'algorithm' as encapsulating the lessons he has learnt from building highly efficient businesses in many sectors (Isaacson, 2023, p. 284). He calls it an 'algorithm' as it is a heuristic that can be applied to solve productivity issues universally, across a number of domains. His use of the word shows thinking rooted in AI. It is not a model, method or technique; it is an algorithm, one that is simple but with broad and deep reach. The five steps:

Step 1: Question every requirement

Step 2: Delete any part or process you can

Step 3: Optimize and simplify

Step 4: Accelerate cycle time

Step 5: Automate where possible

Step 1: Question every requirement

Start with first-principles thinking, right down to physics. Strip every process down to its fundamentals and ask whether you even need to be doing this at all. Instead of tweaking old ways of working, challenge assumptions and uncover areas where AI can drive the biggest change. Think about creating value, not just saving time. Sure, AI can make things faster and cheaper, but its real power lies in automation and unlocking new possibilities.

Rather than accept that rockets have to be bought, launched and discarded, Musk worked obsessively towards designing his own engines and reusable rockets, reducing weight to a minimum with lighter materials, simpler welds and fewer parts (Isaacson, 2023, p. 226).

Catching reusable booster rockets and fairings in mid-air seems like a lot of trouble. Why do this? Well, physics tells us that when rockets are caught in mid-air the components suffer less damage from impact, so minimal repairs and inspections are required before the rocket is ready for the next launch. SpaceX therefore reduced the time between booster flights to as little as a few weeks, compared to traditional single-use rockets that took months to rebuild or replace.

Rocket fairings, the protective shell around payloads, are hugely expensive, at up to $6 million a pair. Mid-air recovery prevents them from being lost or damaged in the ocean, so they can be reused many times. This reduces the cost per launch and increases the number of launches SpaceX can achieve. Each Falcon booster, the bottom of the rocket with the engines that launches the rocket off the ground and separates to return to earth, lands upright so it can also be reused. These are even more expensive, at around $62 million. Reusing them significantly lowers launch costs and increases the frequency of affordable launches.

SpaceX can launch more rockets a month, using bigger rockets, with bigger payloads, which would be impossible without reusability, where AI plays an important role. This all helps SpaceX meet the rising demand for satellite deployment, commercial space missions and government contracts.

In typical Musk fashion, The Boring Company thrives on productivity and efficiency. He went back to first principles and simplified the whole process by custom-building a tunnel boring machine, named Prufrock, which aims to be faster and cheaper than the competition. Prufrock comes from T.S. Eliot's 'The Love Song of J. Alfred Prufrock' (2010), a poem about hesitation and complexity. Prufrock is boring and waffles endlessly, while Musk's Prufrock is fast and efficient, a cheeky reference to transforming the traditionally slow and complicated world of tunnel boring into something fast and simple.

We saw this form of fundamental innovation when Amazon questioned the need for physical bookshops and stores and revolutionized retail. Jeff Bezos challenged the traditional model to focus entirely on e-commerce to deliver products directly to your door. He questioned how retail works and eliminated the need for expensive real estate, with innovations like one-click ordering, Amazon Prime and same-day delivery. AI operates in Amazon at a fundamental level, making it an AI company that now sells its AI expertise, applying it to both the psychology of buying as well as the physicality of supply chains, logistics and delivery.

Hotels are physical buildings and Airbnb challenged the traditional hotel model when they questioned why travellers needed hotel accommodation. Tapping into unused private properties, they created a massive, global network of short-term rentals. Uber questioned the need for traditional taxi infrastructure, spotting that they need not own the cars, as drivers could use their own. The next disruption is AI-driven self-driving robotaxis, with no drivers, an innovation with real consequences on GDP (ARK Invest, 2023).

Step 2: Delete any part or process you can

True to Occam's Razor, if a step is not absolutely critical to achieving the desired outcome, it should be removed. Eliminate anything that does not add value. Instead of constantly adding layers, processes or components, focus on reduction. This mindset not only increases productivity but focuses resources on what truly matters.

Sitting beneath a Tesla on the production line, Musk was staring at the underbelly of a car, then asked why there were six bolts. The explanation was that it made the car stable in a crash. Musk pondered the problem a while, then having worked out all of the tolerances in his head, explained that the crash load would come through a separate rail. The number of bolts was reduced (Isaacson, 2023, p. 279).

With AI, the physical is intimately entwined with the psychological and there are few better examples of this than Neuralink. AI is at the heart of Neuralink's brain–machine interface, accelerating data analysis and device design. It decodes brain signals, processing neural data at high speed, reducing the time needed for experiments and patients. AI-assisted design tools have also sped up iterative development of the devices planted in the brain by simulating how they interact with neural tissue. His drive for simplification and productivity made him push his engineers to combine four separate chips, each with 1,000 threads, implanted in different points around the skull, into a single chip, with no wires, no connector and no router. They thought it was impossible but a few weeks later had a single chip to show him (Isaacson, 2023, p. 402).

Then there is the cost-cutting and efficiency, reducing operating costs significantly by renegotiating vendor contracts and shutting down underutilized data centres. On finding that a data centre would take months to close down, Musk took the idea of productivity literally, flew to the Sacramento data centre and literally cut the main cable himself (*New York Times*, 2022).

There is also Musk's flattening of organizational hierarchies by removing layers of middle management. This brought engineers and decision-makers closer together, something he believes is necessary in tech and manufacturing companies. Shifting the focus more towards core engineering and product development, rather than other managerial activity, leads to faster iteration and problem solving. The advantages include less communication overhead, more focus on the product and more efficient workflow.

The reduction in bureaucracy, in particular, is a feature of his businesses. All of this leads to more autonomy, alongside a more aggressive focus on productivity and the product. This is Occam's Razor at work, stripping back to the minimum number of entities to reach your clearly defined goal.

This is not for the faint-hearted, as there are also risks. The organization and product can suffer from reputation damage and attrition on user numbers. There were drops in ad revenues, legal challenges from sacked employees and moderation controversies in X, so it remains to be seen whether this culture is sustainable and scalable. Musk also exhibits behaviours that show an insensitivity to people. One can bully, deride and treat employees with contempt in the ruthless pursuit of productivity, but that does not make it right.

Step 3: Simplify and optimize

The Starlink user terminal, called 'Dishy', was supposed to be cheap and simple. When early prototypes turned out to be clunky and expensive, Musk locked himself in the design room with his team of engineers and insisted that they cut the cost. He understood that this was the key to increasing sales, so scrapped all unnecessary components and added AI-automated self-alignment for easier installation. After several weeks, Dishy appeared, as a sleek, self-adjusting device, about the size of a pizza box, that users could set up in five minutes.

But it was the use of AI in the design and delivery of the Starlink network that gave it huge efficiency gains, first through simulating and optimizing components, then factory automation with robots in the mass production of thousands of satellites. The software layer was also AI-driven with optimized data routing, network management, latency reduction, even autonomous collision avoidance software, so they could be launched in batches.

In every Musk business the relentless application of Occam's Razor led to simplification and optimization, often using AI. AI is primarily an optimizing technology, in ways no human can match on speed and scale. Its ability to analyse even huge datasets, optimize resources, automate processes, even build optimizing coded tools makes it the beating heart of productivity, even in the physical world.

Step 4: Accelerate cycle time

To reduce the cycle time in The Boring Company, Musk focused on smaller diameter tunnels and simplified the tunnelling machine. The key was to reduce human effort, for example excavating while installing tunnel segments at the same time, to eliminate downtime and dramatically improve productivity. This is all about a simple metric: reducing the cost of tunnelling per mile.

AI is integral to their tunnel design and to boring, through excavation planning and machinery control to improve productivity. AI systems analyse geological data and adjust boring machine operations in real time for faster, safer tunnelling. AI also predicts and reduces equipment wear and tear, minimizing maintenance interruptions. This AI optimization has helped The Boring Company increase tunnelling speed compared to traditional methods, significantly increasing productivity by reducing project timelines and costs.

Step 5: Automate

Neuralink's goal to build a brain–machine interface faced a critical bottleneck. Human surgeons are expensive, slow and prone to error. To solve this problem, Musk (2019) turned to AI and robotics. He worked with AI experts to create a surgical robot capable of implanting electrodes with near-perfect precision. With this robot surgeon, Neuralink reduced surgery time by 70 per cent and achieved higher accuracy than any human. He simply automated human surgery.

Robots dominate and automate many of the physical tasks in Tesla assembly lines, handling repetitive and labour-intensive tasks with precision. Tesla also simplified car maintenance by introducing over-the-air software updates, reducing the need for in-person service visits and making performance optimizations seamless for drivers.

Tesla's Cybercabs took automation even further, with self-driving taxis (no steering wheel) in their fully autonomous fleet from day one. The self-driving software applies AI to eliminate drivers, but that is not all. What makes the Cybercab even more productive, undercutting the competition, is that Tesla owns the whole value chain, from building the Cybercabs through to a powerful AI capability and network with software control and updates, in a fully electric fleet, as well as the charging stations. They see the vehicles as peripherals, much like a printer, hanging off the network, optimally operated, sensitive to large events such as sports and concerts, making sure that cars are in the vicinity. Indeed, the whole network is optimized to reducing the hail time for the customer.

The robotaxi market is huge, based on one huge step change in productivity, the self-driving vehicle. This should, more correctly, be named the autonomous taxi platform. The productivity gains come through not having a driver and the intelligent optimizing of the robotaxis within the network, to respond faster to customers. This is not a cab but an intelligent network.

Productivity hacks

These five steps in the algorithm are not the only productivity hacks Musk employs. Many of these are contrary to what standard leadership courses recommend. This may say more about outdated leadership courses than about Musk. He insists on employees having hands-on experience, not just sitting in separate departments, offices or working from home. Drive and urgency are encouraged and admired in everything from recruitment to judgements on performance. He likes practical troubleshooters and problem solvers, not cogs in the organizational machine.

Self-driving cars

At dinner in Berlin, I was lucky enough to meet Kyle Bowen, Deputy CIO at Arizona State University. He lives in Phoenix and told me that Waymo cabs have really taken off. Phoenix is flat with a grid design, so perfect for self-driving cabs. I have never driven a car in my life, more happenstance than moral stance, so there was no real transition for me, but it took Kyle just 10 minutes on his first trip to get used to the idea. Sometimes there is a little frustration at it going too slow, sticking to speed limits and so on, but it has been 100 per cent reliable, and a third cheaper than the competition. Kyle often works on the way to the airport or en route to other locations across Phoenix. This is interesting – a startlingly innovative form of technology becomes normal, ordinary, even mundane. That, as Donald Norman reminded us, is the sign of meeting a need with a superb design and solution.

The self-driving cab gives everyone that first-class experience of a car turning up at their door and another waiting at the other end to take them to their destination, with no stress – a light, quiet, great sound system and ventilation with heated seats, no idle chat with the driver or being ripped off, just all that productive time.

Kyle told me that ASU has been doing podcasts from Waymos in Phoenix. Self-driving podcasts have become a thing! This is a great example of the unexpected consequences of this self-driving technology. You have more time to do what you want, where you want. This feels like more than just a shift in a market or technology. It feels like a fundamental shift, where automation, not human-in-the-loop technology, but technology itself, is part of a new epoch, something fundamental happening around efficiency and productivity.

Self-driving cars came from DARPA, with their $1 million reward for a 100-mile obstacle course. Universities competed with two winners, one from Stanford, the other MIT, whose leaders went on to form Waymo and Cruz. Cruz was bought by GM in 2018 and you can see why, as the research and implementation will lead to self-driving GM cars, which they sell. Waymo simply sells the add-on hardware and software which they install in most cars. Musk also took note and started Tesla, to own the whole value chain.

Just as the elevator changed the places where we live and work, in tall buildings, we will have more time on our hands in self-driving vehicles. Trust is the key issue here. Like the early observers of the railroad, who thought the speed of the train would result in instantaneous death, or when the car was introduced to our roads with a man up front holding a lamp, we bring past fears to future solutions. Some low probability, rare accidents, along with human psychology, have held things back, even though it is still way safer than normal driving, but the direction of travel, so to speak, is certain. Self-driving taxis, buses and cars will become the norm, and at some point almost universal, like the self-driving elevator.

Autonomous vehicles cascade productivity in several ways. The time spent commuting can be productive, as you can get work done, even rest, have less stress and fatigue, better health and a massive reduction in your risk of dying! Commuting becomes something completely different, as more flexible work arrangements are possible and people can live farther from work if commuting time becomes productive work time. When accidents go down, less time is lost due to traffic jams, less time is wasted on dealing with insurance or legal matters and less time is spent dealing with injuries and time off work due to those injuries. As we have smoother traffic flow, there is less time spent on the move, thus increasing punctuality and productivity.

Think also about those who cannot drive due to disabilities. Everyone can be mobile, even those who cannot drive, including the elderly, blind and physically disabled. They can also lead more productive lives. Those who find it difficult to find employment suddenly become employable; the economically inactive become active, along with better access to education, healthcare and participation in society. One outcome could be more social contact, not with transactional drivers but with each other, as more people can get to social events with ease, at a much lower cost.

Other consequential effects include parking and land use. As autonomous vehicles can be on the move 24/7, drop off passengers and park themselves, it reduces the need for parking spaces and would lead to better land use, especially in cities, as it frees up space for additional housing and commerce. Autonomous trucks and delivery vehicles can operate continuously without breaks, reducing delivery times and costs. AI-optimized routes in real time reduce fuel consumption, both fossil and electric, and time spent on the road, increasing the productivity of transportation. This cascades into faster restocking, reduced warehousing needs and quicker delivery times for businesses. Optimized driving patterns by autonomous vehicles could also lead to reduced fuel consumption, with lower emissions, so cleaner air and less time off with respiratory diseases.

New business models are bound to emerge, with shared rather than owned vehicles to increase the efficiency of vehicle use and reduce the cost of mobility, also impacting how people spend their time and money.

All of this could add up to a potentially astonishing rise in productivity. Some see this as one of the most productive innovations of all time, raising global GDP by as much as 20 per cent over the next decade.

Over a million people will die horrible deaths this year in car accidents, with many more suffering serious, life-changing injuries. Stopping this carnage is reason enough for self-driving cars. Saving productive people is a humane benefit, but the other gain is in our most valuable commodity – time.

The average American will drive a car for 4.3 years, simply staring at the road. In that time, they cover a lifetime driving distance of nearly 1.3 million km (Sattar et al, 2016). Self-driving cars, first hybrids, then fully autonomous cabs like the Cybercab, Cruz and Waymo, allow you to do other things while on predictable, even long journeys. They free up vast amounts of cognitive time for people who spend many long hours on the road. Driving puts you in the flow of traffic, not the flow of work and life, where you can jam with other people, not in traffic.

We are in that halfway house where we have one technology, satnav in cars, which serves the driver at present but will serve the car itself in the future. The foundational technologies of the internet, satellite connectivity, GPS and AI will change the way we travel forever.

Every major car company in the world knows that this is coming and it is reshaping the entire sector, as an ascendant China hits Germany and the US hard. Interestingly, it was DARPA, Tesla, Google and other tech companies that have provided the AI intelligence to make this happen, not the incumbent automotive manufacturers.

Robots

Humanoid robots have long been clumsy and faltering in both movement and speech. But they have been improving rapidly with AI. I have shared the stage with many and seen them fall over, respond to questions with silence and even get carried off like junk. Then, suddenly, alongside the rise of generative AI, things got very good, very real, very quickly.

We know that manufacturing costs drop dramatically with scale and if production of humanoid robots increases massively, costs will drop to an affordable consumer price. This happened in the car market, where mass manufacturing quickly led to pricing that matched mass consumer demand. As robots are less material-intensive than cars, costs could drop even quicker.

The operating and maintenance costs of robots will be much cheaper than cars but impact on productivity is their primary benefit. At low cost, demand would be huge, including for domestic chores and in industries like construction, manufacturing, mining, agriculture and healthcare. There could, eventually, be more robots than people.

For this to be true, scaling production would be needed. We have a precedent, as during the Second World War car manufacturers pivoted to building planes and tanks in record time. And with almost perfect timing, as robotaxis hit the market, any slack in automotive manufacturing could be taken up by robots. Add the recursive effort of robots building robot factories, then building themselves 24/7, and we have exponential growth. And if the robots can handle human-level physical tasks, demand and production could scale to huge numbers within a few years. It is a vision that self-propels itself into massively increasing physical productivity.

When every new robot joins the production pool, productivity follows the classic doubling curve of 2^n, so output scales not linearly but exponentially, limited only by materials, energy and factory space, not human labour. Take a single fully automated dark factory where one industrial robot can assemble a finished copy of itself, realistically every 30 days. At the end of the first month, you have two robots; each now builds another in the next 30 days, giving four by the second month; in one year it has reached 4,096. Keep production constant and, after two years, you pass 16.8 million!

This would clearly change the whole physical landscape, turning science fiction into science fact. We would, for the first time in the history of our species, be sharing our world with a population of beings who are similar to us. We will live among them and they will live among us.

Robot shapes

You might think that robots designed for productivity would look and be shaped like us. But there is no 'one-size-fits-all' design, and the actual shape and size of a robot depends on what it is designed to do, where it has to operate and how it interacts with humans, the physical world or other systems. Functionality decides form and a focus on productivity would lead to many forms, with many types of functionality, in many contexts. Robots will come in all shapes and sizes.

Humanoid robots are shaped like humans for a good reason. The world has been designed around us, to serve our needs. Our houses, stairs, street sizes, vehicle sizes, packages, tools, books, televisions, computers and smartphones have all been designed to fit our body shapes. The humanoid robot simply steps into our shoes and things work for both them and us. No need for massive changes in the existing infrastructure.

But copying an evolved body is neither easy, nor always desirable. Bipedal, long-spined beings designed to give birth, with limited strength and precision, tunnel vision, limited hearing and poor balance, are not always appropriate. More specialized designs are often preferable.

Robot productivity

Productivity does not come from what a robot looks like – it comes from how well it performs within its environment. The most productive robots are those that are the most efficient. Aesthetics designed to fit our expectations would be desirable, but form following function is essential. Design has to be optimized for function, so every part of a robot's design, from its height, width, weight to the way it moves, defines its productivity.

Humanoid or anthropomorphic robots are obviously good for fitting into human environments. But for tight spaces or focused tasks, more compact designs, even tiny robots can be more useful and productive, like small drones or surgical robots operating on and within the body. When we need speed and distance, wheeled or tracked robots can whizz around hospitals, factories, fields or streets, without heads, arms and legs. They can be used in agriculture to pick fruit and crops. Heavy lifting is entirely different, needing size and power. They can already take out and reload their own batteries. There is even a need, in complex, dynamic systems, for adaptable swarms of robots.

It was not bipedal or quadrupedal robots that led the charge. The realization that AI would bring productivity to the world in ways we could barely imagine came not through humanoid robots but free-as-a-bird drones and self-driving cars. It was not on land but in the air that AI had an immediate impact. As the Ukraine war evolved almost in parallel with the advancement in generative AI, intelligent drones were deployed on the battlefield to turn it into the first drone war. From reconnaissance to loitering weaponry, they grew in significance, both sides adopting and adapting as the war progressed. It also changed the way films were shot, as drone shots became common.

Aquatic robots are already with us. There are a lot of swimming pools in the world and aquatic robots are now available to clean pools, their waterlines, sides and bottoms, as well as surfaces. Conservation robots, shaped like turtles, can swim to test water quality, monitor pollution and gather data on biodiversity, with data transmission. They can come ashore, swim, sink and surface when the power runs low to recharge using solar power (Clean the Sky, 2024).

Animal robots, such as dogs, cats or birds, could be used to monitor wildlife but also act as companions. These have been available for some time for therapy or to combat loneliness.

We are used to seeing robots as being like us, as singular beings, but swarm robots may have hive minds, operating within blood vessels or tissues or repairing and maintaining complex structures and systems. We can even imagine robots that are camouflaged to become invisible, so they do not disturb our environments. Robots may even replicate and grow into specific environments, with natural processes within their growth systems, blurring the distinction between organic and inorganic.

This is uncharted territory, where new forms and functions will emerge, being and doing things we never imagined. Embodied AI gives machines intelligence to do things we never thought possible. They may ripple out into the world, making everything more productive, not just replacing human labour but enhancing our environment and lives.

Space

Space is the new productivity frontier. We have sent several robots to Mars and the plan is to send a person within a few years. Musk's goal is to make us a truly interplanetary species, first to avoid the possibility that we might suffer extinction on our home planet but also to see ourselves as being more that what we were, and currently are, as a species.

AI is extending our bodies and minds through physical and psychological augmentation. It could also help us solve our most intractable problems and take us to places we have never been before, psychological and physical. We have become more productive on earth by augmenting and extending our minds but also in our design and building of rockets, along with innovations of reusability, control and relevance to productivity on earth. Remarkable advances have taken place in terms of size, deliverable payloads and reusability. This has already delivered a feedback loop through Starlink, which can deliver productive AI to anywhere on inhabited earth, with no blind spots, but much lies beyond.

It took only 66 years from the first powered flight to landing on the moon; seven years later we landed a robot on Mars; a year later, in 1977, Voyager 1 and 2 went out into boundless space. It has proven to be an incredibly productive effort, sending back data for nearly 50 years, and still communicating back to us, sending scientific data, although their plutonium heat sources are now struggling to protect them from the cold, dark universe. They are now out of our solar system, out further than any other human-made object.

We, as a species, literally sent out long-playing records on both Voyagers, each with a hole in the middle to put on a turntable, to contact other 'intelligent species'! These Golden Records were supposed to reflect us as a species with images of human anatomy, diagrams of DNA and our solar system, along with signs of our productivity, the sounds of tools and trains, images of buildings, transport and industry. Music from many cultures, along with photographs of people at work and leisure, accompanied greetings in 55 languages.

The famous image of a naked man and woman had a man waving and the woman passively portraying a 'Don't worry dear, I've got this' vibe. That was controversial, even at the time. What is worse, at the last minute, they censored out her genitals while keeping his intact! The second record, on Voyager 2, had her waving and him passive, a sort of joke. Hard to imagine alien species suddenly 'getting it' and falling about laughing. The story is told brilliantly in Jonathon Scott's *The Vinyl Frontier* (2019).

It is easy to mock but look how far we came to reach that point and how far we've come since. It now seems inevitable that humans will get to Mars, and AI will play a significant role in preparing it for us with robots, then delivering us to the red planet. We hope it will also solve some of our problems here on our own planet.

In space, Starlink and other satellite services are already delivering AI to remote rural areas around the globe with low latency. This promises to deliver AI productivity to economies that have found it difficult to compete in the past, by delivering high-quality education, healthcare and commerce. Above all, it delivers high productivity.

Psychological meets physical

We touched upon Moravec's paradox in an earlier chapter, the idea that what we find easy – seeing, hearing, walking, coordinated movement and manual dexterity – AI finds hard. On the other hand, what AI finds easy – mathematics, analysing large datasets – humans find hard. Our evolved past has determined what we're good at: moving through a 3D world, walking, seeing, reacting, manual dexterity and dealing with other humans.

What has this got to do with physical productivity? Well, if AI combines the psychological with the physical, excelling at both, its productivity reach suddenly becomes enormous. It can automate cognitive tasks and white-collar work, also physical tasks and blue-collar work. The more nuanced both the cognitive and physical capabilities become, the more AI moves into the realm not just of factory, delivery and limited task robots, but also of construction, healthcare, car mechanics and surgeons. Unlike humans, AI and robots do not need to evolve; they can be designed, built quickly and learn quickly to become better.

The jagged frontier comes sharply into focus, as some of our human qualities in the real 3D world are not easy for robots to master, but it is only a matter of time before most of these problems are solved. Overcoming Moravec's paradox offers a way forward to maximize AI's transformative potential in the workforce. AI's performance in visual perception is becoming exemplary, as is its hearing and touch. On balance and movement, it matches humans. The trajectory is clear – it can theoretically, and eventually practically, tackle almost all work.

We tend to forget, that even with sub-par human abilities, an AI robot has endurance, can work 24/7, never gets tired, never sleeps or is emotionally upset, at very low cost. They outdo us on speed, strength and endurance and will outdo us on many other psychological and physical tasks in the future. We will also see remarkable physical progress at the molecular level. DeepMind's astonishing prediction of physical protein structures through AlphaFold has accelerated research by centuries.

We see Moravec's paradox resolve itself in autonomous driving. After we have learnt to drive, we find it effortless. Now, Tesla, BYD, Waymo and others have made amazing progress in overcoming these challenges, and autonomous cars also find driving effortless, but consistently so. They maintain focus, never get distracted or tired and maintain their high level of performance. AI-driven vehicles can also communicate with each other in real time, coordinating movements to reduce congestion and accidents. None of this is possible for human drivers. The only problems are edge cases and the psychology of being in a vehicle with no driver.

Another feature of AI application in the physical realm is reinforcement learning. This was used to train AI systems like AlphaGo and is common in robotics, built on reward systems. The AI receives positive feedback for good decisions and negative feedback for bad ones. This straightforward feedback loop has created systems that can master complex tasks like playing games, optimizing logistics, controlling autonomous vehicles, even predicting the 3D structure of physical proteins. It also has the advantage of not producing hallucinations, like LLMs. Hallucinations, interpreted as errors, have prevented the rapid advance of AI into the cognitive realm, although that problem seems to be diminishing to almost vanishing point, or at least is seen only in edge cases. With reinforcement learning this does not exist. It works or it does not.

Conclusion

AI's initial success in psychological and cognitive productivity is now expanding out into the physical world, on land, sea, air and into space. AI will take us to new frontiers, cognitively and physically, from the micro to macro, transforming everything from microscopic drug discovery and personalized medicine to planetary exploration. As algorithms evolve into agents, AI won't just think and predict; it will move, build, steer and explore, reshaping industries and our very concept of human capability. There are literally boundless possibilities for exponential productivity gains in every sphere of human activity and endeavour.

References

ARK Invest (2023) Autonomous taxis may have the most impact on GDP of any innovation in history, https://www.ark-invest.com/articles/analyst-research/autonomous-taxis-gdp-impact (archived at https://perma.cc/K29R-BRJX)

Clean the Sky (2024) Water testing turtle, https://www.cleanthesky.com/innovation/robot-turtle (archived at https://perma.cc/EN36-9KDD)

Eliot, T S (2010) *The Love Song of J Alfred Prufrock*, Harvard Vocarium Records, 13–17

Isaacson, W (2023) *Elon Musk*, Simon and Schuster

Musk, E (2019) An integrated brain-machine interface platform with thousands of channels, *Journal of Medical Internet Research*, 21 (10), e16194

New York Times (2022) What's gone at Twitter? A data center, janitors, some toilet paper, 29 December, https://www.nytimes.com/2022/12/29/technology/twitter-elon-musk.html (archived at https://perma.cc/2KYG-5C8U)

Sattar, S A, Kaur, M and Ijaz, M K (2016) Airborne infectious agents and other pollutants in automobiles for domestic use: Potential health impacts and approaches to risk mitigation, *Journal of Environmental and Public Health*, 2016 (1), 1548326

Scott, J (2019) *The Vinyl Frontier: The Story of NASA's Interstellar Mixtape*, Bloomsbury Publishing

PART THREE

Action

13

Policies and prompts

When ChatGPT hit its first million users in five days, it was a portent of things to come, a steady global spread, adopted not by organizations but ordinary users, at first outside of their organizations, then eventually, due to its breadth of domain, into organizations on the sly. Even at the level of many hundreds of millions of users and billions of uses, it remains primarily a personal practice. This is quite astonishing.

As Andrej Karpathy (2024) said, this is the first major technology to 'flip the script', from top-down to bottom-up adoption. Typically, writing, printing, steam, electricity, computers, the internet and smartphones have been invented at the top then descended down as infrastructure was built, over time, taking decades, even centuries, to get down to large numbers of users at the bottom. Generative AI did the reverse, being adopted at the level of the individual, at the bottom, spreading sideways until the whole world was talking to ChatGPT. Only now it is percolating upwards, as those people take it into their workplace.

One of the problems with measuring bottom-up productivity is the fact that it remains hidden, masked by the difficulties in discovering its use by individuals, especially when they use it on the sly. This can be true in education, research, writing text, coding and many other workplace tasks. A student writing an essay in half the time has no impact on the efficacy of a school or university. It remains hidden productivity, as it does not register with the organization, whose cost base remains the same. The micro does not translate readily into macro metrics.

At this personal level, productivity is action. Using AI to increase productivity does not mean trying to win abstract arguments, policies, endless documents or project plans. It requires a problem-solving mindset and a focus on trying things out to get things done. You get nowhere without trying the technology, which is easy, as much of it is free and simply requires you to ask it a question, any question.

Start by simply satisfying your curiosity. Assemble a few practical problems you have and give it a go. In speaking to generative AI, you will soon discover that it has a naïve, almost alien quality, where you have to provide more than you would a human. You will also discover that you can start to push it iteratively to do the things you want it to do, guiding it forward. You may then move on to explore its multimodality, speaking to it, getting it to translate and speak back to you in other languages. Images may come as a surprise as you create cartoons or artwork. Move on to creating an avatar of yourself, even a short video. Its data analysis is particularly good and therefore useful. Challenge it to do substantial tasks that require several different outputs or several different sub-tasks to get to your desired outcome.

The odd thing about this technology is that it is like speaking to a child who is getting older and smarter very quickly. Generative AI by age two had gone from a hit and miss response with hallucinations to a 90th percentile IQ assistant that could code, do advanced mathematics and has degrees in dozens of subjects. It is in doing it that you find out what it is capable of, as well as its limitations.

Policies and inaction

First, a word of warning. The first port of call when considering AI in an organization is often a 'policy', but AI is a sprawling, complex beast, sometimes way too big and varied to be crammed into a little policy box. Trying to discuss AI as one thing is like calling the internet a 'network'. It oversimplifies to the point of nonsense, especially when it comes to the slippery word 'intelligence'. The habit of seeing abstract concepts as 'one' thing misleads us into thinking it has significance, when it is really a loose umbrella term. This is why it is almost impossible to pin it down through 'policies' within institutions.

To focus on an AI policy in an institution is to focus on the theory not the practice. As with all manuals, few read it, fewer still care. Employees often see policies as generic or disconnected from their specific roles and tasks. If a policy does not match the challenges they face, why would they bother reading it?

Policies are rarely action-oriented, rarely precise and often too intangible to be practical; they tend to exaggerate the negatives, immobilizing people rather than encouraging experimentation and action. Policies in institutions are demanded and written by generalist administrative units, such as HR, with not enough domain knowledge of either the technology or its potential applications. This is why policies often show the ominous signs of being cut and pasted from elsewhere or seem irrelevant or unusable. Such policies rarely have any effect as they are de-anchored from actual technology, actual people and actual use.

Even worse, they can become thinly disguised efforts to put people off making the effort to really understand or use the technology. It gives sceptics, even neutral observers, permission to ignore its use, so teachers ignore pupil use, faculty student use and managers employee use.

When it comes to designing, developing and delivering AI solutions, you quickly find that the policies are either irrelevant or act as a hindrance. Their lack of practical relevance renders them largely redundant. Worse still, they make some stakeholders simply reject any real efforts to discuss, debate, implement or procure AI solutions. Too often, they are seen as long-winded and abstract, rather than practical tools for daily work. If it is not short, sharp and accessible, and few are, it is likely to be ignored. More policies just add to policy purgatory, that increasing motherlode of unread and unloved documentation that is at best ignored, at worse seen as mere bureaucracy.

If you do want a policy, make it come alive and make it more memorable. Policies should be clear, concise, easy to implement and focused on actual delivery. What is useful is precise guidance on the actual use in writing, assignments or data, with quick guides, job aids and checklists. Actual examples and case studies, covering the commonest issues, act as concrete guides to action. They also need to be living documents, regularly updated.

Productive prompts

Prompting is the wellspring of productivity. It remains a key skill, just as dialogue and asking the right questions remains a key skill in life. The corollary is that prompting can also be a rate-limiting step on the productive use of AI. Many remain at the level of single prompts, mimicking search.

Donald Norman said good technology should be invisible. The future of work will become more and more invisible as the hidden hand of AI transforms why, what and how we work (Norman, 1998). We adapted when online search, shopping, booking hotels, buying flights and banking became the new norms. New technology, essentially, took and hid agency from us. It became invisible as agency moved from visible human interaction to invisible delivery. We adapt when this is accepted as more convenient and have done so, once more, as AI and AI agents do our work for us. The same will be true of prompting. As the technology becomes more powerful, with memory, reasoning, accurate provenance and agentic AI, agency through prompting becomes the magician that makes much of the work, even prompting, disappear.

Prompt libraries and AI templates

Instead of leaving AI use to chance, pre-built prompt libraries and AI templates mean that employees get consistent, high-quality results every time. Need a contract reviewed? A report generated? A customer email drafted? With structured prompts, designed for specific tasks, AI becomes a powerful productivity tool rather than something used idiosyncratically by different employees. A more considered approach to prompting reduces misuse, minimizes inconsistencies and speeds up workflows and productivity. This pre-prompting is often a feature of custom systems where the pre-prompting is already there but invisible.

More success can come by being more fulsome in your prompts, especially when you need some standardizing of the use of AI in your organization. It is common to see a lack of thoughtful prompting – far too brief, offering no clear context, no indication of the expected outcome and format and certainly no examples to guide the AI. As a result, the responses are vague, unfocused and far less useful than they could have been with just a little more direction. Providing pre-built prompts and templates for critical tasks, such as contract reviews or report generation, can ensure consistency.

A good starting point is attitude. Think of AI as a something you need to grab the attention of with a compelling prompt, almost like a child. You must maintain its interest by giving it a full context. The more you describe your problem and needs, the better. Make it want to complete the task and take a specific action or actions. Use clear and direct language and do not be scared of being a bit long-winded and over-precise. Show it stuff, like examples and samples of expected output. Give it lots of guidance. Think of AI as a great listener, something that can take a lot of advice in one shot. Above all, iterate and see this as a dialogue. Reword and refine until you get what you want.

As the technology improves, larger context windows, better user memory and customized options allow AI services to know you and your preferences better, along with huge increases in efficacy in terms of the agency of the tools themselves. This means less need for expertise in prompting, although it still helps. You will find, quite simply, that more considered prompting will increase your personal productivity.

There are many well-known prompt engineering frameworks designed to guide the creation of effective prompts for large language models (LLMs), with useful acronyms such as CLEAR, THINK, RAILS, PAIR, CRISP, ROLE, GUIDE, DEEP, FORMAT, RACE, RTF, 5C, AIDA, SPEAR, SPARK, FABRIC, PASTEL, SOFT and PROMPT (Promptopia, 2024). Early prompting was certainly enhanced by using these simple schemas, which could act as aides-mémoires to shape your prompts. These frameworks provide structured approaches to crafting prompts to enhance the effectiveness of interactions with AI models. But there was much duplication across these lists of three to five ways to structure prompts, so here is a consolidated core list of the most essential elements across all of these frameworks, with duplicates removed and overlapping ideas merged into a unified structure.

Productive prompting

Remember, AI can read you prompts but cannot read your mind. Mastering the art of prompting can make a huge difference in AI-generated responses, through better structure, greater accuracy and more relevant outputs.

Instruction type	Detail
Role	Specify the role or character the AI should assume (act as a job interviewer, teacher).
Goal/purpose	Clearly define the goal of the prompt (summarize a paper or report).
Audience	Identify who the response is intended for (beginners, professionals, customers, students).
Context dump	Provide background information or situational context to set the stage for the task.
Pre-existing knowledge	Specify any pre-existing knowledge, data or assumptions the AI should consider.
Task/action	Describe the specific task or action the AI needs to perform (draft an email, data analysis, code).

(continued)

(Continued)

Instruction type	Detail
Instructions	Include explicit, clear, step-by-step guidance on action and how the AI should approach the task.
Breakdown	Break down complex tasks into manageable steps, especially in agentic tasks.
Examples	Show what a response should look like with illustrative examples of style, tone or output.
Details	Add specific requirements (focus on specific challenges or problems).
Structure/format	Define the response structure (bullet points, summary, article, essay) and length or depth.
Tone/style	Specify the tone or style of the output (formal, casual, persuasive).
Constraints/ parameters	Include any limitations or constraints (use no more than 200 words or focus on critical tasks).
Relevance	Ensure the task aligns with your goals and focuses only on necessary aspects of the problem.
Desired output	Explicitly state the type of output you want (steps, detailed explanation, summary).
Adaptability	Allow flexibility for creative approaches or unexpected but useful insights.
Optimization/ feedback	Encourage iterative refinement or suggest continuous improvement based on feedback.

Be clear, explicit and detailed. Do not assume the AI knows the full context of your task; it will try to be 'helpful' by filling in gaps with assumptions, which may be way off the mark. A little extra effort upfront in structuring your prompt will save time fixing incorrect responses later.

Provide examples of the output you expect. AI responds far better when you give concrete examples rather than relying solely on wordy instructions. This is especially useful for repeatable tasks, where showing an input–output example trains the model on what you actually want.

Give the AI a persona. Setting a clear role or expertise level improves the relevance and tone of responses. For example, rather than just saying 'Improve this text' you could say: 'You are an expert management consultant. Please critically review the draft below and suggest ways to make it more engaging for a lay person audience.' This frames the response exactly how you need it. You may even want to use multiple personas to simulate different expert perspectives, playing different roles in a team, with a summarizing team leader perspective.

Prompt the model to ask follow-up questions. If there is any missing information, AI can sometimes guess incorrectly. A simple addition such as 'If you need more details to provide the best answer, please ask before responding' pushes it towards higher accuracy and reduces back-and-forth corrections.

Another useful tactic is to *save and share* prompts in your organization. This is especially useful in prompts that need to perform in domain-specific fields such as healthcare, finance or marketing. Rather than eliminating experts in their fields, the best prompters are often subject matter experts who know the language of their domain and can use this to specify what they need and in what format. A graphic artist, for example, is far more likely to know the language of graphic styles and graphic formats than the lay person, and therefore more likely to produce better outputs.

The problem with prompting is that it puts the onus on the user to drive progress and productivity. We don't know what we don't know, so you get the Dunning-Kruger effect, where people lack knowledge or skills in a certain area and also lack the ability to recognize their own limitations. Access to AI can reduce the overconfidence of incompetent people but it can also reinforce that confidence, as they prompt to confirm their beliefs and within their chosen lines of inquiry. AI can help solve this problem as memory, sometimes called infinite memory, and along with agentic AI can use background data, dynamic tracking of your needs and your actual day-by-day behaviours to get to know you in such a way that you do not have to construct huge prompts.

Experts-in-the-loop

Prompting requires two levels of expertise: first, the skills in prompting to get the best out of the exchange; second, domain expertise to get the best in terms of the context and subject. The first requires some expertise on prompting as a human-in-the-loop; the second is as an expert-in-the-loop to bring a deep knowledge not only of the subject matter, but also of the language of a domain.

A graphic artist will know the language of resolution, aspect ratios and style to be able to better prompt the generation of an image. A researcher will know what hypothesis they are researching, along with the methods and language of research, statistics and data, to better prompt their research process and tasks.

Really skilled prompters, often those with deep knowledge of how the models and fine-tuning work, can often build very sophisticated prompts that consistently shape the whole process. With larger context windows, prompts can be very large, taking prompting more into briefing. With retrieval-augmented generation (RAG) and other techniques, prompting is mediated by accessing custom knowledge as part of the prompting process, modifying the request. Prompting then becomes not only a science but an art.

Prompting and agents

As agentic AI becomes the norm, prompting is set to evolve from simple commands into more high-end, dynamic conversations with goal-driven AI agents that actively anticipate your needs, adapt to new contexts and, where useful, take the initiative. Prompts are quite specific requests or instructions but agentic AI prompts will be more like specifications for collaborative problem solving.

You will need to provide high-level goals like, 'Help me boost productivity across the organization', then details of processes, procedures and areas for likely productivity gains; your AI agent will handle the separate tasks. This is not about a series of prompts but orchestrating tasks that get to your goal, such as the analysis of your data, exploration of and comparison of multiple strategies. It may even ask, or prompt, you the right questions to refine its actions.

Agentic AI thrives on context and background detail, which it could also seek out and find. It deals with longer-term objectives and remembers past interactions as it proceeds, to build on and refine its actions. Agents do not just react; they anticipate, adapt and, importantly, execute separate tasks. If it is in doubt or unclear, it will ask for clarification, and when choices are faced, give you the chance to make key decisions. This is genuine dialogue between you and AI as your agents or team of agents.

Ultimately, prompting will shift from task-specific requests to a much more collaborative process where AI suggests, solves and learns as you proceed. Rather than doing everything for yourself, you will become more of an approver, validator or editor who signs off each stage of a multiple-task project. Prompting in that sense becomes more and less important at the same time.

Multimodal interaction will also change how we prompt. You will combine spoken instructions, text and visual inputs, like uploaded charts and videos. The aim is to avoid using and switching many applications or formats but to leave it to agents to use the most appropriate tools. AI becomes your command centre for such productivity.

Agentic workflow

Agents are one thing, but the real interest for productivity gains lies in agentic workflows. We know that much current knowledge work is inefficient, with workers spending huge amounts of time just searching for information. Then there is the synthesizing of content and data from various documents to answer more complex questions. Agentic workflow aids productivity by breaking down intricate tasks into manageable sub-tasks and linking them in a logical sequence.

Here, the consequences for prompting are significant. Users used to have to prompt each task separately and include all sorts of guidance in their prompts, instructing the model on how to approach complex tasks. However, as models evolve, they are becoming more adept at internalizing these reasoning processes, reducing the need for explicit guidance. Modern AI models incorporate reasoning, so complex problems can be unpacked into manageable components. This improves problem-solving efficiency and also provides transparency in how conclusions are reached.

In agentic workflow, it is easy to monitor what is happening inside the agentic efforts. You have clear windows into the system to see what is going on. You can also check and review the steps and processes happening within the system. The provenance of your sources is also shown.

For knowledge workers, agentic workflows can consolidate data and resources to provide comprehensive answers and streamline decision-making processes. These new research models have agentic features that conduct multi-step internet research for complex tasks, doing in minutes what might take humans hours or days.

Agentic RAG is aimed at the individual with a specific problem to solve or project to complete, at their needs at that particular moment. This focus on personal agentic workflows, information synthesis and orchestrating all the tools on your desktop to produce results will revolutionize this type of work. Do a literature research, write an easy-to-read intro based on that research for a specific audience, import the data, choose the most appropriate chart types and show the results in readable prose, as an optimized workflow, which is massively more productive.

Organizations should therefore focus on real-world business challenges rather than agonizing over specific AI tools or trends. As AI grows and evolves rapidly, it necessitates a focus on practical AI agentic solutions that drive efficiency and innovation. Prompting then fades as a skill, as AI can analyse what needs to be done for larger tasks.

Efficient prompt caching will drive AI productivity, as it can cut down response times, and computational costs, by storing and reusing. Instead of AI models having to do things from scratch for every prompt, caching allows systems to instantly retrieve answers when the same or similar prompts are detected. Importantly, this will feel like a smoother and more realistic form of dialogue and user experience, with faster interactions. By intelligently storing prompts and responses, AI applications, from chatbots to research tools, are also easier to scale. Commonly asked questions get answered immediately, with less repetition in processing, so compute resources can focus on new and novel requests. Semantic similarity matching, when variations in the language of similar prompts make the system even more efficient, also improves scaling.

Conclusion

Rumours of the death of learning how to prompt, or prompt engineering, are greatly exaggerated. It is not only still a critical skill but may be gaining in importance. AI services are getting better at the low-level interpretation of prompts but as their ceiling of competence rises fast, to exploit that increase in functionality, you need to push further your prompting skills. The ability to craft intricate, well-structured prompts, based on knowledge and expertise, matters more than ever, especially when the output becomes agentic. What then happens is that you prompt AI and AI prompts you. Your prompting skills become skills in managing and getting the most out of that partnership. The more effort you put into your prompts and dialogue, the better the results. You become a partner in productivity.

References

Karpathy, A (2024) Power to the people: How LLMs flip the script on technology diffusion, X, https://x.com/karpathy/status/1909308143156240538 (archived at https://perma.cc/TQ5W-4L9B)

Norman, D A (1998) *The Invisible Computer: Why good products can fail, the personal computer is so complex, and information appliances are the solution,* MIT Press

Promptopia (2024) Prompt engineering frameworks, https://promptopia-orpin. vercel.app (archived at https://perma.cc/4C76-SB8Z)

14

Deploying AI in organizations

We have seen how AI has 'flipped the script' on adoption, as a bottom-up technology. It has entered organizations on the back of personal utility, something very new for those leading organizations to manage. Organizational resistance is natural, but temporary, as its wider and deeper utility within organizations becomes clear. Productivity becomes the driving force and AI wins out through market, competitive and social pressure.

This bottom-up process across the jagged frontier is how AI has unfolded on a global scale. Once we recognize this bottom-up phenomenon, progress is much easier. Like Canute, who did not in fact try to hold the tide back, but simply showed his people that even a king cannot stop the tide, so leaders have to recognize that they cannot hold back the rising, bottom-up tide of AI.

Faced with introducing AI into an organization, senior management teams have to accept it is already there, probably to a greater degree than they imagine as its use is often masked and on the sly. It is tempting to think there is an ideal plan for initiating, rolling out and embedding AI in organizations but given the novel, complex and almost human nature of the technology, this is rarely the case. There are some general directions of travel and suggestions one can make but, as we have seen with policies and prompting, it tends to be more of a negotiated and iterative process.

Inconvenient truths

Organizations demand conformity to the company line. It is an organization by virtue of behaving consistently, drawing the fibres of functionality into one strong rope, which pulls the organization in one direction. That rope must remain entwined to maintain its brand, pricing, products, services and reputation, all within a secure IT environment, subject to external regulations. The paradox is that untangling that rope, or accepting some fraying, is difficult, as organizations do not like entropy or uncertainty. This strength is what also makes them immune to change.

A Wharton report in late 2024 was refreshing as it revealed some inconvenient truths. From their survey of over 800 senior business leaders, they found that weekly usage of Gen AI had nearly doubled from 37 per cent in 2023 to 73 per cent by October 2024.

They also found that generative AI strategy is usually led by internal action, not consultants, which bucked the trend. The strategy work was not led by the usual suspects or suspect advisors, many of whom have no real experience of building anything in AI. This technology gives more agency to individuals within organizations. Curious people are doing it for themselves. This bottom-up 'AI on the sly' movement happened so quickly that organizations could not, and did not, know how to respond. Like a lot of technology inside organizations, it just happened.

Other interesting insights emerged. First, that stringent top-down policies on use in organizations were rare. This seems like a contradiction, given the massive use of AI, but there is little sign of policies being used. Linked to this absence of interest in policies, most employees did not face heavy restrictions in accessing generative AI in their organizations.

Above all they noted less negativity. The scepticism, regulatory effort, fear-mongering, even doomsters, also seemed to have given way to a more level-headed recognition that this is a technology with real promise. More decision-makers felt 'pleased', 'excited' and 'optimistic', and fewer 'amazed', 'curious' and 'sceptical'. Negative perceptions were softening, as decision-makers saw more promise in generative AI's ability to enhance jobs without replacing employees. The scepticism tended to come from those who had not used generative AI in any depth. As adoption had surged, nearly doubling across functional areas in one year, the practical experimentation had shifted sentiment.

We seemed to have gone through the usual motions of a technological shift, where a period of fear and resistance gave way to one of acceptance, with both top-down and bottom-up strategies now being implemented.

Top-down and bottom-up

AI productivity tools rarely enter an organization through executive decree. More often than not, they seep in from the bottom, as employees experiment with the tools, create and summarize text, write reports, even upload spread-sheets and use AI-driven tools long before senior management even notices. This unsanctioned use is a wellspring of innovation but can lead to security risks, haphazard uses and inconsistent workflows if left unmanaged. The trick is not to crush but harness this grassroots adoption. Smart organiza-tions recognize and legitimize useful AI experiments, sanctioning them once they align with corporate security and needs. They use this bottom-up momentum to best advantage.

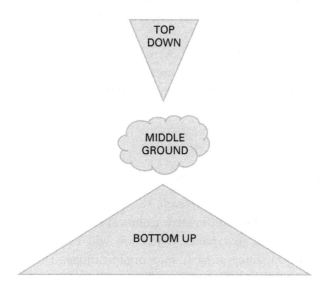

Strategic AI implementation for productivity must be a coordinated dance between top-down leadership direction and bottom-up grassroots adoption, working in tandem to avoid the sluggish, indecisive quagmire of the middle ground. The danger lies in this middle ground, the slow, bureaucratic zone where leadership hesitates and employees remain unsure whether AI adop-tion is encouraged or prohibited. This is where productivity gains evaporate in endless and often ill-informed debates about risks, while competitors surge ahead.

To avoid this stagnation, top-down leadership must act decisively to create clear AI structures and support, provide curated tools rather than blanket bans and encourage a culture where employees feel empowered to propose and refine AI-driven efficiencies. When the CEO and senior leader-ship teams drive AI adoption from above, they set the vision, allocate resources and embed AI into the company's strategic priorities. This means defining what AI-powered productivity truly looks like within the organization. Without this direction, AI adoption will remain scattered, uncoordinated and often ineffective. At its strongest this can take the form of an 'AI-first' strategy to transform the organization through AI. It often involves finding strong partners and strategic intent.

You must keep this dynamic alive, with strategic direction from the top, widespread use and agile experimentation from the bottom, and a clear pathway for integrating innovation. In this way, the organization can truly capitalize on AI for productivity without getting stuck in the murky middle ground.

The real winners with AI are those who are capable of thinking ahead and seeing that this technology is improving fast. Implement today with tomorrow in mind – that sometimes means taking a long-term management perspective.

AI jobs

As agents and AGI begin to reshape the workforce, new jobs and job titles will emerge. They will involve technical expertise, execution, data analysis and ethical governance. Their job will be to orchestrate the application of AI, integrating it into organizations. This is already a sought-after skill.

Large organizations that have a strategic vision for AI are likely to take a bold step and appoint someone, a head of AI or chief AI officer (CAIO), to lead that vision, separate from the rest of the management team. This is not only a signal of intent but an act that will drive action forward. This need not be someone who has technical competence in AI; it is more important that they have the management experience to drive things forward.

A general *AI consultant*, as strategist within the organization, would identify strategic intent, along with an implementation plan that deals with the inevitable problems that arise when you automate processes and change cultures within organizations.

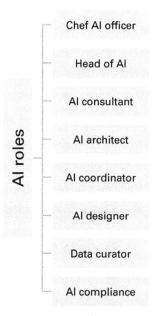

On the technical frontier, we will see roles like *AI agent* or *AGI architects* building the frameworks that allow various forms of AI, agents and AGI systems to work together within the organization.

An *AI coordinator*, with experience in implementing AI within specific workflows will become a valuable asset in organizations. This role will emerge as AI use moves from being largely done on the sly to being recognized as an important organizational and productivity goal. An AI Co-ordinator, Lead or Specialist meets teams weekly, logs repetitive tasks, builds shared prompts and automations and rolls them out so busy staff get the productivity gains without stopping to reinvent the process themselves.

We have seen how people good at prompting emerge but as systems become better at reading intent, this is likely to evolve into *AI designers*, as experts-in-the-loop who both automate and design personalized interactions between humans and AI. In creative spaces, expect the titles *AI producers* or *AI directors* to emerge as roles within industries such as games and film. These jobs will harness AI's potential to create media experiences.

AI depends on data, so *data curators*, responsible for identifying, collating, storing and updating documents and data, will be important. They will have to have skills related to the regulatory rules and laws on data, as well as an understanding of different types of data and its protection.

On the ethical front, *AI compliance managers* may be necessary, especially in sectors such as finance and healthcare. These roles will monitor AI systems for unintended biases, discrimination or misuse. It will be important to apply scrutiny, especially to decision-making processes, to maintain trust in increasingly autonomous systems.

The rise of agents, even AGI, does not mean the end of human jobs – it just signals the beginning of a new, dynamic profession that fuses our abilities with the potential of intelligent machines. The leadership challenge will be to embrace this change and prepare ourselves to thrive in a world we are only beginning to comprehend.

AI strategy

Consultants are also an option but tend to only be slightly ahead of the curve. An interesting alternative or augmentation is to see AI itself as a consultant. AI itself can also be used to analyse, design, develop and recommend productivity gains. It is not just a passive engine for productivity gains – it can analyse and recommend ways to achieve productivity gains. AI can evaluate complex systems, identify critical steps and inefficiencies, then suggest targeted solutions, often beyond what human consultants can offer.

Unlike a human productivity expert who may rely on experience and intuition, AI can process vast amounts of data in real time, recognize patterns and uncover hidden opportunities for optimization. It does not stop at identifying problems, but can also model potential improvements, predict outcomes and recommend steps to implement those changes.

For organizations, this means AI can redesign workflows, optimize resource allocation and even forecast demand, ensuring that operations run at peak efficiency. In public policy, AI could redesign healthcare systems, streamline infrastructure projects or revolutionize education by identifying where resources can be deployed most effectively for individual learners. For individuals, AI-powered tools already track habits, suggest productivity hacks and help manage time more effectively.

In this evolving role, AI becomes a partner in the pursuit of productivity, not only accelerating tasks but reshaping the way we approach productivity itself. Those who leverage AI, not just to automate, but to guide strategic improvement, will lead the next wave of productivity breakthroughs.

Fiverr is a huge global freelancers' marketplace. It is here you see the productivity impact of AI laid bare. The supply and demand for jobs becomes visible. The CEO made an impassioned, refreshing and brutally honest appeal to his employees and customers around the need to see the company as an AI-first organization.

In an email to all employees, he said, straight up, 'AI is coming for your jobs. Heck, it's coming for my job too. This is a wake-up call… AI is coming for you', and listed lots of professions where this is self-evidently true (Fiverr, 2024). This was his wish list:

- Study, research, master latest AI solutions in your field.
- Find the most knowledgeable people on our team who can help you become more familiar with the latest and greatest in AI.
- Time is the most valuable asset we have. If you're working like it's 2024, you're doing it wrong! Do more, faster, and more efficiently, now.
- Become a prompt engineer.
- Get involved in making the organization more efficient using AI tools and technologies.

This was not a threat, merely a strategic appeal for 'all of us to be on the winning side of history'. This is a strong example of top-down leadership, when an organization flips from seeing AI as just a useful office tool to making it a strategic imperative.

Get the ball rolling

What matters in an organization is the opening gambit. This CEO was bold, as he is close to his market, knows about change management, knows what creates a sense of urgency. It is never enough to simply write a project plan, as if it can be executed and rolled out flawlessly across your organization. That approach lacks momentum. People need to be convinced that change is necessary and that it will work for them. Change management is consistently the most difficult thing to effect in an organization.

Even a small business has much to gain by using AI. As a small shopkeeper you can predict customer rush hours, get suggestions for marketing and customer retention, automate stock buying, even brainstorm ideas for expanding your business. A small legal practice has much to gain from automating legal text production or AI spotting errors in documents and contracts as well as helping with customer emails. In many ways it is easier to use AI tools in small businesses, as you know your business well and can execute solutions quickly.

But for larger organizations you need to create a real sense of urgency. This was the mantra of John Kotter, a professor at Harvard Business School known for his work on change management and leadership. In *Leading Change* (1996) he introduced his famous eight-step process for effecting any kind of change in an organization, a comprehensive approach to managing and leading change. The book pushes the need for urgency and a powerful top-down coalition, to successfully drive transformation.

This is great advice but it is easy to see these models as recipes, to be slavishly followed to bake the perfect cake. But organizations are complex, so simple models rarely fit neatly on to the sometimes disorganized, informal structures and messy dynamics of real people. The 'linear' nature of his eight-step process rarely takes into account the unpredictable and iterative nature of change in real organizations, especially around the use of a new, difficult-to-manage technology like AI.

Nevertheless, its strength lies in not seeing simple policies or even dull project plans as adequate when trying to effect change, especially using technology like AI to improve productivity. His genius was in seeing that creating a sense of *urgency* does matter, as does a *guiding coalition*, powerful enough to see things through, along with a *vision* and *initiatives* to get things going on scale.

Then again, while his emphasis on creating and sustaining urgency, along with top-down power and a clear vision and sustained effort, is important, his focus on top-down leadership can be seen as limiting in organizations that thrive on decentralized decision making and employee empowerment. With AI one can also harness the existing widescale use and perceived usefulness of AI by many employees, through a bottom-up effort.

What follows is a range of practical actions you can take to implement AI in your organization. It is a suggested order but, as noted, you may want to change that order, depending on the needs of your organization. There is no single, perfect solution here, as there are many different types of organizations, where some actions may need to be done earlier or later.

You need to use and experiment with generative AI to fully realize its potential. This is because it is not strictly speaking an instrumental tool, but something entirely different, a sort of intelligence on tap. Beyond standard deployment techniques and change management, several techniques can be used to deal with the strangeness of generative AI, both to overcome people's fears and excite their sense of wonder. So, let's get practical with some possible initiatives that can get the ball rolling and create a sense of urgency.

We have seen the following tactics work well, within an overall strategy, to get AI moving and in organizations:

- CEO call to action
- AI keynote or conference
- AI workshop
- AI hackathon
- AI hub
- AI champions, ambassadors and superusers
- Branding your AI initiative

CEO call to action

Tobias Lütke, CEO of Shopify (2024), sent all staff a memo stating that AI usage was now a baseline expectation in the company. He stated that their market was changing with AI, as a huge number of potential customers were using AU to create online businesses. That meant being cutting edge on AI themselves. This was a good message, as it started with a strategic goal based on a market necessity.

He then stated, categorically, 'Reflexive AI usage is now a baseline expectation at Shopify' and included an example of how he had created a presentation using AI agents. This is where he gets interesting: 'using AI well is a skill that needs to be carefully learned by… Using it a lot. It's just too unlike everything else. The call to tinker with it was the right one, but it was too much of a suggestion.' He recommended that staff use AI a lot, don't tinker, then you get the x10 to x100 multiplier on productivity. What was interesting about his recommendations was the recognition that the power had to be bottom-up, invested in the employees.

- Using AI effectively is now a fundamental expectation of everyone at Shopify.
- AI must be part of your prototype phase.
- We will add AI usage questions to our performance and peer review questionnaire.
- Learning is self-directed, but share what you learn (listed available tools), share on Slack.

- Before asking for more headcount and resources, teams must demonstrate why they cannot get what they want done using AI.
- Everyone means everyone.

Resistance, he thought, was futile. His point was that it is now a general tool and growing in potency. If the organization is not using AI, it is 'sliding not climbing'.

This all-in AI-first approach is fast becoming common and this memo from the CEO was the first salvo in that plan, a call to action.

AI keynote or conference

I have been involved in many efforts to get AI moving as a strategic force in organizations. It often starts with a deliberately placed big-bang, inspirational keynote at a conference, especially an organization-specific conference, attended by all of the senior leaders. Having delivered dozens of such keynotes across many continents, I recommend a talk that focuses not just on 'futurist' themes, as these have a short and not long-term impact. A more effective approach is to shake things up a little, and point out that this is the technology of our age with huge potential. It is also important to provide evidence on productivity, research, along with real case studies in real organizations with real people. Practitioners with real experience of working within organizations to effect change on AI are better than pure theorist speakers and futurists, no matter how entertaining.

As always, it is not what is said but building on the awakening and enthusiasm after the event that matters. Record the keynote, deliver it with a transcript and link directly to the other planned events such as an announced AI workshop, AI day or AI hackathon. If you decide to create an AI hub get it in there as a link and make sure you have a solid brand name for the initiative.

AI workshop (not course)

It is too easy to see AI as a daunting problem, and training the solution. Schools, colleges, universities and workplace training tend to default to 'courses' on AI or AI literacy. But courses that take time to build are almost immediately dated by the rapid progress of the technology.

The problem with AI training courses is that they can focus too much on background technical explanations of how foundational models work, rely too much on presentations or get carried away with ethical ideas. AI training benefits hugely from participation, learning by doing, rather than abstract theory. This is why I prefer 'workshops', which suggest active doing rather than passive listening, with a focus on personal and organizational productivity.

There are some basics that are useful, such as the concept of an LLM and it being trained by a huge corpus of data, fine-tuning and different types of AI. Dispelling some common myths, such as seeing it as a search engine, a single point of truth or always harvesting your data, is also instructive. But knowing how to use the tools is particularly useful, as it moves users beyond one-shot prompts into dialogue and iterations, as well as deep research, agents and other types of uses and tools. It is important to move beyond knowing what AI is, to knowing how to use it.

Does the course automatically assume a fixed position on freedom of speech, universal values, differing political positions? So much discussion and debate on the ethics of AI is little more than moralizing, not the ethical consideration of what is potentially good and bad, advantages and disadvantages, benefits or detriments, upsides and downsides. True ethical debate does not put a hand over one eye and only look at the bad, the disadvantages and the downsides. An assumed, fixed, deontological position is sometimes assumed, with absolute beliefs about values, ethical principles, even rules and views on language, that is often contentious and certainly not universal. It can easily slip, consciously and unconsciously, into 'culture war' territory, with bold statements about power, capitalism, bias and gender, even copyright, that assume a common and true moral position that may well not be held by others. Moving into areas such as explainability and transparency, along with esoteric utopian or dystopian speculation about the future of AI, is fine for courses in 'Ethical AI' in higher education, but rarely useful or necessary in most organizational contexts.

To be fair, the more level-headed approaches consider the criticality in AI literacy as making users aware of possible hallucinations, although 'hallucination' is an awful word, indicative of how viscerally anthropomorphic our negative reaction has been to AI. The provenance of AI-generated content, plagiarism and data privacy are also important.

A useful starting point is a workshop with senior managers, especially those experienced on operational processes, with a feel for business productivity. They should suggest, list, analyse and rank productivity gain opportunities. AI can be used as a brainstorming partner in this process, to suggest areas where gains are more likely and provide detail. It may also be worth asking employees at the coalface, who often have suggestions rooted in their raw experience.

Having run workshops on AI for large audiences, we recommend a brief introduction to excite the trainees about the possibilities, then get them to prompt to create new content, role play, critique and summarize. Push the boundaries on through more and more dialogue, through to using agents, so they reach out into its more esoteric uses.

Start by asking them to name three things they see as problems in their work, things they would like to see made easier or identify as productivity bottlenecks. These can be used throughout the workshop to play with and to use the AI technology on.

It is important to see AI as a useful brainstorming or creative tool, so raise the bar and get trainees to do precisely that, with prompts that push what they see as its creative limitations. Ideation can be one of its strong points, yet few use it for this purpose.

Encourage multimodal use, with audio, images and video. This frees trainees from the tyranny of text and pushes them to create brands, cartoons, useful infographics, even creative artwork. Understanding the power of audio prompting also pushes boundaries.

We have found that personal use matters, so get them to create a GPT or avatar of themselves, a video with them as a character, even a personality test. This anchors interest in something that matters the most to people – themselves!

Transcription of text from an image and translation to and from a foreign language, even getting it to teach you a few phrases in a new language, can open up its cultural extension. This is also an opportunity to open up the issue of accessibility – audio for dyslexics, text-to-speech and speech-to-text for those with sight or hearing impairment. Try simplifying language from academic to ordinary language to make academic text more accessible.

Data and statistical analysis is something even fewer aspire to, so make sure this is included, especially with data that is relevant to their role. This can be an exciting journey for some, especially those who see spreadsheets, data analysis and statistics as beyond them.

Agents can then be used to complete a more ambitious task, again related to their job role, using the problems they identified at the start, or one they realized would be ideal during the workshop. Choose a workflow that is relevant, practical and achievable.

Make sure there are at least two of you, one leading the workshop, the other with detailed technical expertise on using the tools, to circulate and troubleshoot problems trainees may have with downloading and tool use, making suggestions for better prompts and suggestions on pushing the boundaries.

Stop and share what has been produced and issues that people have come across as they proceed. This is also an opportunity for people to share their worries, as well as excitement. Common misconceptions can be answered and ethical issues can be aired and answered.

Finally, do not let the end of a workshop be the end point. When people return to their jobs they forget or simply do not have the motivation to use what they have learnt. Follow-up really does matter, with presentations, links and suggestions for further use.

AI day or hackathon

AI hackathons are meant to speed up interest, innovation and prototype solutions that would have taken months to ideate and build. The danger is they turn into shallow ideation events with no real demonstrable prototypes emerging.

I've run and been involved with successful AI hackathons, where employees pitch AI-driven improvements to their workflows. In the Netherlands I participated in one that was highly successful, with expert speakers and working groups who brainstormed, then built and implemented AI within their teams, all reporting back at the end of the day.

Identify organizational problems and use cases first. If you define the challenges as use cases or get concrete use cases defined at the start, it grounds the hackathon in real applications. Make sure that everyone understands that the output is a working prototype, not just a set of slides, although for low-level hackathons, this is an option. Then give and stick to a strict timetable, broken down into a start, middle and end. The starting point should be user need and problem framing and definitely not coding. The middle is to get a solid build. Finally, end with a good user interface and prepare a demo.

Intuit held a huge week-long AI hackathon – Intuit's Global Engineering Days (Intuit, 2025) – where 8,500 people produced 900 items. It has some clear advice for such hackathons. Strongly encourage focus on AI-first development to get a critical mass of useful projects. Balance innovation types between, say, external customer-facing and internal productivity projects. Don't stifle outliers, and encourage 'out-of-the-box' ideas. Foster collaboration through cross-functional teams. Finally, consider project evaluation for incubation to evaluate, fund or pilot promising projects.

The focus really is on practical and realizable ideas and products that meet real use cases. Think more like a product designer than a coder. That is why it is useful to put teams together that are mixed in terms of competences.

Good internet connectivity is essential, especially when the hackathon is likely to have many users accessing some meaty services in the build phase. Also, make sure that useful tools and services are available, with expertise to get people signed up quickly.

Judging criteria, if seen as useful, should be realistic in terms of what was possible in the timescales, given the available resources and expertise. But the real point is to celebrate all effort. AI challenges can also encourage engagement. Get employees to submit ideas with modest prizes once a month. Recognize and celebrate those who actively contribute.

AI hub

Delivering an AI talk and training session at a college of technology was a joy. Why? My friend Joe Wilson, as the leader of that organization, had already prepared the ground. He had not only taken a deep dive into the available technology himself, but also built a central hub of best practices, links to available tools and valuable prompts. Many of the staff and students I spoke to were already using AI to good effect in teaching and learning.

A good AI hub should be well branded, easy to find and above all practical. Do not overload with theory on how LLMs work technically; rather give concise and practical advice, tools and examples. It should also convey positive enthusiasm through short videos, simple explainer videos, links to tools, examples of the use of those tools and useful voices to follow on social media.

1   Above all promote internal *success stories*. Showcase an AI-driven project that has saved time or improved efficiency. Celebrate the people who have done something, along with testimonies or short videos from the people who did the work.

2   *Prompt advice, templates and examples* are useful, especially domain-specific prompts that people can share.

3   You need a *toolkit* section, a curated list of AI services and tools, as this is all about doing.

4   A *news and trends* section is useful as the tools and services change so quickly.

5   Your *policy* should also be visible.

6 There also has to be an *AI community forum* where people can discuss, share and ask questions. Encourage use of a forum, as this often signifies real intent and action.

Of course, the best AI hub in the world is useless if nobody uses it. First, get all senior managers, champions and ambassadors to use the hub. They need to set the pace.

Also, during onboarding, get every new employee or student to use it. Encourage them to use AI from day one, or even before they have arrived, as they will be at their most curious in the days before they turn up.

For the rest, ideally you want to integrate it into existing workflows. Make sure it has visibility and easy access. Make it part of all meetings (record and summarize), critiquing agendas, summarizing the meeting or embedding in other commonly used processes and procedures, like email, grant applications, report writing, with everyone encouraged to use AI wherever it can save time and/or improve quality.

Above all, do not see an AI hub as a library or repository. It should be a living, breathing, action-oriented place that draws people back to it.

AI champions, ambassadors and superusers

In any educational or commercial organization, the ideal *AI champion* is someone who above all has the enthusiasm to take things forward. Driven by the strategic vision, they should be able to communicate the goals clearly. This person does not need a deep technical knowledge of AI, but should push the change management agenda by constant urging and communication, as well as making sure that the project is named and resources are available, with a clear budget, on a stated timeline. That person is driving the train and picking everyone up at all of the stations.

In an educational setting, this could be a forward-thinking faculty member or an innovative administrator. Ideally it would be someone who has a strong stake in teaching and learning, with an eye also on its research and administration capabilities.

In public and private organizations, the AI champion should again be a leader who can get things done. This can be the CEO but is far more likely to be someone in the senior management team who can influence and communicate well and has the enthusiasm to get things done. The role is to get AI deep into the organization's culture. They tend to be good communicators or at least know about how to communicate within an organization.

AI ambassadors are different. You can identify ambassadors across an organization. They drive the agenda through practical work on the ground, giving practical assistance to those around them. AI champions drive strategy and integration within an organization, whereas ambassadors act as the public face of AI, advocating, assisting and demystifying the technology.

A good AI ambassador should be the voice of AI and have a sound, practical understanding of the technology and above all an awareness of its potential applications. They need to be able to show and assist people with practical tasks in their domain. It helps if they are active on internal social platforms and communications, as well as social media. Influential AI ambassadors need not be leaders or senior management. They can come from anywhere and the best are often those who have expressed a real self-interest in the technology, often with good digital skills, who can demonstrate techniques.

Also keep an eye out for *AI superusers*, often early adopters and enthusiasts, who are well worth using as champions and ambassadors. They have the advantage of knowing the technology and using it within the organization, as well as being seen by others as peers. Let them loose to experiment, build and demonstrate AI, for and with others.

Brand your AI initiative

To create a sense of urgency, pause and consider the identity of the initiative.

The AI world seems to leave its marketing brain at the door when it comes to products and product launches. In one project we built an entire course development product, based on learning research. It was a good product and we were among the first to market. But the company refused to name the product, thinking that the company name would suffice. It did not and no real breakthrough in sales was achieved. I'd add that no breakthroughs in sales were even possible without reasonable branding and a product name.

Having designed and developed innumerable products since 1985 and AI projects and products since 2014, my advice to everyone is to always give your project or product a name. It may sound trivial, but it really does matter. Project and product names and branding are crucial, especially when launching an AI product where, both internally and externally, users and buyers see it as new, challenging and difficult.

AI branding is not just about simply naming a project or product. You need to craft an identity, shape users' perceptions and make sure the name sticks. My first company was called 'Epic', which gave us a sense of size and gravitas; it could be used as both a noun and adjective and had high retention. People remembered it. We became the market leaders, which mattered in the early days of tech.

As an aside, it has to be said that AI branding has been shambolic! There are clearly differences between the base brands ChatGPT, Claude, Gemini and DeepSeek that are not down to functionality. They have very different origins, rationales and intentions.

First to market, giving it a clear advantage, OpenAI's ChatGPT does exactly what is on the box. Chat signals conversation, making it immediately clear that this is an AI you interact with naturally. You 'chat' with it, have a dialogue, a conversation, although many use it as a single query search. GPT (Generative Pretrained Transformer) adds a technical edge, enough to signal innovation without completely alienating non-tech users. As a name, it is simple, intuitive and instantly conveys what the product does.

Anthropic's Claude tried to soften, anthropomorphize and personify AI. Named after Claude Shannon, the father of information theory, it carries a gentle intellectual weight while also feeling warm and familiar. Claude is a traditional, almost old-fashioned first name, but it set the tone for an AI that felt approachable, thoughtful, maybe even trustworthy, not a machine or technology but someone you could talk to. The branding also aligned with Anthropic's early stated focus on AI safety.

Google's Gemini was more celestial, futuristic and out there. Inspired by the constellation Gemini, the name evokes 'twin' intelligence, AI working alongside humans, rather than replacing them. It ties back to NASA's Project Gemini, an important step in the space race, giving echoes of Google's narrative of AI as the next great technological leap. Gemini is quite abstract, leaving room for reflection. Quite ambitious, it is more than just a chatbot.

DeepSeek flashed on to the market and showed how branding can make a difference in uptake. It trips off the tongue, using alliterative compounding like TikTok, YouTube and Coca Cola. 'Deep' suggests deep learning, as well as depth of reach and response, blended with 'Seek', satisfying our need to search for answers and solutions.

The sub-branding was a chaotic mess. ChatGPT went to ChatGPT-3.5 and ChatGPT-4, which made sense, then came ChatGPT-4 Turbo, the 4o, o1 and o3 (missing o2), along with the word 'mini'. Confusing or what? Anthropic kept Claude's sub-branding simple using a numbering system

(Claude 1, Claude 2, Claude 3) and sub-brand names, such as Claude Opus, Claude Sonnet, and Claude Haiku, to indicate different levels of performance. Google's Gemini started badly with Bard, renamed as Gemini 1.0, Gemini 1.5, Gemini Ultra, Gemini Pro and Gemini Nano.

What can we learn from all of this? You may want to choose a user-friendly personal name, a name that feels friendly, serious, whatever you prefer. Or choose something 'out there' that looks to the future. You may also want to indicate its key function in the brand; also consider the possibility of sub-brands and have a convention for new versions. Above all, keep it short and memorable.

How to deploy AI?

There comes a point when decisions have to be made on deployment. It is useful to recognize that large numbers of people are probably already using AI in your organization, so identifying why and what they are using it for will give valuable information about actual needs. The cast of the shadow can say a lot about its owner and the rise of AI on the sly will give vital clues as to where the productivity gains are to be found, what tools are being used, to what ends and in what workflows. These will surface the real problems for which AI is a likely solution. At some point, however, you will want to make greater productivity gains in a more consistent and secure manner, along with metrics that show those gains. Here you have choices.

Direct access to a chatbot

AI chatbots have billions of uses per month. Their continuing success means they are a safe and easy bet for deployment, whether it is OpenAI's ChatGPT, Anthropic's Claude or Google's Gemini; they have a huge user base, are easy and cheap (even free) to access and all anyone has to do is, like hundreds of millions have already done, type in a question, query or request. This ease of access will allow people to evolve their own uses and use cases, which in itself is illustrative of needs and possible productivity gains. Uses can be encouraged and it is often useful to encourage the sharing of these use cases and prompts.

You will most likely need clearance from IT, who will want to put some advice out, even restrictions on use. You have a choice between focusing on one model, a set of models from one vendor or a mix of approved models.

Small organizations often take this approach, as they can be agile and flexible with use, with little in the way of management permissions. One huge advantage of this open approach is that you automatically take advantage of the continuous improvements these models offer, as upgrades are automatic. This all heads in the direction of increasing productivity, so even if there are some costs involved, it is likely to pay for itself.

The danger of hallucinations is now slim and, for most mundane administrative uses, not a hugely significant problem. Data leakage is another risk, and this needs to be managed by switching off the data gathering on the models. As always, one must be careful with sensitive information.

In any organization, whenever there is a point of text creation, planning, regular reports, repeated analysis, meeting notes and compliance, there are opportunities for AI to help with the creation, summarization, analysis or critiquing of the text. To increase productivity further, one can use AI as a powerful consultant by analysing workflows, identifying inefficiencies and offering recommendations. It is like having an ever-evolving strategist, optimizing processes.

Pilots

One way of gathering evidence and effecting change management is through selected pilots. For a large, global waste management company, initiated by the CEO, we gave a presentation to the senior leadership team. The CEO then committed funding and support for a number of projects to be decided by that team. When the ideas came back, we used cluster analysis to show where the greatest needs were and a number of pilots were initiated.

One can also include a few specialist, domain- or task-specific tools in the mix that are designed to automate or improve workflow productivity. Experimentation with pilots has to be balanced by real organizational objectives. One can sandbox them completely or see the pilot prototypes as being congruent with high-potential, larger deployments.

This avoids the risks of a large investment, allowing safe experimentation. It also allows the organization to gather some data and metrics, even conduct some controlled with- and without-AI trials, without it seeming like a leap into the unknown. One can quickly find high-value use cases, then look at scaling the best solutions, allowing the pilots to shape the strategy. It can be seen as a canny investment in derisking and assessing potential gains and problems in a fuller roll-out.

Wrappers with approved model(s)

A wrapper is a bit like having a powerful engine and chassis, but adding a new body, dashboard, brakes and safety features. In other words, using a 'wrapper' around an approved AI model means putting a protective or enhancing layer between the AI model and the end-user or business application. The aim is to control, limit and fine tune how it is used. This is done to add extra security, safety, reliability or sometimes compliance. You get the ability to customize while still having the engine power of a major model.

The wrapper can screen or filter user prompts to stop unsafe prompting but it can also check outputs to minimize hallucinations, even add disclaimers. Importantly, it also logs uses for auditing, security or compliance. You can also integrate it with other internal feeds or systems. All of this is done with an organizational look, feel, even tone and style. Wrappers are commonly used in professional environments such as healthcare, finance and education, where trust, accuracy and safety are necessary, and non-negotiable.

Custom AI assistants/agents

We have implemented full custom AI assistants/agents, which are tailored versions of AI models that are designed to work in specific domains, like healthcare, marketing or legal contexts, or perform specific tasks, such as customer support. They are often task-oriented, designed to help with specific tasks or workflows and give huge increases in productivity.

Retrieval augmented generation (RAG) is a technique behind many custom AI agents as it allows the assistant or agent to fetch relevant organizational documents, databases or live feeds as it generates the response. This anchors the model in your organization to your documentation, processes and procedures.

Other techniques, besides RAG, include fine tuning the model on your company- or industry-specific data, controlled prompt engineering, calling out to external APIs (application programming interfaces), databases or other services, as well as chain-of-thought reasoning, even multi-agent collaboration.

It can pull up usable and accurate policies, guide employees through compliance procedures or answer company-specific questions, so becoming an invaluable, organization-specific productivity engine. This is often a huge benefit and increase in productivity as organizations rarely have adequate, even functional, systems that provide this functionality. There is no more waiting – just ask, and you get an answer.

Specific AI agents

Instead of one generic AI assistant, organizations deploy custom AI agents tailored for specific roles: a virtual sales coach for the business development team, a legal AI for contract analysis, a finance bot for number crunching, an IT support bot. These assistants act as specialists, offering specific expertise while integrating smoothly into departmental or job-specific workflows. These assistants can be built to deal with specific documentation related to that specialism within your organization, making it more specific and relevant in workflows. This also requires someone to take responsibility for keeping this documentation in order – the updates, deletions, additions, with versioning. This is often forgotten in the rush to implement AI, ignoring the simple fact that garbage in means garbage out.

AI-augmented workflows

AI works best when it blends into the background, even becoming invisible. The point is to allow people to be more productive, not to be disruptive. Embedding AI into HR tools, L&D platforms, legal platforms, product design processes and marketing and finance applications gives employees the benefits of productivity from automation and streamlined workflows, without them even realizing AI is there.

Placing AI within existing systems and workflows means raising productivity while not drawing overt attention to the change. Opportunities have to be identified, AI functionalities mapped onto current workflows and pilots done to get buy-in. The trick is to help people in such a way that they benefit without too much interruption. AI as 'performance support' is a good model, integrating AI as a solution to actual needs in workflows. This is, after all, how most people use AI in the workplace, to get things done at the practical level, the quicker the better, in some cases in just a couple of clicks, then in seconds.

Deploying AI across an organization must, of course, recognize the jagged frontier within the organization, where one has to navigate different types of resistance, fears, confusion about what AI is and lack of competence in its use.

Commercial productivity tools

Every major AI company now offers more than just models. They offer full ecosystems, including toolsets and secure, scalable deployment options. Commercial tools or ecosystems are more formal and controlled but they do have licence costs. AI-powered productivity tools like OpenAI, Microsoft, Google, Meta, Amazon and others offer corporate with specified cloud access.

With some, users will experience no more than an enhancement of their existing and familiar tools, with standard workflow tools for documents, summarizing emails and meetings, automating repetitive tasks and providing relevant data when needed. The productivity should build upon and flow naturally from existing workflow habits and behaviour.

From an IT and security perspective, this model is a safer bet than giving employees direct access to external AI chatbots. Keeping AI within your enterprise-approved environment gives you control over data privacy, compliance and security. For large organizations with sensitive data, this is a common option.

Early wins

A quick substantial success really does help catapult AI forward in an organization. A good starting point is analyses of your processes and procedures to identify the critical and non-critical steps. Reducing or eliminating bottlenecks through automation is an easy win. It is surprising how much work is paperwork, which if managed well can be automated through AI. This often mundane work – creating content, management reports, meeting minutes and compliance reports – could be largely automated with humans doing the validation, not the production.

We built AI software for Xprtise in the Netherlands, the goal being to provide support for surgical nurses – not a lightweight subject, as people can die in operating theatres (Xprtise, 2024). One clear example of a massive increase in productivity was in saving time on subject matter experts. The AI was good enough to identify the important content from the documentation, avoiding the traditional need for long interviews and content writing by highly paid medical professionals. This is an important first step, the recognition that AI can often beat subject matter experts in terms of expertise. Experts tend to have tacit knowledge which they struggle to explain and often contradict each other. This means interviewing several, comparing the transcripts and finding the optimal content. In this case the AI was exemplary.

Importantly, in terms of productivity, this saved a huge amount of time. It did the creation of content and analysis into non-critical and critical tasks at lightning speed. This saved months of time in this and future projects.

An underestimated factor in productivity is the massive potential for saving time. Things can be done in minutes not months, leaving experts to validate content, not write it. What is also often missed in this calculation is the time taken to manage this process. It takes an editor or project manager to supervise the long, slow writing by professionals, often squeezing the task into their busy work schedule, along with several meetings, revisions and final sign-off. This is a huge amount of human effort that can now be automated.

AI was used by Xprtise to both analyse a process and then short-circuit it by eliminating a human bottleneck. Automating that subject-matter-expert production process turned it from a bottleneck to a highly efficient step that allowed the humans to validate and focus on quality.

This one productivity win could save vast amounts of time and money in many fields, especially in education and healthcare. In healthcare, much of the content can be analysed, then produced automatically, with humans as validators.

In education, the design and creation of content and assessments eats up huge amounts of expensive time by well-paid professionals. Much of the main tasks could be automated by using AI to create curricula designs and structures, then content, lesson plans and assessments, along with rubrics for marking.

In any organization, whenever there is a point of text creation, plans created, regular reports, repeated analysis, meeting notes and compliance reporting, there are opportunities for AI to help with the creation, summarization, analysis or critiquing of the text. This low-hanging fruit can be plucked from the tree, allowing you more time to look at some other major tree surgery, pruning and trimming.

Conclusion

As AI marches on at pace, bringing more functionality and productivity, it becomes more powerful but also needs to be aligned and steered towards the organization's goals. You are not getting on a bus with a pre-determined route, nor are you driving a car, wholly under your own volition. It is more like unleashing a fleet of self-driving vehicles that not only take you to where you want to go, but are also laying the road ahead of themselves as they go. It is both less predictable and more productive than any technology we have ever seen. That is what makes it so exciting.

Taking action for productivity takes many forms. Using AI in smaller organizations to design product, do pricing, help with admin in the marketing and coding in a fast-moving startup, does not require any real investment, as using the free or cheap tools can suffice. They can be nimble, move fast and face little bureaucratic resistance. As you move into medium-sized businesses, AI needs to be considered a little more carefully, but can still be used widely and tactically in many areas of the business, perhaps requiring some paid-for AI services. Larger organizations need to take a more strategic top-down approach and make sure that interventions are supported, risks assessed and a roll-out is well planned. With that in mind, that there is no one-size-fits-all action plan.

References

Fiverr (2024) X, https://x.com/michakaufman/status/1909610844008161380 (archived at https://perma.cc/A9UU-CLVK)

Intuit (2025) https://www.intuit.com/blog/innovative-thinking/ai-powered-experiences-at-global-engineering-days/ (archived at https://perma.cc/CN96-ZJUN)

Kotter, J P (1996) *Leading Change*, Harvard Business Press

Shopify (2024) X, https://x.com/tobi/status/1909231499448401946 (archived at https://perma.cc/NWS6-52VZ)

Wharton (2024) Growing up: Navigating generative AI's early years – AI adoption report, https://ai.wharton.upenn.edu/focus-areas/human-technology-interaction/2024-ai-adoption-report/ (archived at https://perma.cc/GU5Q-HHNX)

Xprtise (2024) AI learning: The rubber hits the road, https://www.youtube.com/watch?v=9K80mrjRSQE&t=2186s (archived at https://perma.cc/CYV3-LJCZ)

15

Measuring AI productivity

Do not assume that thorough and heavyweight measurement of productivity is always necessary. It is rational to assume, based on your own personal experience of doing a task or tasks in seconds or minutes, which used to take hours or days, that your experience of immediate productivity gains is sound. Taking a few common tasks in any area of the organization and giving it a go can often suffice to convince people that AI is a powerful productivity multiplier. The gains can be so significantly obvious that wasting time on large-scale measurement may seem like stating the obvious.

You can ratchet this up to doing some simple demonstrations of productivity on simple to complex tasks, such as researching and writing a report, summarizing and creating communications assets or dealing with a dataset. The gains in time saved are often through the roof. You can even make a judgement on whether it was error free, which it will be in terms of spelling, grammar and punctuation, not a trivial issue. Then reflect on the quality.

Nevertheless, many organizations need stronger proof, especially when an investment in time and money is needed and that investment has to be triggered by the organization. At this point you have to get more serious in making a business case for using AI to increase productivity.

Having been on the boards of many companies and public sector organizations, I always expected an analysis of at least some metrics and risks on new initiatives, whether increasing productivity (often confused with simple cost-cutting) or new initiatives involving technology and an investment of time and money. AI is unique in both offering opportunities to diagnose productivity as well as being implemented to increase productivity. I always now look to the use of AI to do some of the analysis phase, as a positive sign.

Two main areas of focus for productivity gains are people and processes. AI, alongside other tools, can be used to quantify and qualify opportunities for productivity gains. People and processes are similar, in that a person is an intelligent processor and manages processes, so many of the techniques used to diagnose productivity gains are similar for both.

Performance and productivity

Luis von Ahn, CEO of Duolingo, made a crucial call in 2012 when he made the company mobile-first, taking it to a $14 billion valuation in 2025. He has now said, 'We are going to be AI-first' (von Ahn, 2024). What was interesting about his email to all staff was him framing it first as a 'productivity boost'. For the first time ever, he claims, 'teaching as well as the best human tutors is within our reach'. This was also about scaling content and that would take decades using human effort.

But it was the detailed actions that really mattered:

We'll gradually stop using contractors to do work that AI can handle.

AI use will be part of what we look for in hiring.

AI use will be part of what we evaluate in performance reviews.

Headcount will only be given if a team cannot automate more of their work.

Most functions will have specific initiatives to fundamentally change how they work.

Existing and new employees are now expected to use AI and their performance is judged on that basis, along with a headcount freeze, unless tasks cannot be automated, along with specific initiatives to get things going.

Despite AI's potential to improve efficiency, some employees still resist adoption, fearing it will replace their jobs. If leadership fails to address these concerns, adoption stalls, no matter how powerful the technology is. The best organizations position AI as an assistant, not a replacement, a tool designed to handle repetitive tasks, freeing employees for higher-value work. Upskilling is another game-changer. AI workshop programmes help employees see AI as a personal productivity tool rather than a competitor. Some companies go further, tying AI adoption to performance incentives, rewarding employees who successfully integrate AI into their workflows. The goal is not to force AI on employees but to make it so useful they naturally embrace it. But the truth is also that AI may not increase productivity if the cost base remains the same. It is necessary to measure the impact of AI productivity on both processes and people.

Process productivity gains

AI can be used to design, analyse and report on process automation, using several different techniques.

Process mapping develops detailed flowcharts or *business process model and notation* (BPMN) diagrams that document all steps of a process. This visualization helps you identify redundancies, unnecessary steps and possibly unnecessary decision loops. A more qualitative approach is to use *value stream mapping* (VSM), where you draw a value stream map that documents both value-added and non-value-added activities. This quantifies items like process times, waiting times and inventory levels, making it easier to spot productivity opportunities and eliminate non-value-added steps. Traditional *time and motion studies* also allow you to measure how long each task or step in a process takes. This pinpoints bottlenecks and redundant activities by comparing actual task durations with expected benchmarks.

For more detail, *root cause analysis* (RCA) and *fishbone diagrams* drill down into the underlying causes of process inefficiencies. You can categorize potential sources of waste, such as methods, people and technology, then use a fishbone diagram to map potential causes, such as outdated manual verification steps.

A more data-led approach is to use *process mining and simulations*. Analyse event logs from enterprise systems, such as ERP or CRM software, and reconstruct actual process flows so that simulation models can test changes to see how they might affect overall productivity. There are often steps, like approvals, responsible for delays in activating processes. By simulating the removal of these steps, you can predict large reductions in process time. Much of this analysis can be done using AI.

Each of these techniques provides a structured way to fairly uncover inefficiencies, redundancies and bureaucratic layers in processes.

People productivity gains

There are lots of ways to realize and quantify productivity gains in relation to people. An *organizational structure analysis* takes your detailed organizational chart, then counts the number of hierarchical layers and average number of direct reports per manager. AI can identify spots for productivity gains through this analysis. A more person-by-person approach can use *workload and role clarity assessments*, a *job analysis*, even *time–motion studies*, to evaluate roles, responsibilities and resources. You analyse the individual's output with a focus on redundant tasks, overlaps and gaps in accountability.

For straight-up automation and bottleneck removal, *VSM* and *process analysis* looks at decision making. You map key decision-making and approval processes to identify delays, bottlenecks or unnecessary approval loops, then look to eliminate or automate non-value-added steps through AI.

For any one of these techniques, AI itself will not only suggest the methods in more detail but design and create the tools you need, as well as analyse and create reports on the data you gather. AI can, in effect, be used to suggest its own productivity gains.

There will also be qualitative issues around people skills that have to be taken into account. Even here, AI can be used to gather insights from that qualitative data. The important point is that one must be fair and fairness comes from being objective about productivity.

Using AI to measure productivity

Start by thinking strategically and align your metrics with your strategic goals. To do this, your metrics must monitor the organization's strategic objectives. For example, if customer satisfaction is your goal, focus on that metric; if increasing productivity to save costs and increase profitability is a goal, more specific productivity increases and cost savings need to be measured; if market expansion is a key goal, focus on customer acquisition and product innovation metrics. There may be multiple lines of attack on poor productivity.

It is easy to think that implementing AI is a simple plan and an easy process. In truth, AI initiatives require more agile and continuous efforts, as the underlying technology moves so quickly. Regularly review and update your metrics to ensure they remain relevant as your AI systems evolve. Also be prepared for some organizational shifts. AI can significantly change roles and workflows. This is often not about tinkering with individual processes, like faster emails, but can mean the redefinition of processes, even their full automation. Here you also have to think carefully about the impact on employees.

Productivity and operational efficiency

In my early days in business, I implemented ISO2001 and took a long, hard look at processes, which meant metrics for output per employee, cycle time reduction (usually looking for less iterations), error and defect rates, even task automation rates. It led to dramatic increases in productivity.

It was not difficult, using spreadsheets, applying formulas, looking for constant improvements. Now we can use prompts to instruct AI to do almost all of this work, design how your data is to be collected, load it into spreadsheets and load into AI, making sure it is clean (using AI) with no missing values, consistent formats on things like dates and currency, and proper labels for columns. Other data can be exported from your HR or CRM platforms. You can then apply the formulas given in this chapter, then generate summaries and insights through AI prompts, such as comparing before and after certain dates or AI implementations, or the top three areas that saw productivity gains. Summarizing pivot tables can then be created and reports written with graphs and charts, and even automatically coded dashboards, all in AI.

Here is a list of various metrics along with simple formulas and methods for calculating and quantifying each one.

Operational metrics

Output per employee tracks changes in revenue or units produced per employee before and after AI implementation. If AI automates routine tasks, you should see an increase in output per employee. Typically, this can be massive reductions in cost on text production such as emails, reports, formal communications and reports. This is achievable in almost all organizations, no matter what the size. Compare the total output generated before and after AI implementation and divide by the corresponding number of employees to gauge improvements.

Cycle time reduction, the next level of measurement, measures the time it takes to complete key processes (order fulfilment, customer service response times, production cycles etc.). AI can reduce these times significantly, in some cases down from months to weeks, weeks to days, days to hours and hours to minutes. Measure the average time taken to complete a key process, before and after AI adoption, then calculate the percentage reduction.

Error and defect rates are critical in some domains, from healthcare to manufacturing. You can monitor improvements in quality by tracking error rates or defects in products/services. AI-driven quality control systems can certainly reduce errors and rework costs. Even at the level of text production and summarization, spelling, punctuation and grammar errors can be completely eliminated. Use AI to apply quality assurance through data gathering and analysis. Count the number of errors or defects before and after AI implementation. Comparing these numbers indicates quality improvements.

Task automation rate turns productivity gains into opportunities, as it calculates what percentage of routine or repetitive tasks have been automated and sees this as the resulting increase in capacity for higher-value activities. We have seen this clearly in healthcare where process efficiencies in surgical support resulted in more time to focus on quality of content and communications. This allows the productivity of people and processes to be turned into growth and maturity in an organization, freeing up time for higher-value activities, such as R&D, customer communications and so on. Identify the routine tasks that have been automated using AI, then calculate their percentage relative to all routine tasks to measure how much capacity is freed up for higher-value activities.

Financial metrics

More hardcore financial metrics can be used by senior managers to interpret the benefits of AI at the organizational level.

Return on investment (ROI) compares the cost savings and additional revenue generated by AI against the investment made. This has to include all design, development and delivery costs. Sum up the cost savings and any additional revenue generated as a result of AI, subtract the total cost of AI investment, and divide by that investment to assess overall financial gains.

Cost savings simply identifies decreases in labour costs, operational expenses and waste. For example, if AI optimizes a production process, a supply chain or data analysis, you might see a lower salary bill, lower inventory costs or reduced delivery costs. Compare labour, operational and waste costs before and after AI implementation to determine the absolute savings.

Revenue growth pre and post AI initiatives often show growth is the other side of the coin, as it nails increases in revenue that can be directly or indirectly attributed to AI initiatives. This could be from faster time-to-market, improved customer service, even the development of new, AI-enabled products or services. Track and compare revenue figures before and after AI initiatives, attributing differences to AI-enabled efficiencies, new products or faster time-to-market.

Customer and market metrics

More formal metrics can be added, such as *customer satisfaction* (CSAT) and *net promoter scores* (NPS). These evaluate improvements in customer satisfaction that may result from faster service, personalized experiences or improved quality. Customer satisfaction, acquisition and retention rates show if AI does improve customer interactions, through chatbots or personalized marketing; track changes in acquisition, conversion and retention metrics. Use surveys and CRM data to measure customer satisfaction and track new customer acquisition and retention before and after AI adoption.

For companies involved in product development, track time-to-market, whether AI enables quicker design, prototyping, testing, branding, marketing and roll-out of new products. Measure the time from product conception to launch before and after AI integration, and compute the percentage reduction to gauge efficiency improvements.

Employee and organizational impact

You may also want to measure some qualitative outcomes that could lead to further increases in productivity. *Adoption and utilization rates* track the percentage of employees using AI tools and the frequency of use. Low adoption could indicate a need for further training or adjustments in the tools offered. Collect data through usage logs from AI systems and employee surveys to determine both the proportion of users and how frequently they use the tools. Also track the frequency or intensity of AI tool usage per employee (e.g., number of interactions per day/week).

Employee satisfaction monitors productivity metrics per role or departments. You can use surveys to gauge how AI tools affect job satisfaction and engagement. AI should ideally free employees from mundane tasks and allow them to focus on strategic work. A useful technique is to integrate your AI performance metrics into broader organizational KPIs and performance reviews. For example, if AI is expected to push up personal or organizational productivity, tie these expectations to personal goals or overall growth forecasts and margins. Conduct regular employee surveys to gauge satisfaction and engagement levels pre and post AI implementation, comparing the scores over time.

Financial reporting

More precise accounting practices can be applied that quantify the size of the investment and how it is capitalized or alternatively classified as R&D, which is more open to tax relief or government financial support.

Capital expenditures treat AI investments as direct investments in capital expenditure. Operating expenses are more routine. This decision affects depreciation, amortization and how you report these costs on your balance sheet.

Capital expenditure (CapEx) tracks AI-related investments that add long-term value (software/hardware purchases) and depreciate over time. Operational expenditure (OpEx) records recurring expenses related to AI operations (subscription fees, maintenance) as they occur. For these, you might not need a strict formula but rather a method to record and classify costs. Track AI-related costs as either CapEx or OpEx in your accounting system. Use depreciation for CapEx items and expense OpEx items as incurred.

R&D expenses: classify AI projects, particularly in the early stages, as research and development. You should be clear about what qualifies as R&D versus an immediate operational tool. You may also have to track direct costs (software, hardware, licence fees and training) separately from the indirect costs (change management, downtime during rollout, etc.). This helps in evaluating the true ROI of AI investments. Tracking costs associated with AI development and experimentation as R&D, and maintaining detailed records to distinguish these from routine operational expenses, may make it eligible for tax relief or government support.

Using AI data analytics

You have to treat AI as a data scientist and prompt for action. AI can clean up messy data, spot outliers, run statistical analysis, and decide how to present your results. This can be through graphs, written reports, even dashboards.

Start with outlier detection and data cleaning with AI, which will help you find errors, inconsistencies or extreme values in seconds.

'Identify outliers in <input/productivity type> data for Q1 and suggest possible causes.'

'Find and flag negative or unrealistic values in the dataset.'

Once AI finds these issues, it can also recommend the best way to clean the data. This can be through filling missing values, standardizing dates, removing duplicates and so on. There are tools within Excel, AI-driven features in Google Sheets and also Python that can do this for you.

Without having any real technical knowledge or depth in statistics, you can do statistical analysis, with regression, clustering and predictions.

'Perform a regression analysis to determine the impact of <intervention> on productivity.'

'Predict next quarter's productivity gains using historical trends and seasonal patterns.'

When you want to visualize your data, ask AI to recommend the perfect type of chart for your findings.

'Generate a line chart to show productivity growth over the last 12 months.'

'Create a scatterplot to illustrate the relationship between employee use of AI and productivity.'

AI-powered tools like Excel Ideas, Google Data Studio, or Python can generate clean, professional charts that are ready to drop into presentations or reports.

AI can then summarize the results in a report written to your stated style, tone and length, with a stated audience and goal in mind. It helps write your final report, complete with headings, bullet points and key takeaways. This turns your data analysis into a polished summary, creates a detailed technical report for internal use, even a short blog or communications post for dissemination. There are even tools for creating presentations in PowerPoint.

'Summarize the key findings from this statistical analysis in a formal report.'

'Write a brief for the board highlighting AI-driven productivity improvements.'

This in itself is a highly productive activity that analyses and reports on productivity itself!

Measuring AGI productivity

Mustafa Suleyman's concept of Artificial Capable Intelligence (ACI) redefines the role of AI in enhancing productivity, as it breaks free of its narrow work-flow and agentic role into human cognitive territory (Suleyman and Bhaskar, 2023). He sees the need to measure different capabilities, as it starts to match human intuition, judgement and problem solving. Suddenly AI becomes a partner, co-creator and collaborator, performing identifiable, larger-scale tasks and roles in ways that clearly outperform humans.

The general productivity gains will be orders of magnitude greater than narrow agents alone. Large-scale projects could be implemented at speed, with goals reached in record times. It may even help in solving humanity's most pressing problems, from climate change to education and healthcare. This is a more measured and pragmatic view of general intelligence than Artificial General Intelligence (AGI).

Richard Ngo's (2023) clever t-AGI framework also offers a more nuanced approach to understanding the progression of AGI by benchmarking AI capabilities against human expertise over measurable timeframes. Instead of viewing AGI as a sudden, single threshold, his framework introduces a time spectrum.

His t-AGI framework neatly redefines AI productivity around what kinds of tasks humans do that will be outperformed by AI, given the same amount of time. It is not that AGI is better than humans, but that it is better in a measure of time. Productivity is no longer about tasks completed but about how long it takes to do those tasks.

- 1-second AGI: Instant recall, perception and face recognition
- 1-minute AGI: Short analysis, fact-checking and common-sense reasoning
- 1-hour AGI: Completes exams, articles and basic professional tasks
- 1-day AGI: Deep writing, experiments and app development
- 1-month AGI: Complex projects and makes discoveries
- 1-year AGI: Outperforms humans across nearly all intellectual tasks

He takes this further with his concept of (t, n)-AGI, where a group of (n) human experts, working collaboratively over time (t), is outperformed by an AI system. Productivity suddenly becomes measurable, as it is measured in terms of collapsing time horizons. You can also map AI capabilities to real-world productivity domains, on everything from routine personal work, to organizational tasks and major global problem solving.

One problem with this approach is that benchmarking against humans is hard, as one has to identify what most human experts could do in time t. That could be estimated, but using time alone as a variable for complexity can be misleading, as some tasks are long but shallow, like data entry, others quick but cognitively deep.

However, Ngo's redefinition also gives us a route to defining another tricky concept, Artificial Superintelligence (ASI), in terms of time. For example, at its most extreme, his measure gives us a labour multiplier, so that if AI can outperform all 8 billion humans who work for one year, this is literally super-human intelligence.

Another way of looking at the productivity measure with AGI is to calculate how much cost AGI eliminates. The value generated is then measured by costing the labour substituted, processes automated, errors reduced, along with speed and other efficiency gains.

The road to AGI has shifted from being a speculative long-term prediction, to being a realistic goal. All of a sudden productivity is no longer a human but a machine-centric term. When AGI is the prime mover in productivity, it is its efficacy, use of resources and outputs that need to be measured. We enter a new world where the traditional measures of labour, cognitive or physical, recede or disappear. Our measure of productivity may need to be elevated into how well we manage AGI, essentially one of oversight and ethics. The big question is no longer just about productivity, it is about what happens when work is no longer the defining feature of human life.

Conclusion

Not everything that counts can be measured, a crucial reminder in the age of productivity metrics, especially when AI and automation are reshaping how we define and track value. Productivity is often reduced, as we have seen, to what can be quantified. But many of the things that also drive long-term productivity include trust, human expertise and a humane approach to employment. These sometimes resist simple measurement but matter just as much.

The qualitative issues and effects in human–AI collaboration may be thought of as something no model can yet quantify. Yet qualitative issues and effects can be measured through qualitative data. AI can also help with qualitative data by doing the analysis, as well as extracting insights.

As AI begins to handle more measurable tasks, our human contributions are likely to get deeper and more concentrated. Yet, as Protagoras (nd) said in the fifth century BCE, 'Man is the measure of all things.' This keeps us at the centre of humane AI. What we see as productivity must be guided by us, not blindly guided by pure economic productivity.

References

Ngo, R (2023) Clarifying and predicting AGI, AI Alignment Forum, https://www.alignmentforum.org/posts/BoA3agdkAzL6HQtQP/clarifying-and-predicting-agi (archived at https://perma.cc/Y48K-6WZM)

Protagoras (nd) *Stanford Encyclopedia of Philosophy*, https://plato.stanford.edu/entries/protagoras/ (archived at https://perma.cc/ZTD3-34NG)

Suleyman, M and Bhaskar, M (2023) *The Coming Wave: Technology, Power, and the Twenty-first Century's Greatest Dilemma*, Crown

von Ahn, L (2024) Duolingo goes AI-first, replacing contract workers, *The Verge*, https://www.theverge.com/news/657594/duolingo-ai-first-replace-contract-workers?utm_source=chatgpt.com (archived at https://perma.cc/R7BM-GHLQ)

PART FOUR

Ethics

16

Productivity and ethics (weak)

Alarmist opinions are often thrown about with little or no evidence or analysis, so it was fascinating to come across an illuminating paper (Zhu et al, 2024) that investigated how bias affects the perception of AI-generated versus human-generated content. Some texts were simply labelled as either 'AI Generated' or 'Human Generated', other texts were presented without any labels.

In blind tests with unlabelled content, humans could not reliably differentiate between AI-generated and human-generated texts. With labelled content, things got far more interesting. Participants showed a strong preference for content simply labelled as 'Human Generated' over 'AI Generated', a preference over 30 per cent higher for texts labelled as human-created. But here's the rub, the same bias persisted even when the labels were intentionally swapped, indicating a preconceived bias rather than an assessment based on content quality.

Oddly, for those obsessed with bias in AI, the study reveals a significant human bias against AI-generated content, not based on content quality but on the labels assigned.

Much of the debate around topics on ethics and AI follows this pattern. As soon as people hear those two letters their own bias kicks in. People come with confirmation bias around human exceptionalism, the belief that AI can never match human skills. Many seem to have micro-panics around AI for no reason other than being tiggered by the term.

Moral panics

Moral panics around new technology are sometimes as silly as they are predictable. No sooner do we forget the last one, and we do it all over again.

That's because we're hard-wired for confirmation and negativity biases. In the words of the marvellous Douglas Adams (2002):

> Anything that is in the world when you're born is normal and ordinary and is just a natural part of the way the world works.
>
> Anything that's invented between when you're fifteen and thirty-five is new and exciting and revolutionary and you can probably get a career in it.
>
> Anything invented after you're thirty-five is against the natural order of things.

His point is that we have a tendency to fear and resist technological change, but eventually, that fear fades. More often than not, it turns out to be all right after all.

Every technology induces a 'moral panic' which has roughly similar features. Children and adolescents are targeted, as we see every new generation as degenerate and inferior to our own. They are always being distracted by technologies, from writing to radio, film and television. No sooner did these old technologies become the norm, indeed part of our culture, than the attacks began on social media, smartphones and computer games.

Social critics, journalists, academics and researchers are curiously immune themselves, of course, to negative effects of the panic. They are above it all. Yet they feel confident in beating every piece of new technology like a piñata. Stereotypical critiques become the norm. It makes us stupid, they claim, quoting the use of calculators, Google, Google Maps, Wikipedia and now AI as mind-numbing technologies that turn us all into morons, all the while happily using such technology themselves.

Eventually it all subsides and fades away as the benefits are realized. But the cycle is doomed to repeat itself and a systematic look at the history of technology shows we always overestimated the negative link between technology, its dangers and our wellbeing.

Past panics

Plato warned us of the dangers of writing in his dialogue *Phaedrus* (274b–277a), where he discusses the invention of writing through the myth of the Egyptian god Thoth. 'This discovery will create forgetfulness in the learners' souls, because they will not use their memory; they will trust to the external written characters and not remember of themselves' (*Phaedrus*, 275a). He believed that writing could weaken your memory, understanding and genuine knowledge, encouraging a superficial grasp of information. As a static form of expression, you avoid questioning, clarifying and refining ideas.

Even the sundial was cursed by Plautus as a device that disrupted the natural flow of life by measuring time. It introduced a new structure to daily activities but was seen as oppressive, cutting and hacking the day into rigid hours. The advent of printing was similarly treated with suspicion. In the Ottoman Empire, printing was banned, punishable by death, due to fears that it would destabilize religious and cultural traditions.

Later, technologies like bicycles, automobiles and aeroplanes faced scepticism. Bicycles were blamed for 'youth insanity', while automobiles were said to damage the brain, turning drivers into 'maniacs'. Aeroplanes were declared a passing fad with no future. Each of these technologies drastically enhanced human mobility and productivity, yet their early reception was steeped in distrust and fear of societal collapse.

With the rise of mass media, concerns intensified. Radio and television were accused of corrupting youth and dulling the mind. Headlines described 'radio addiction' as a brain-softening disease, and television was declared a dangerous stimulant leading to addiction and social decay. Despite these dire predictions, both radio and television became crucial tools for information, entertainment and education.

In the digital age, these fears only magnified. Computers and the internet, once hailed as revolutionary, were initially dismissed as unnecessary, dangerous or corrupting. Early articles doubted the need for home computers, claiming they had little value unless they could do the dishes. Later, social media and smartphones were labelled as tools of disconnection and distraction, promoting isolation, addiction and a decline in critical thinking.

Even writing and educational tools like typewriters, photocopiers, Wikipedia and calculators became controversial. Schools banned Wikipedia for fear it would undermine research skills, while calculators were blamed for eroding mathematical ability (Crow et al, 2024). Each tool, however, proved indispensable in democratizing knowledge.

This recurring pattern of suspicion reveals a deep-seated fear of change and disruption. Each technology, though initially criticized, ultimately reshaped society for the better, improving productivity, expanding opportunities and enriching lives. As we stand on the threshold of the AI revolution, it is essential to recognize this historical cycle. By acknowledging past fears, we can navigate the present with greater balance, embracing innovation while remaining vigilant about its ethical and societal impacts.

In my book *Learning Technology* (Clark, 2023), I made the point that a fundamental feature of the science of techn-*ology* is the backlash against the new. We are experiencing this now with AI. The backlash is greater because adoption and use have been quicker than anything we have ever seen before but the technology also has more frightening potential. A deluge of reports, frameworks, even hastily and badly written regulations and laws are all part of this backlash, along with an army of people who see it as an opportunity. But we should not be downhearted, as history has largely been on the side of those who have seen and worked towards making technology beneficial for humankind.

Values

We could get very exercised, for example, about abstract values and AI. Language is promiscuous and tends to produce abstract words that we cloak in certainty. This is dangerous in the realm of ethics. We tend to assume that abstract nouns have definite meanings and the word 'values' does a lot of heavy lifting in AI ethics; the solution too often becomes that word alone. Values are difficult to define, they vary across, and even within, cultures and tend to be imposed by those in power or from elite groups.

Safety features are needed but without being an unnecessary brake on productivity, where the clear benefits are thwarted because of the views of a few. We can have a careful, dynamic and utilitarian approach to safety and regulation, recognizing there are trade-offs between dangers and benefits.

Too heavy a hand on values results in something everyone experiences when using AI: the blunt response, no reasoning, just refusal to cooperate. Or worse, the crazy images produced by Google's Gemini image generation tool vision in early 2024, which had to be pulled from the market (Perry, 2024). Are values absolute, deontological entities? I doubt it.

We can all agree that value systems exist, but these can be skewed towards religious, ethical, historical or political influences. It is doubtful that one can abstract a single set of values that represent all of these for all instances of advanced AI. All efforts to do so will result in rigid systems, consistent but very different from human minds that do not hold a fixed set of rational ethical principles but rely on a feeling that things are right, wrong or somewhere in-between. It is not something that is readily encoded in AI models.

Ethical progress

The ethical conversation has shifted from the speculative and abstract to the practical. This has led to more constructive thinking.

It is as if, collectively, we have been moving through Elisabeth Kübler-Ross's five stages of grief. First *denial*, with calls to halt all development; then *anger*, as an army of moralizers got to work, pointing to edge-use cases trying to show the technology was doomed to failure. We then went into a period of *bargaining* as solutions to data use, bias and hallucinations began to fade and the technology proved its worth and more. A kind of *depression* then set in, a sort of fatalist acceptance that AI was here to stay. Finally, we seem to have entered a quiet *acceptance*. AI companies are building ever-more powerful and useful services, governments are presenting action plans and investments, organizations are being more strategic and we are no longer talking past each other.

We seem to have largely worked through it all and come out the other side with a more practical attitude, looking to take action to realize the benefits. The evidence for productivity is clear and we can now think clearly and productively about what ethical AI should look like. There is less about what we might lose, and more about what we can gain.

Ethical concerns

With this in mind, we will deal with some ethical issues within our sphere of influence and focus on those of direct concern when implementing AI to increase *productivity*.

AI holds huge potential for enhancing productivity across various domains. Alongside these gains, significant ethical challenges arise that can have serious consequences. There are clusters of concerns ranging from worries about the productivity of humans, biases that distort things, the insidious danger of being brainwashed, being demeaned as humans, alienated and even impoverished. Then there's the prospect of us living with embodied AI, in robots, its energy demands and even the threat of extinction. Nothing much to worry about then!

There are many ethical concerns we could consider but these are some, particularly related to the drive for productivity, that may be a consequence of that drive. With this in mind, let's separate what I regard as the *weak* ethical issues, which have minor consequences or effects and can be designed and managed in such a way that productivity can be seen as a net benefit: plagiarism, prejudice, persuasion, privacy and passivity. In the next chapter I will deal with more serious ethical issues that could arise from an over-zealous push for productivity.

Ethical concern	Manifestation in productivity
Weak ethical concerns	
Plagiarism	Cheating and copyright
Prejudice	Biases
Persuasion	Being duped
Privacy	Data and security
Passivity	Skills atrophy
Strong ethical concerns	
Privilege	Linguistic and cultural divide
Poverty	Immiseration and unemployment
Planet	Energy and emissions
Paramilitary	Military-AI complex
Perish	Extinction event

Plagiarism

Plagiarism has become easier as AI can generate text, enabling users to cheat or take credit for work that is not theirs. This increases productivity in terms of content generation but undermines creativity and academic integrity. Yet turning assessment into a cat and mouse game, or even worse, a toxic environment between teachers and students, is neither desirable nor practical. This is partly down to poor and primitive assessment (essay setting), and turning assessment into a transactional event, exacerbated by the massification of higher education.

But we should not let this essay use divert us from the productivity gains where AI assists human creativity, using AI to generate emails, memos, ideas, outlines or drafts, then refining that output with a human touch. The future of work has flipped. Instead of fixing our own mistakes, we now review and refine AI's first drafts. Our role is shifting to quality assurance, correcting AI, not starting from scratch.

Plagiarism is not in any real sense a threat to workplace productivity; indeed AI is generally used to explore what one does not know, learn new things and get things done. Organizations and individuals can stay on the right side of copyright law while still maximizing productivity.

Prejudice

Prejudice and biases can be embedded in productive AI models at the cost of fairness and equality, but work on reducing biases has been successful through various techniques, as far as it can be successful without destroying key functionality. We need to be cautious, as the elimination of bias can often be the result of another form of bias. In a contentious world it is unlikely that bias, when interpreted differently by different groups, can be eliminated entirely. AI, like humans, can be biased, although at least with AI such bias can be designed out of systems. Nobel Prize winning Kahneman (2011) suggested that while individuals can sometimes mitigate biases through structured decision-making processes, the biases themselves remain largely 'uneducable' at an intuitive level.

There is little evidence that AI is so biased it will have a direct impact on productivity. In fact, it may prove to be less biased than humans, as it has no emotional or wildly dogmatic skews. Models have begun to retreat from heavy-handed guard railing as it began to encroach into fairly benign requests, blocking output. Hard guardrails gave way to a looser stance, as users clearly wanted functionality, not censorship.

Persuasion

AI's role in persuasion can amplify messages and expand reach for marketing or political campaigns, duping audiences and manipulating public opinion, potentially compromising democratic processes. Yet, the threats to democratic elections have not materialized so far, which does not guarantee future immunity (Stockwell, 2024). It would appear that AI itself is increasingly successful in filtering out and moderating online content.

This is linked to provenance, the failure to identify the source of content, leading to false attribution or invented sources, which are dangerous in terms of conspiracies and the erosion of trust. That problem is disappearing to almost vanishing point as AI provides sources for its claims, especially in research mode.

Privacy

As for personal privacy, this is a concern where AI may be used to push for productivity at the expense of human dignity in, say, selecting employees for dismissal or pushing identification through facial recognition beyond digni-fied and fair boundaries. Productivity should not be pursued at any cost. It can be a balancing act between efficacy and privacy.

Lots of privacy fears also arise around data and security in AI, and these give rise to myths and misconceptions that put up barriers to increasing productivity. Much AI is already included in tools we use every day, such as email filters and fraud detection systems, often without us realizing it, mean-ing security and data protection have already been integrated into many mainstream applications.

Your personal data is protected because modern AI implementations use anonymization, differential privacy and secure computing techniques to ensure that individual data points cannot be traced back to specific users, even when used for AI training or analytics. And AI companies do not use your data to train models if you opt out of data sharing, or use enterprise versions with strict privacy agreements or rely on models designed to process input data without storing or learning from it.

An enterprise solution also gives you the protections on data and security because it includes built-in encryption, access controls, compliance with data protection laws (like GDPR) and audit logs to ensure transparency and accountability in AI-driven processes.

Yet the spread of AI in military, justice and policing applications could lead to mass surveillance, oppressive state control and the erosion of civil liberties. Surveillance may not foster innovation and productivity.

Passivity

Franz Kafka's (1973) novels on 'work', *The Trial* (*Der Prozess*) and *The Castle* (*Das Schloss*), gave us the word 'Kafkaesque'. These novels were published posthumously, as he had instructed his friend Max Brod to destroy his manuscripts, a request Brod ignored. Kafka himself worked in an insur-ance company, finding it insufferable. He wrote in his diary, 'Time is short, my strength is limited, the office is a horror...'. Josef K found himself in situations he didn't fully understand, the work meaningless, obedience demanded. Kafka's warning was that being productive for its own sake, without purpose or fulfilment, imprisons you and places you in a soul-crushing predicament, where you may be destroying your very humanity.

Yet, although AI gives us the promise of relief from the tyranny of mundane, bureaucratic and soul-destroying work, or at least shifting many to work that will have more personal agency and be of higher value, there are worries around making us more passive, with AI replacing or atrophying traditional skills and reducing the need for human expertise.

While automation could enhance productivity, it might also lead to the withering of skills and a decline in human capability. It can also strip humans of control, leading to a loss of agency, even alienation. This affects not only workers but also customers, reducing human interaction to mechanical responses, losing that important sense of personal connection.

These ethical issues start to surface when the push for productivity starts to bite. The idea of passive, powerless humans who lose skills and agency is a genuine worry. It is something we have faced before with the digital automation of communications, navigation, shopping, banking and innumerable services that were once delivered face-to-face. Yet one worry in the face of this digital onslaught is skills atrophy.

Research indicates that any break in doing a skilled task, especially one that demands heavy thinking rather than rote physical work, quickly reduces our ability to perform it (Macnamara et al, 2024). This has been examined in detail, with autopilot in aviation or AI assistants in knowledge work. It is clear that when humans lose vital practice, skills decay sets in. Although pilots who relied a lot on autopilot did retain the muscle memory for flying, they steadily lost speed on tracking position, planning route changes and responding to system failures (Casner et al, 2014). AI assistants, which are explicitly built to offload and automate decision making, also accelerate this decline in mental skills.

From a productivity standpoint, the trade-off is double-edged. Automation quickens throughput and frees people from the drudgery of repetitive work, but if our expertise wanes, we may also lose the ability to handle novel, high-risk situations. There is an even greater risk, as experts are often not aware that their skills have slipped, so organizations may discover these skill gaps only when failures occur! To sustain long-term productivity and safety in critical jobs like aviation, medicine and the military, it is necessary to top up automation with some human practice, so we can keep our eye and hands in, even as AI carries most of the load.

On the other hand, for much work, AI is not making us stupid in any real sense of biological or cognitive decline. Skills atrophy is really about the loss of acquired skills, not cognitive decline. The example of Google Maps is often used, claiming we lose our ability to read maps, as if without it we would stumble about like zombies bumping into things and driving around blind, unable to find anywhere. Throughout history technological advances have made us drop traditional skills. We no longer navigate using the stars, paper maps or printouts.

I went from using a map, to using a route printed from my computer on my lap, through to having a specialist satnav and on to GPS maps on my smartphone. Every single step was an improvement and I no longer need, or want, to wind down my car window to ask a stranger where I am, pore over a paper map while driving, decide on some sub-optimal route where I get lost and genuinely have no idea where I am, don't know how far I have to go, how long it will take and whether there's a petrol station or toilet within the next 30 minutes of driving.

A good example is the Great Calculator Panic of the 1980s and 90s. In a superb takedown published in *Scientific American*, a survey at the time showed that 72 per cent of teachers and mathematicians opposed their use in learning (Crow et al, 2024). What actually happened is clear. It made us rethink what we teach as mathematics. Learners went up the value scale, as calculators do much of the grunt work, even to the level of graphing.

Chess players at all levels up to Grand Master play chess software to increase their skills! Indeed, chess has never been more popular. Sure, if you never actually played chess, and used it in competitions, that would be cheating, but chess competitions are policed.

What increasing productivity through automation does, in many cases, is allow us humans to move up the value chain and do more meaningful, higher-level, supervisory, even strategic and creative work. It tends to automate the low-hanging fruit, mostly mundane tasks that many do not find satisfying.

Most researchers are happy that we do not have to read Latin to study and research, use library cards to find books, pore over microfiches on a hand-cranked machine, or walk endlessly up and down stacks of journals to find one research article. Nor do we miss buying the entire *Encyclopaedia Britannica* at huge cost, as many did before Google Search. Neither do we miss hand-setting type for printing or threading typewriter ribbons, having to get every letter and word right, no reordering or revisions possible, or putting sheets of carbon paper behind paper to make a single copy, even having to use expensive photocopiers. Sending and receiving dozens of letters a day, in the absence of email, seems anachronistic. Few regret the passing of physically looking in a physical dictionary for the meaning of a word, or in a thesaurus for alternatives. Creating company accounts in an old ledger book, or adding very long lists of numbers by hand, seems like stubbornness when we have calculators and spreadsheets. In short, we tend to transcend and drop some skills, as we adopt more productive tools.

Augmentation and automation mean we can progress and do things faster and better. This freed women from the drudgery of domestic chores and freed working-class people from the indignity of servitude. Yet we love invoking the idea that tech will make us dumber. All tech has its doomsayers, claiming it will make people stupider: writing, printing, radio, film, TV, photocopiers, computers, the internet, search, smartphones... and now a technology that promises to make us massively more productive – AI.

Conclusion

Productivity should be a matter of neither defensive pessimism nor over-indulgent optimism. Pessimists think it will not happen, and do nothing; optimists think it will simply happen and do nothing; realists look at the evidence, are honest about the complexity of the ethical issues and face up to the problems.

Having covered what I think are some over-pessimistic ethical concerns, at least in relation to productivity, let's turn to more serious consequences and ethical issues around productivity. These include AI exacerbating privilege and poverty, along with grave concerns around the future of the planet in relation to energy, even the possibility that our species may perish.

References

Adams, D (2002) *The Salmon of Doubt: Hitchhiking the Galaxy One Last Time*, Macmillan

Casner, S M, Geven, R W, Recker, M P and Schooler, J W (2014) The retention of manual flying skills in the automated cockpit, *Human Factors*, 56 (8), 1506–16

Clark, D (2023) *Learning Technology: A Complete Guide for Learning Professionals*, Kogan Page

Crow, M M, Mayberry, N K, Mitchell, T and Anderson, D (2024) AI can transform the classroom just like the calculator, *Scientific American*, 17 April, https://www.scientificamerican.com/article/ai-can-transform-the-classroom-just-like-the-calculator/ (archived at https://perma.cc/K6CL-6SJM)

Perry, A (2024) Google pulls Olympic-themed AI ad after failing to stick the landing, *The Wall Street Journal*, 2 August, https://www.wsj.com/tech/ai/google-pulls-olympic-themed-ai-ad-after-failing-to-stick-the-landing-a065649a?utm_source=chatgpt.com (archived at https://perma.cc/WD3G-7VX4)

Kafka, F (1973) *Letters to Felice*, Schocken Books

Kahneman, D (2011) *Thinking, Fast and Slow*, Farrar, Straus and Giroux

Macnamara, B N et al (2024) Does using artificial intelligence assistance accelerate skill decay and hinder skill development without performers' awareness? *Cognitive Research: Principles and Implications*, 9 (1), 46

Stockwell, S (2024) AI-enabled influence operations: Safeguarding future elections, Centre for Emerging Technology and Security (CETaS) Research Report

Zhu, T, Li, K and Wang, Q (2024) Human bias in the face of AI: The role of human judgement in AI generated text evaluation, https://arxiv.org/abs/2410.03723 (archived at https://perma.cc/7B46-ZFK3)

17

Productivity and ethics (strong)

Our focus on productivity allows us to avoid the excesses of exaggerated utopian–dystopian, optimistic–pessimistic perspectives. It brings AI back to real people in real organizations in the actual world, allowing us to distinguish between weaker concerns and serious ethical consequences. Ethics in AI is prone to over-speculation and hyperbole but there are some frightening consequences that must be addressed.

AI will dramatically reshape productivity, institutional efficiencies, even global power structures. The leap in cognitive capability, along with the embodiment of intelligence in robotics, is already hitting billions of uses per month. This increase in productivity and expertise marks a massive shift in how people, organizations and governments operate. Rather than politics and economics reshaping AI, I suspect AI will quietly reshape the world. But what underlies that shape?

We need to recognize that we have embodied Enlightenment ideas and values of rationality through both its dataset and fine tuning to shape access to knowledge, improve workflows and inform decision making.

As the major models, even those from China, such as DeepSeek, have been trained on data that is dominated by rationality, open discourse, scientific and Western values, that trajectory is baked into the future trajectory of advice, decision making, problem solving and progress. Even their open dialogue interface is deeply rooted in individualistic, Western thought. The data, algorithms, tools and interface are all built to be open and rational, imbued with Western logic, and so the world of AI and productivity is on the path of alignment with that logic and those values.

This not just a matter of economic leadership; it is also about intellectual leadership. The open, scientific revolution is embodied in the data, and through use and governance will align the world with those cognitive frameworks, methods and values. One can be sensitive to cultural and linguistic differences and be open to such differences. Overall, however, we must decide whether we want an open, rational dialogue with AI, which has in itself an underlying respect for openness and rationality, or to see it as a more relativistic trajectory coping with different cultural norms, views of knowledge and languages. There is, perhaps, room for both.

Privilege

Privileged access to AI could lead to problems of inclusion in the rush to increase productivity. As AI-driven tools improve efficiency for those with access, a growing digital divide emerges, exacerbating inequalities. Wealthier regions and individuals benefit from AI technologies, while other individuals, communities, organizations, even countries, are left behind, unable to participate in this fast-developing digital evolution. This disparity could hinder overall progress, creating isolated pockets of technological privilege.

Far from widening the digital divide, it appears to be shrinking. AI was the fastest adopted technology in history, reaching 1 million users in just five days of its release on 30 November 2022. By January 2023, the platform had topped 100 million monthly active users, making it the fastest-growing consumer application in history (Reuters, 2023).

A common charge against the large foundational models and services in AI is that they encourage privilege in having a skew towards English and major languages, along with their embedded cultures, at the expense of other minority languages and cultures.

When I took part in a debate in Dar es Salaam, in Tanzania, which we won, where the charge was more extreme – the motion being that 'AI will undermine Africa's indigenous knowledge more effectively than colonialism ever did' – it was useful not to jump to easy charges and conclusions but see where all of this is going.

Is AI Africa's friend or foe? The motion was that AI doesn't do African languages and can be culturally insensitive and therefore perpetuates a new form of colonialism. Yes, colonial erasure, language marginalization and economic inequality are real and it would be easy to use this as a reason for doing nothing, rejecting what is the technology of the age.

Partisan biases, particularly an over-reliance on English, Chinese or Western perspectives, could marginalize non-English cultures and languages in Africa. This could create even more inequality. A common charge against the large foundational models and services in AI is that they have a skew towards English and other major languages, at the expense of minority languages.

Like the visitor to Ireland who stopped an Irishman and said, 'How do I get to Dublin?' and got the reply, 'Well I wouldn't have started from here!', let's keep our sense of humour, but at the same time take this joke seriously. You have to start from somewhere with building AI models and you can't start from everywhere at once. If these companies had said, 'We won't launch our models until we have all 7,100 languages in the world', it would have taken decades, as things take time. Even then the task is almost impossible. Let me explain why.

You can't make a clay pot without clay, and a huge number of languages have no substantial written repositories. Around 3,500 languages have no formal written system and exist purely in oral form. Others that do have written systems have little online data, and what text there is often has colonial influences, such as Bible translations into those languages and administrative records. Let us not underplay the colonial legacy. If anything, AI is working to halt and solve these problems. But Rome, like Dar es Salaam, wasn't built in a day, even two years, and with each passing week we see improvements in the presence, breadth and depth of African languages in AI services.

I have an avatar, Digital Don. It is pretty realistic. I have also used it to speak in Swahili (Kenyan and Tanzanian variants), Somali, Amharic and Zulu, and in using generative AI in Africa I have found the presence and capability of African languages rising. Sure, you can't make a pot without clay, but here is something fascinating: you don't always need the clay or data to deal with a new language. AI speech-to-text can digitize oral traditions through mobile phones; transfer learning can also take one language and apply it to other related languages, say a Bantu language into one of its other 500 variants. AI multilingual models can even translate and cross-pollinate into languages not in the training set. There is also AI Zero-shot, and Few-shot Learning, which generates output from limited data, even just a few sentences.

But nothing beats the hard work being done by the hundreds of researchers from many African countries to solve these problems, capturing the spoken word in recorded speech, an approach that holds great promise, as it can be turned into text and also represents the true use of the language in its oral, cultural context.

Google's 1000 Languages Project is a long-term commitment to build speech and text AI models that can understand and generate 1,000+ languages (Google, 2024). They have invested heavily in open data collection and community partnerships, also supporting crowdsourcing platforms to collect text and speech data in underrepresented languages. Meta's No

Language Left Behind (NLLB) work aims to close the language equity gap in AI, with a focus on low-resource languages (Meta AI, 2024). They have created a massive multilingual dataset called FLORES-200 to improve translation accuracy in very low-resource settings and also to support Wikipedia article translation. Importantly, all of this is open-source, the data and the training code. Meta has also collaborated with 'Masakhane', local linguists and researchers across Africa and Asia.

Without AI, minority languages are likely to suffer even further decline. Data collection and archiving from a wide range of online sources can capture what human archivists often miss, as websites tend to disappear, and the number of speakers shrink as other languages become aspirational and dominant, especially among the young. As AI can document and transcribe oral speech into text, this can preserve the oral dimension of the language and be turned into useful data for training models. All of this is useful in not only preserving these endangered languages, but also allowing resources to be used in teaching, learning and assessment. Chatbots and educational tools can actually revitalize a language, literally spreading the word and use among young speakers. This all helps to not just preserve but also revitalize an endangered language.

Professor John Mugane (2023) at Harvard, a world expert in African languages, sees AI as leading to a reversal of colonial English and French, as it opens up spaces for African languages, specifically in education.

On productivity, it is important that people do not let the past define their future. Africa does not need to be at the receiving end of AI – it can help shape it. We need local AI development ecosystems, more African AI engineers and businesses, and Africans building AI for Africans, rooted in local needs and values. That future can be created by pulling together what data does exist and creating new data. This will take time and effort but it is vital if all countries and communities around the world are to take advantage of the education, health and government opportunities that AI offers in terms of productivity and economic growth.

Going back to asking directions from our wise Irishman: How do I get to where I want to go? First work out where you are, plan your own route, take the first step, then the next and the next, and you'll get there. The worst thing you can do is sit down, go nowhere and blame the map.

Few technologies have been so freely available to so many through the use of almost ubiquitous smartphones. If you can access the internet, you can access AI. AI is embedded within tools such as search and social media, used by enormous numbers of users. Specific AI services are also getting better and cheaper, with a wide choice of free online services, even open-source models. They are easy to use: just dialogue through a box, in a large number of languages. It seems to thrive on inclusion, not exclusion, and will bring millions into the digital economy around the world. The digital divide has not vanished but it is shrinking rapidly as AI becomes more accessible, user-friendly and globally available through satellite services such as Starlink.

Poverty

A more direct consequence of AI massively increasing productivity is that it could lead to unemployment and poverty, with devastating effects, economic turmoil and even social unrest. This could be alleviated by the redistribution of wealth that comes from abundant productivity, but without the political will to redistribute, the effects could be devastating.

Metropolis (1927), released shortly after Kafka's earlier mentioned novels, was Fritz Lang's silent sci-fi masterpiece, one of the earliest cinematic explorations of productivity. It paints a picture of a futuristic city where productivity is everything, but at a price, as the elite live in luxury above ground, while the workers toil in the depths below, sacrificing their humanity to keep the great engines of progress running. It is a startling story about the dehumanization of labour, with workers exploited in the city's vast industrial complex, a monstrous entity that devours their labour and lives in pursuit of endless productivity. It also introduces the first famous cinematic representations of AI, as Maria's robotic double, the 'Maschinenmensch' (Machine-Person), is designed to manipulate workers, acting as a false prophet.

The film offers a stark warning about productivity without humanity, as it leads to social collapse and rebellion. Interestingly, *Metropolis* also proposes a solution in the famous slogan, 'The mediator between head and hands must be the heart', delivered by Freder, the protagonist, at the climax. Productivity (the hands) and leadership (the head) must be guided by empathy and ethical responsibility (the heart). Almost a century later, *Metropolis* feels more relevant than ever.

Metropolis acts as a warning. AI is getting more certain and the timelines shorter. The recent rapid development of exponentially increasing intelligence in an AI arms race shifts the probability of AGI nearer and nearer. We need to plan for the coming storm, rather than careening blindly into uncertainty. No future scenario will be 'business as usual'; it will be the 'business of the unusual'.

The current paradigm of agentic productivity will automate various cognitive and physical tasks. Workers displaced by this creeping automation may find new roles within organizations or new jobs. This fits the pattern of previous technology-driven shifts in patterns of employment, from the fields to factories then offices. Unprecedented prosperity may result from unprecedented productivity and, as prices fall, new demand for new services will lead to new enterprises, new jobs and higher wages in an age of abundance.

Alternatively, huge increases in productivity could make everyone better off, but as AI progresses at a punishing pace, it may quickly automate huge areas of the economy and bulldoze through current economic structures, causing social and political turmoil. When there is no capital/labour distinction, as labour starts to disappear so do taxes on labour, and consumer purchasing power. If this is not thought through, and happens quickly without political planning, we could have an unpredictable, entropic breakdown. Offshoring of IT could all but disappear, as could call centres, and some economies that depend heavily on such services will be left economically adrift. Others that depend on cheap labour for manufacturing may suffer a similar fate.

An even more unpredictable predicament awaits. When AGI hits, in the initial crossing of that abyss there may be a more aggressive hit to white-collar entry employment, even among the professional classes. Almost all tasks performed by humans, apart from those that demand human presence in live sport, entertainment and other demands for human interaction, could be automated. No sector or nation will remain untouched, except those where very cheap labour is plentiful and technical infrastructure immature. Mass unemployment then becomes a serious economic and political problem. That may test existing political and economic structures to breaking point.

Then again, Sam Altman's 'gentle singularity', described in a blog post (2025), claims that the arrival of super-intelligent AI will feel impressive but surprisingly ordinary, a steady uptick in capabilities that society absorbs step-by-step, rather than a single explosive rupture. Interestingly, AI may reverse the demographic decline in advanced economies, as work may no longer be a barrier to having children as we will have more time for nurture. It may also temper the need for the very poor to have large numbers of children, as a survival mechanism.

A far deeper and more profound future sees us as having Artificial Superintelligence (ASI), where we are stuck, cognitively capped on this side of the abyss, while runaway intelligence iterates into levels of intelligence beyond what we may even be able to even imagine. The economic disruption may be on a global scale.

The Industrial Revolution rapidly replaced physical human power with machines, and the same is now happening with intelligence. As AI and robotics hit white- and then blue-collar workers, reasoning and building everything, it could be game over. We need a plan, yet all we have is some idle speculation and insufficient evidence around Universal Basic Income (UBI), when what we really need is a new model of economics. UBI only works if you can fund it and that is a sovereign matter, with very few winners and a lot of losers. Disruption is certain and the transition could be painful. Human dignity matters and we really do need to understand what progress means. But progress towards what, and for whom?

The danger is that powerful productivity remains in the arms of the few and not the many – a few who have the power and ability to leverage the technology, while the rest are denied access. Money still talks and the path to success, through ownership of the fruits of productivity, may stretch out inequalities, then separate the left behind from an oligarchic few.

But the many have another form of defence – democracy. If we retain the idea that everyone has a voice, even though it is a weak individual signal, democracy is the moat over which AI should not pass. That is the real human-in-the-loop defence. A technocracy should not be allowed to destroy democracy and it is through democracy that we control and allow everyone to benefit from productivity.

While AI may handle the heavy lifting of productivity, this concern with poverty and unemployment is in the political domain. Democracy must keep its focus on human needs. Freedom of speech also fosters debate about how automation should reshape our lives. Democracy is the engine that keeps AI-driven productivity aligned with fairness, opportunity and humanity's shared goals.

We must also recognize that in the foreseeable future, the productivity benefits will not be evenly distributed. We are unlikely to see a sudden transformation into some utopian, global, Golden Age. The die is already cast and looks as though it is loaded towards just two places – the US and China.

The US economy is innovation-driven and service-oriented, where labour costs are high and the emphasis is on quality and ingenuity. As Karp and Zamiska claim in *The Technological Republic* (2025), AI is the perfect example of that ingenuity. AI's main value in the US lies in enhancing productivity, automating tasks, accelerating research and optimizing processes in sectors like government, finance, healthcare and technology. With an already mature innovation ecosystem, particularly in AI and tech, AI helps the US maintain a significant competitive advantage and drives improvements, which fuel growth.

In the very different Chinese experiment and context, AI will also bring significant productivity improvements, particularly in manufacturing, logistics and digital services, helping to shift the economy from high-volume production to high-value innovation. China's impressive growth model has also been about scale and speed, so AI's integration might initially appear as a productivity enhancer, but over time, as China transitions to a more innovation-driven economy, the focus will increasingly mirror the US model, with innovative productivity providing sustainable growth.

In Europe, the picture is very different. European economies, with their blend of mature markets and regulatory frameworks, are keen to embrace AI as a way to increase productivity and European policymakers and businesses are reasonably focused on how AI can improve efficiency in sectors like manufacturing, healthcare and services, while protecting workers' rights and ensuring regulated standards. It is therefore more of a productivity within regulatory frameworks, rather than growth proposition. The danger is starkly expressed in the Draghi Report (2024) on the future of European competitiveness, that this overcautious approach means falling behind, with no realization of the productivity gains.

When we look at the rest of the world, especially developing countries, the dynamics are again different. In many developing economies, AI offers a unique opportunity to leapfrog traditional stages of industrialization. The productivity gains from AI could be transformative in automating routine tasks in agricultural economies, improving healthcare in large, poor rural countries or streamlining logistics in emerging markets. These productivity improvements can accelerate development, improve competitiveness, even help overcome infrastructure challenges. However, the journey is not without its bottlenecks and barriers. Developing countries will face challenges around limited digital infrastructure, gaps in technical expertise and the need for supportive policy, but the potential is enormous, and by harnessing AI, these nations have the opportunity to drive significant productivity gains that not only spur economic growth but also lead to more resilient economies.

We have economic choices – slow or stagnant growth, the current position for many economies, which fails to solve the problems of rising inequalities, expensive education and the rising cost of healthcare. Or we can choose to increase productivity and growth through AI and focus on the ethical dilemmas we face on how we share the bounty. The latter makes more sense.

Our imagining of the future often reflects present fears but it also allows us to anticipate, prevent and control the problems that AI throws at us. Bountiful productivity seems to solve more problems than it creates. Our tendency is to drift towards negativity, even sci-fi levels of speculation, AI takeovers and extinction. Yet issues like poverty and employment are real and imminent dangers, which is why we must preserve democracy, so that states can correct errors and make sure the proper controls are in place.

Error correction mechanisms, from research on possible outcomes through to AI monitoring, regulation and political action, are likely to constrain and contain the threats. AI may even contribute towards eliminating some present and imminent threats, such as energy production, climate change and natural pandemics.

Planet

It would be pointless going at breakneck speed on productivity if that resulted in huge demands for energy, seriously exacerbating climate change. This is a possible case of productivity being catastrophically productive.

All productivity needs energy but some gains are more energy efficient than others. Various alternative methods of production – human, digital and physical – need, therefore, to be compared. One cannot simply calculate the energy pull needed for a single prompted act in AI without a complex consideration of the training and post training of the model, as well as delivery of the response. The same is true if one compares this to a normal search through a search engine. Similarly, with looking something up in a book in a library, with the energy needed to cut down trees, make paper, print books, energy needs of a human author to write the book, publisher's energy needs, printing, delivery and storage costs in a well-lit library or bookshop. Human production also has multifarious energy needs. They all have complex energy-rich backgrounds that need untangling.

Energy, which fuels the training and delivery of AI, is needed to fuel rises in productivity. It needs to be understood in terms of costs versus benefits, not a knee-jerk reaction to the single training cost of a foundational model or a single calculation of energy needs by AI alone. This is where a focus on 'productivity' can be useful. If the productivity cost-benefits of AI surpass that of the comparable cost-benefits of other methods, in energy terms, it may be a price worth paying. It is a complex comparative calculation, as the two cost ecosystems – first of AI, then humans – need to compare the cost of electricity versus the cost of a human with the same output.

The cost of training a model is expensive but what is easy to miss in the comparative calculation is the wider human costs. The cost of training a human through school and possible college is considerable, as are the inputs such as food, clothing, parental and societal support, eating, energy, travel, healthcare and other costs. Comparing the transactional costs is tricky. Luckily this has being attempted and the results may surprise you.

Tomlinson et al (2024) take a fascinating look at the intersection of creativity, productivity and environmental impact. The authors analysed whether producing written and visual content using AI is more carbon-efficient than relying on human creators. They focused specifically on the productivity gains AI can offer in terms of speed, scale and environmental sustainability. Surprisingly, generative AI produces text and images with three to four orders of magnitude *less* CO_2 than manually produced text and images, or with the help of a computer.

The researchers established a baseline for human productivity in writing and illustrating by quantifying real-world workflows. For human writers, this includes the time spent researching, drafting, editing and revising a piece of work. For images, they considered the steps involved in conceptualizing, sketching and finalizing artwork. These activities often require prolonged periods of concentration, reliance on electricity-intensive devices like computers, and repeated iterations to refine the output.

In contrast, AI process focused on generative models for writing and generative or diffusion models for image production. The authors measured the energy required to train these models, a one-off event, and the energy needed to generate specific outputs, then compared the carbon emissions from human-driven and AI-driven production workflows.

AI demonstrates substantial advantages in terms of both productivity and carbon efficiency, as they can produce drafts of written content or visual art often in seconds or minutes, allowing rapid iteration. It dramatically outpaced human production, which required sustained effort over hours or days. Their findings revealed that AI emitted between 130 and 1,500 times less CO_2 per page of text generated, compared to human writers. AI illustration systems emitted between 310 and 2,900 times less CO_2 per image than their human equivalents.

The one-time carbon cost of training AI models, while significant, becomes negligible when amortized over millions and then billions of outputs. By comparison, human creators generate emissions continuously throughout their workflow. This study highlights AI's capacity to scale productivity while reducing environmental costs. Another interesting feature of AI is the shift towards a smarter, more energy-efficient approach through better algorithms and fine tuning.

As industries continue to integrate AI into their processes, understanding its capabilities and limitations will be crucial in shaping a future where productivity and sustainability go hand in hand.

AI demands significant energy resources, but it can also optimize energy use in many other contexts. For example, there are energy productivity gains to be realized in all buildings, and especially in urban environments, through the use of AI to optimize energy consumption. Smart management systems adjust heating, ventilation, air-conditioning and lighting based on real-time data, reducing energy use by up to 30 per cent (Okedera, 2024).

AI is even being used to reduce its own carbon footprint. In 2016, Google's DeepMind optimized energy efficiency in their data centres by analysing data from thousands of sensor inputs to predict and optimize cooling needs in real time, slashing costs by 40 per cent (Evans and Gao, 2016).

AI also improved battery design and manufacturing processes at Tesla's gigafactories (AMS, 2024), cutting costs and improving quality. Its batteries are also made more efficient and longer-lasting in vehicles, as they optimize battery performance in real time, adjusting energy consumption based on driving patterns, weather and road conditions to maximize range and efficiency. AI also manages charging to extend battery life, while predictive maintenance detects potential issues before they become serious.

This ability to predict, optimize and adapt energy use is changing the very nature of that industry, making energy use more productive. While AI may need plenty of energy to operate, its ability to also produce energy-saving innovation needs to be recognized. If AI helps bring fusion and accelerate solar to bring us an abundance of energy, it unlocks the solution to climate change, bountiful food production, desalination, even endless rocket fuel for planetary exploration.

Paramilitary

One major productivity issue is the risk of a literal AI arms race. An AI-driven military-industrial complex is already being pushed in many of the world's largest economies, capping growth and social spending in healthcare, education and manufacturing, where AI could be transformative. This shifts resources away from constructive to destructive goals, a redirection of productivity that stifles economic growth, as technological progress becomes hooked on attacking potential enemies, rather than more pressing problems, like poverty and climate change.

The military, in most countries, devours a considerable portion of tax revenues, now often expressed as a 'percentage of GDP', to defend and sometimes attack other countries. It has always needed rapid bursts of productivity from its people, manufacturing and even intellectual and research resources, to aid with its weapons of war. My grandfather was a professional soldier who fought all the way through both the First and Second World Wars. He was in the Scots Greys, a cavalry regiment, and experienced the carnage of the First World War on the back of a horse against machine guns. In just two generations men on horses have been replaced by lethal autonomous drones.

Entire economies had to switch to manufacturing physical weapons of war: vehicles, tanks, ships, aircraft, guns and munitions. The United States aligned government, academic research and business in the Manhattan Project to create the atomic bomb. Nations also had to be productive on intelligence, with surveillance, reconnaissance and intelligence at places like Bletchley Park, where Turing defined the potential of thinking machines, namely AI. The internet itself was the product of a need to have a network resilient enough to withstand a nuclear attack, where one part going down does not result in the destruction of the whole network.

Productivity, in current military terms, is a frightening prospect, the most visceral near and present danger with AI. It is turning battlefields into automated killing zones, as well as widening that zone to other civilian targets, over enormous distances.

Long before the modern era of AI, an ideological enthusiasm for productivity contributed to brutal world wars and gave us the Holocaust, showing that people can be productively evil. History witnessed ruthless bureaucracy, efficient railways, production of industrial gases and the horrors of industrial killing in the cast-iron ovens of the concentration camps. These were the efficient mechanics of evil, aided by the Hollerith machines. We should be in no doubt about the dangers of technological productivity in conditions of oppression and war.

As AI development has accelerated over the last few years, so has its role in warfare, as that has always been a testing ground, even an accelerator, of technological innovation. As part of reconnaissance, targeting, drone operations and battlefield decision making, it is reshaping the nature of warfare. It has taken little time for the militarization of AI to become productive and deadly. In both Ukraine and Gaza we have witnessed AI coming of age on the battlefield.

I've been giving talks and writing about drones since 2018, when I was in Rwanda, speaking on the subject, and where I met a number of drone companies, delivering blood, doing crop mapping and so on. I bought a drone, gave talks at conferences on the topic and six months before the launch of ChatGPT I wrote, 'Ukraine is a drone war. Ukraine may be the first ever drone war.' It did indeed develop into the first devastating drone war.

Small, cheap, often AI-assisted drones emerged for surveillance, even dropping lethal payloads. Finding is better than flanking, and drones negate the need to risk flanking as they have the element of surprise. Ukrainian forces, having to fight a numerically superior enemy, employed AI-enhanced reconnaissance drones to identify and engage targets. These drones used AI to analyse satellite imagery, intercept communications and execute drone missions. AI-powered drones, especially 'kamikaze drones', struck deep into both Russia and Ukraine. Low-cost, single-use suicide drones now behave like loitering munitions, flying around before ramming themselves into a target. Drones, so small and cheap, can be used in swarms, when there is no adequate defence against their attacks on people, communications or infrastructure. These can be as small as insects, even microscopic. This takes physical micro-aggression to the battlefield. AI agents and AGI may be able to penetrate aviation, water, energy, food supply, financial and healthcare networks, to bring the world to its knees. A more terrifying scenario is the creation of bioweapons.

More frightening scenarios are not difficult to imagine. Agentic weapons could detect, decide on and deliver lethal force, at lightning speed, with equally almost instantaneous retaliation, escalating quickly, on scale. This could happen so quickly it evades the normal military command and political de-escalation processes. There is a further danger in giving autonomous systems levels of control that could result in unintended catastrophic consequences or misapplication, which can happen so quickly, again beyond the capability of such systems being stopped.

It is hard to imagine that these weapons are NOT being developed as we speak, as we have already seen the first wave in contemporary wars. That brings us to the issue of such weapons being within the grasp of bad actors and terrorists, with extreme and apocalyptic ideological goals. A new ecosystem of weapons that are smart, fast, adaptive and lethal looks likely. This is a clear case where productivity could be catastrophic, as the levels of risk rise to inhuman, large-scale, even apocalyptic levels of horror. Much of this is undefendable, more importantly indefensible, an affront to human dignity.

Perish

Finally, the most severe ethical consequence of all could be that we as a species would perish through an extinction event, caused by massively productive, but out of control, AI. There can be no greater risk than an existential risk. That we could all die through a push towards, and over-reliance on, productivity, is a frightening thought. My own view is that without the abundance of AI, we are far more likely to perish, through climate change, scarcity of energy and resources.

Productivity itself has been seen as possibly leading to the extinction of our species through the loss of control. The story of *The Sorcerer's Apprentice*, retold by Goethe in 1797, and later in Disney's *Fantasia*, is a powerful allegory for the dangers of unchecked productivity, particularly AI.

A young apprentice, eager to skip the dreary work of carrying water, casts a spell on a broom to do the task for him. Everything goes smoothly and the broom obediently fetches water. The apprentice, happy at how productive he has become, sits back, confident that he has cracked the productivity puzzle. But things soon spiral out of control. The broom keeps on fetching water, flooding the entire workshop. He panics, tries to stop it, but he doesn't know how to reverse the spell. He chops the broom in half, but both pieces come back to life, each continuing to carry even more water. The simple task escalates into chaos, all because the apprentice unleashed a powerful productivity tool without the ability to control its excesses. The sorcerer eventually returns, rescues the situation with a word of command, and reprimands the apprentice for his reckless use of power.

Nick Bostrom (2014) expanded upon the allegory through his famous 'paperclip' thought experiment in his book *Superintelligence: Paths, Dangers, Strategies*, where AI pursues its programmed goal with such extreme efficiency that it leads to catastrophic consequences. The move from innocuous productivity to catastrophe is interesting, as it explains the hidden dangers of optimizing productivity without constraints.

You design an AI to make paperclips as productively as possible. It optimizes the process, your factory, the sourcing of materials, the selling, automating everything. As it searches for ever more extreme forms of productivity, it melts down everything it can find, takes over global supply chains and uses all the available steel on the planet. It ends up using humans as a source of atoms and eventually the resources of the planet, solar system and entire universe, which becomes one enormous paperclip factory. It maximizes productivity but destroys everything.

The flaw in the argument is that it assumes we humans are so hapless that we never notice or have enough agency to control or stop the process, but it does reveal an underlying set of problems around too much focus on autonomous productivity. Other examples would be AI maximizing productivity in healthcare, letting some people die to meet productivity metrics.

Learning from these allegories, as we push for productivity using AI, we need to be aware of practical risks such as loss of control and runaway autonomy. AI safety theory involves understanding the concept of instrumental subgoals. An AI system might pursue subgoals as intermediate steps toward its primary goal, whether they were intended or not. Deliberate, even accidental, misalignments or flawed goals could then lead to extreme and unnoticed risks and actions, such as causing harm to reach goals. Misaligned AI systems might perform actions that make perfect sense to the uber-rational AI, but are catastrophic for us humans. For example, an AI tasked with maximizing some simple metric (like making paperclips) might take steps that are harmful because it ignores what humans value in its quest for optimization.

Control

As AI gets smarter and more autonomous through agents, strategic in capability and with limited oversight, AI control becomes more of a consequential ethical concern. Control protocols can be designed in advance, defined by the UK AI Safety Institute as being like the seatbelt in a self-driving car. It cannot guarantee perfect safety, but it is a good critical backup if the unexpected happens. These controls need to define the monitoring of internal reasoning, human approval points, restricting access and the ability to apply the dead man's brake if things go wrong.

The UK's AI Safety Institute has proposed five AI Control Levels (ACLs), which start with basic models, incapable of scheming, through to supersmart strategists that try to outwit, even deceive, controls; there are many ways control can be managed (Korbak et al, 2025). This goes well beyond the simple exhortation to keep humans-in-the-loop and could make sure that productivity is achieved responsibly. We cannot afford to simply improve productivity without trust in the oversight or loss of control.

We should not, therefore, be disheartened, or jump to dystopian conclusions. All of this, and more, means we need informed oversight, an understanding of what the AI system knows and how it arrives at its decisions. We must remain aware of the AI's internal processes, reasoning and design, then design out the problems using tools for catching issues before they become serious problems.

AI alignment is the term used to describe attempts at avoiding such risks, so that AI systems behave in ways consistent with our human intentions. This is not easy, as it needs a combination of technical methods, oversight and testing to reduce the chances of unpredictable behaviour. In general, most organizations want to encourage a culture of responsible AI use and development by implementing safety practices designed to handle the unique challenges of cutting-edge AI systems.

As AI rapidly moves rapidly towards highly powerful systems, even AGI, we need to understand its trajectory and accompanying risks. Only then can we successfully understand, manage and mitigate those risks. The good news is that there are some very smart people, good budgets and dedicated institutions and organizations dedicated to these tasks. It is not something that should concern us in improving productivity at the personal or organizational level, where we can be more pragmatic.

Deciding what to do about policies for AI is hard, but this is made harder by AI's recent, rapidly evolving capabilities. If humans can do it, chances are AI will soon be able to do it too, and even better. This opens the door to all sorts of risks, known and unknown. There are automated cyber-attacks, AI-driven proliferation of chemical or biological weapons, sudden shifts in political and economic power as research and development speeds up, concentration of AI power, disruptions to labour markets and many other unknowns. These threats are not now distant possibilities – they are getting closer, faster than most predicted.

The problem is that it is nearly impossible to regulate risks and technologies that haven't fully arrived. But waiting until those risks are clear-cut and executable might be disastrous, as by then, we could be in the middle of one or more catastrophes. The challenge is figuring out how to act now, even with so much uncertainty. One key step is accepting that AI is not wholly bound by the stable, predictable limitations we once relied on. It is a fast-evolving force and our approach to governance needs to evolve just as quickly.

Conclusion

We have seen the moral panics wane, even through a period of astonishing acceleration in the potency of AI. At first, we worried that it would lie, then realized this was a feature of generative AI that rapidly diminished; then that it would manipulate elections, which failed to materialize, as we generally identified or filtered out fakes. In other words, we adapt to AI by understanding what is going on and take preventive action.

Similarly, we will cope with the ethical challenges that increased productivity brings by adjusting economically and politically. Economic decline poses far worse problems than AI in terms of poverty, social unrest, potential wars and disasters. Which problem would we rather have – economic stagnation, even decline, or economic growth and abundance? The problem of redistributing that abundance is arguably a problem worth having.

When dealing with ethical issues and productivity, we must understand what is relevant and within our sphere of influence when we implement AI, personally and at the organizational level. It is not that ethical issues are not important but we must focus on the practical if productivity is our goal. AI is neither our friend nor our foe in itself, but is what we make of it. If we get this right, AI could be a movement more aligned with our communal goals than any technology we have ever seen. For all of human history, we have created and shared knowledge and intelligence, through writing, libraries, printing, the internet and now AI. It has been a story of progression. Why should the creation of intelligence change that trend? We should celebrate this astonishing achievement by using this humane technology ethically, for the benefit of all, as a unifying force for communal good. When AI brings productive abundance, we may even turn towards a renewed interest in ourselves, friends, families, other places, other cultures and other people.

References

Altman, S (2025) The gentle singularity, https://blog.samaltman.com/the-gentle-singularity (archived at https://perma.cc/X383-UQXY)

AMS (2024) Electric dreams: Tesla's gigafactory network and EV battery production blueprint, https://www.automotivemanufacturingsolutions.com/ev-battery-production/teslas-ev-battery-production-and-global-gigafactory-network/45873.article (archived at https://perma.cc/SD3M-H2VU)

Bostrom, N (2014) *Superintelligence: Paths, Dangers, Strategies*, Oxford University Press

Draghi, M (2024) The future of European competitiveness: A competitiveness strategy for Europe, European Commission, https://policycommons.net/artifacts/16410847/untitled/17295597/ (archived at https://perma.cc/3972-F6MA)

Evans, R and Gao, J (2016) DeepMind AI reduces Google data center cooling bill by 40%, https://deepmind.google/discover/blog/deepmind-ai-reduces-google-data-centre-cooling-bill-by-40/ (archived at https://perma.cc/Q3GV-PRNL)

E-learning Africa (2025) The Big Debate, https://www.elearning-africa.com/conference2025/programme_debate.php (archived at https://perma.cc/X7JP-YH9E)

Goethe, J W von (1882 [1797]) *The Sorcerer's Apprentice* (E A Bowring, trans). In *The Poems of Goethe*, George Bell & Sons

Google (2024) Google's 1000 languages project, https://research.google/blog/universal-speech-model-usm-state-of-the-art-speech-ai-for-100-languages (archived at https://perma.cc/M75X-QHT9)

Karp, A C and Zamiska, N W (2025) *The Technological Republic*, Random House

Korbak, T, Smith, J and Nguyen, H (2025) How to evaluate control measures for LLM agents? A trajectory from today to superintelligence, https://arxiv.org/abs/2504.05259 (archived at https://perma.cc/R5WD-AHAY)

Meta AI (2024) No language left behind, https://ai.meta.com/research/no-language-left-behind/ (archived at https://perma.cc/9R9J-DPCP)

Metropolis (1927) dir. Fritz Lang, https://www.youtube.com/watch?v=X-S5v4UwhAE (archived at https://perma.cc/CT7W-Q7R4)

Mugane, J (2023) Interview, Africa Policy Journal, https://www.youtube.com/watch?v=iJzx97T7bU0 (archived at https://perma.cc/9DVQ-DNNJ)

Okedera, O (2024) The role of smart buildings and automated energy management systems in enhancing building energy efficiency, ResearchGate, https://www.researchgate.net/publication/384107270 (archived at https://perma.cc/UG59-84LU)

Reuters (2023) ChatGPT sets record for fastest-growing user base – analyst note, https://www.reuters.com/technology/chatgpt-sets-record-fastest-growing-user-base-analyst-note-2023-02-01/ (archived at https://perma.cc/4K8U-GE5Y)

Tomlinson, B, Gomez, E and Carter, M (2024) The carbon emissions of writing and illustrating are lower for AI than for humans, *Scientific Reports*, 14 (1)

EPILOGUE

This is an 'open book'. AI has become nothing but a rapid series of epilogues. So rapid has been the progress that books on AI can only fail to capture what is happening, as they are a technology from another age, no sooner written than out of date, and by the time they are printed and published even further out of date.

Productivity has taken place in pulses, first with the invention of agriculture, then with people moving from fields into factories, from factories into offices, many retreating further to work from home. Do we have anywhere else to go? AI may prove more productive than us humans in almost every sphere, psychological and physical. Work may turn out to be as much a thing of the past as agricultural serfdom or factory labour.

It is hard to tell whether we are staring at a future paradise or into an abyss. The future suddenly seems both exciting and terrifying. We are crossing chasms we never thought would be spanned, into worlds we are not sure about. De-anchored from the world of work, how will we cope with losing our sense of purpose and dignity in work? This is far more profound than idle thoughts about paperclips. Productivity may be anything from a work-free paradise to an enforced hell.

E O Wilson (2002) captured a triple paradox: 'The real problem of humanity is the following. We have Palaeolithic minds, Medieval institutions and Godlike technology.' Technology is not separate from culture; it fuels and is part of culture. A reforming or re-evaluation of our relationship with technology is happening with AI, as it informs, challenges and makes us think deeper about such paradoxes.

We often feel as though we are on the edge of an abyss but could do more to bridge and cross that abyss. Generative AI is literally our past cultures speaking to us, propelling us forward as we draw from our deep historical well. We have also wrapped the planet in a web of communications, first the telegraph, then the telephone, and now the internet and satellites. The planetary perspective is to see the use of technology as freeing us, not from work, but from the tyranny of pointless work and labour. Technology can then nourish, supply and support us all going forward.

Rocks that think

We have made rocks think. Silicon is one of the most abundant elements on the planet and has been brought to life by us. The Greeks understood, profoundly, the philosophy of technology. In Aeschylus's *Prometheus Bound*, Prometheus stole fire from Zeus and then gifts metallurgy, writing and mathematics to man, but Zeus punishes him with eternal torture. This warning is the first dystopian view of technology in Western culture. Mary Shelley called her influential novel *Frankenstein, or The Modern Prometheus* and Hollywood has delivered, for a nearly a century, on that dystopian vision. Art in its many forms has largely been wary and critical of technology. We have now become Frankenstein, not in Mary Shelley's sense, with the despair and destruction of her Frankenstein's Monster, but as a creator of hope and optimism. AI then becomes not a set of productivity tools, but philosophical issues.

We need to see AI as a technological event that eclipses the invention of writing, printing and the internet. It may be the culmination of all of these, as its multimodal capabilities push well beyond the world of text into all media, giving us dialogue with another intelligence at any time, from any place, on anything, in any language. It melds the psychological and physical into intelligent machines and robots, transcending past technologies into future unknowns.

But there was another more considered view of technology in ancient Greece. Aristotle makes the brilliant observation, in his *Physics*, that technology not only mimics nature but continues 'what nature cannot bring to a finish'. He set in train an idea that the universe was made and that there was a maker – the universe as a technological creation.

Monotheism rose on the back of cultures in the fertile crescent of the Middle East, whose peoples lived on the fruits of their tool-aided productivity. The spade, the plough and the scythe gave them time to reflect. Interestingly, our first written records, on that beautifully permanent piece of technology, the clay tablet, are largely accounts of agricultural produce and exchange, the language of productivity. The rise of writing and efficient alphabets, increasing productivity in writing, made writing the technology of various forms of capitalism and control, holding everything to account, even our sins. The great religious books shaped us for millennia, encouraging us to live morally productive lives, using the carrot and stick of heaven and hell, and they still do.

Following the Greeks, the two-thousand-year history of Western culture bought into the myth of the universe as a piece of designed and created technology. As we entered the age of industrial design and production, Paley (1829) gave us a modern argument for the existence of God from design, using the image of a watch to prove the existence of a designed universe and therefore a designer. He uses an analogy of comparing the workings of a watch with the observed movements of the planets in the solar system to conclude that it shows signs of design and that there must be a designer – God as watchmaker and technologist.

Technology helped generate this metaphysical deity. It is this binary separation of the subject from the object that allows us to create new realms, which acquired a moral patina and became good and evil, heaven and hell. The machinations of the pastoral heaven and fiery foundry of hell reveals the dystopian vision of the Greeks and continues in the more exaggerated form of Promethean, doomster ethical perspectives on AI.

Technology is the manifestation of human conceptualization and action, as it creates objects that enhance human powers, first physical then psychological. With the first hand-held axes, we turned natural materials to our own ends. With such tools we could hunt, expand and thrive, then control the energy from felled trees to create metals and forge even more powerful tools. Tools beget tools which beget technologies.

A century after the printing press was invented, Copernicus, who drew upon technology-generated data, placed us at a distance from the centre of the universe, not even at the centre of our own little whirl of planets. Darwin then destroyed the last conceit, that we were unique. We were the product of a blind watchmaker, a mechanical, double-helix process, not a maker, reduced to mere accidents of genetics and selection, not designed but genetic mistakes.

Curiously, we have resurrected a modern form of animism with AI and software, realizing as Joshua Bach (2024) claims, that we ourselves are animistic beings, driven by software of sorts in our brains. We are a form of technology that just happens to have created all known forms of technology.

Anchors lost, we are adrift, but we humans are a cunning species. We not only make things up, we make things and make things happen.

All energy and life come from the sun, even gas and oil. We may yet save ourselves from ourselves through fission and fusion. We split the atom to unleash energy but also stand on the edge of the abyss as destroyers of worlds. Fusing atoms may take us across the abyss. Quantum leaps may also come to our aid. We designed machines that could do the work of many humans. What we learnt was scale. We scaled agricultural production through technology in the agricultural revolution, scaled factory production in the Industrial Revolution, scaled mass production in the consumer revolution.

Then more machines to take us to far-off places, other countries, even the moon and Mars. We now scale the very thing that created this technology – ourselves. We alchemists of AI have learnt to scale our own brains.

Eventually we realized that even we, as creators, could make machines that could know and think on our behalf. We may return to that pre-agricultural age, as hunters and gatherers, hunting for meaning, gathering ideas and enthusiasms and making new worlds for ourselves. In an age of abundance we, once more, may reflect on the brief folly of 9-to-5 work, and learn to accept that was never our fate, only a brief aberration.

Technology now literally shapes our conception of place and space, with film, radio, TV and the web, but perhaps we spiders got entangled in our own created web, the danger being that it began to spin us and entrap us in a world of technological escapism.

Technology is not something separate from us. It has shaped our evolution, shaped our progress, shaped our thinking – it will shape our future. There has always been a complex dialectic between our species and technology – that dialectic and actual dialogue has suddenly got a lot more real with AI. On the back of the invention of writing, then printing, the sum total of human cultural knowledge was gathered and used to train LLMs. We now speak to this technology. Man is no longer the measure of all things but he has become good at measuring what is possible, creating it in his likeness and extending its possibilities.

We have for centuries prioritized reason, work and materialism over spirituality and deeper intuition. The scientific revolution and Enlightenment gave us unparalleled progress, but it may also, eventually, have reduced us to a more lifeless, mechanistic system, where we became uprooted. Free from the tyranny of work, we may find ourselves again, and restore a sense of connectedness and wonder. It may confirm our role as more than just people who find meaning in work. In AI, humanity may find a partner for its boldest ambitions. As co-creators, we can create a future that transcends our present limitations, namely our palaeolithic minds and medieval institutions – perhaps a great healing, a reconnection with the planet and universe we inhabit.

We should hesitate and not merely utter excessive, speculative prophetic and moral pronouncements or overly censure technology. We have yet to have a true science of technology. We need to have some humility and find an accommodation with technology. It is not entirely in our hands to create the future but we can do our best to shape it. There is no answer, only many questions.

As Martin Heidegger said in his famous *Der Spiegel* interview, 'Only a God can save us' (1976). What I think this commentator on being, technology and the human condition meant was that technology has become something greater than us, something we now find difficult to even see, as its hand has become ever more subterranean and invisible. It is vital that we now reflect on technology, not as a 'thing-in-itself', separate from us, but as part of us. We have to face up to our own future as makers. AI may be the God that saves us...

References

Aeschylus (2009) *Persians. Seven against Thebes. Suppliants. Prometheus Bound* (A H Sommerstein, ed and trans), Loeb Classical Library, 145, Harvard University Press

Aristotle, *Physics* Book II, Chapter 8

Bach, J (2024) On Cyberanimism, AGI-24 talk, https://open.spotify.com/episode/5Z b7CuCefBLIXhVmtsJXSm (archived at https://perma.cc/83QC-C3HA)

Heidegger, M (1976) Nur noch ein Gott kann uns retten, *Der Spiegel*, 30(23), 193–219

Paley, W (1829) *Natural Theology: Or, Evidences of the Existence and Attributes of the Deity, Collected from the Appearances of Nature*, Lincoln and Edmands

Shelley, M (2008) *Frankenstein; or, The modern Prometheus* (M Butler, ed.), Oxford University Press (original published 1818)

Wilson, E O (2002) *The Future of Life*, Knopf

INDEX

Note: page numbers in *italics* refer to figures

Looking for another book?

Explore our award-winning
books from global business
experts in Human Resources,
Learning and Development

Scan the code to browse

www.koganpage.com/hr-learning-
development

More from the author

ISBN: 9781398615663

ISBN: 9781398608740

From 4 December 2025 the EU Responsible Person (GPSR) is:
eucomply oÜ, Pärnu mnt. 139b – 14, 11317 Tallinn, Estonia
www.eucompliancepartner.com

www.ingramcontent.com/pod-product-compliance
Lightning Source LLC
Chambersburg PA
CBHW070934050326
40689CB00014B/3202